AN
ALBUM
OF
MEMORIES

TOM
BROKAW

•

AN
ALBUM
OF
MEMORIES

•

Personal Histories
from the
Greatest
Generation

RANDOM HOUSE
NEW YORK

Preceding photographs:

LEFT: *Celebrating the victory over Japan with
a jubilant kiss in Times Square, August 14, 1945.*
(Alfred Eisenstaedt/TimePix)
CENTER: *Army troops packed aboard the USS Gen. Harry Taylor as it
docks in New York City on August 18, 1945. The transport ship was
on its way to the Pacific front from Marseille, France, on August 7
when news of the Japanese surrender diverted it back home.*
(AP/Wide World Photos)
RIGHT: *Private Samuel M. Cawthon, from Tyler, Texas, writes
a letter home from his pup tent in Italy.*
(AP/Wide World Photos)

To the memory of those
who didn't return

FOREWORD

—— • ——

For the past three years I have been immersed in the stories of
what I call the Greatest Generation, those American men and
women who came of age in the Great Depression, served at home
and abroad during World War II, and then built the nation we have
today. In two books, *The Greatest Generation* and *The Greatest
Generation Speaks,* I documented their stories of bravery and sacrifice, achievement and humility, loyalty and service.

The reaction to these books has been deeply gratifying. Members of that generation, characteristically, are modest and yet quietly proud of what they have achieved individually and collectively,
and proud also to have had their accomplishments recognized at
this stage of their lives. In turn, their children and grandchildren
tell me that they are reexamining their own lives and values, measuring them against the legacy of their parents and grandparents.
It is a kind of symbiotic effect in which the generations, by inter-
acting, are giving new meaning to their lives.

It was a common trait of the Greatest Generation not to discuss the difficult times and how they shaped their lives, but now,
in their twilight years, more and more members of that remarkable
group of men and women are determined to share their experiences.

Frankly, when the second book was finished, I thought we had
exhausted the supply of fresh material, but the stories keep coming in, describing history as it was lived by ordinary people—on
D-Day, on Bataan, during the Battle of Midway, and so on. I have
come to realize that there are still so many stories to be told, so
many lessons to be learned from even the briefest recollections of
that time of deprivation and war, heroism and belief, uncertainty
and peril.

So this album of memories is a way of celebrating more of

those lives and preserving their memories and stories. It is designed to complement the earlier books and also the new World War II memorial in Washington, D.C. Part of the proceeds from the sale of *An Album of Memories* will be dedicated to the work of the memorial.

Again, I am deeply indebted to the men and women whose stories you will find here, and to their children and friends who offered their reflections as well.

I am, as always, especially grateful for the inexhaustible and invaluable assistance of Elizabeth Bowyer and Philip Napoli, Ph.D. This book would not have been possible without them.

I am grateful too for the assistance of James Danly.

At NBC, Diana Rubin, Meaghan Rady, Sara Perkowski, and Eric Wishnie were tireless and extremely well organized in their dedication to this project.

Once again, Kate Medina, my friend and editor at Random House, was the company commander, a cool and insightful mentor and motivator.

Others at Random House without whom this book could not have been accomplished include Frankie Jones, Benjamin Dreyer, Carole Lowenstein, Andy Carpenter, Richard Elman, Susan Brown, and Maria Massey.

I am greatly indebted to the British military historian John Keegan for his masterpiece, *The Second World War,* and to Stanford professor David Kennedy for his monumental Pulitzer Prize winner, *Freedom from Fear: The American People in Depression and War, 1929–1945.* They were invaluable references.

Finally, when I was moved to write the original book, *The Greatest Generation,* it was a labor of love. I did not anticipate the changes it would bring to my own life. It has been, simply, the most fulfilling professional experience of my career and a deeply emotional personal experience. I feel privileged to have the opportunity to share these lives with you.

CONTENTS

———•———

ABOVE: *Bob Barrigan, a fellow sailor, and several Marines witness the aftermath of the Pearl Harbor attack from atop the Naval Operations building, approximately 11:00 A.M., December 7, 1941. "We were fully expecting an invasion and were sent to the rooftop with rifles. One sailor did not know how to load his and had to ask me for help."* (U.S. Navy Historical Center photo)

RIGHT: *Wearing a black armband, President Franklin D. Roosevelt signs a declaration of war against Japan, a day after the bombing of Pearl Harbor.* (TimePix)

B<small>ETWEEN</small> 1929 <small>AND THE END OF WORLD WAR II IN</small> 1945, the world was in economic, political, military, and cultural turmoil on a scale unprecedented in recorded history. Earlier periods of great disruption brought on by the ambitions of the Roman empire or Genghis Khan, the bubonic plague in Europe or the changing of a dynasty in China, were largely regional events. But by the third decade of the twentieth century, air and sea transportation, communications technology—the telephone and radio—and trade had made the world a much smaller place, where regional events had global ramifications. As the United States would learn in painful and costly fashion, the presence of two great oceans east and west did not insulate America from the ravages of economic chaos, the cruelty of nature, and the winds of far-off wars.

The American stock market collapse in 1929 was the beginning of a radical change of fortune for the United States, and it coincided with the rise of sinister political forces in the heart of Europe and in Asia. In Europe, Adolf Hitler was plotting to take over Germany with his National Socialist Party, the Nazis. In Asia, Japan was preparing to extend its political and military ambitions well beyond that tiny island nation.

To the average American, however, those distant developments were of little consequence when measured against the frightening state of the U.S. economy. The numbers were staggering. In three years stocks lost 80 percent of their value. The Ford Motor Company employed 128,000 workers in 1929; by 1931 that number had dropped to 37,000. American farmers who had sold a bushel of corn for 77 cents in 1929 were getting only 32 cents a bushel by 1932. By then the American economy was in a free fall. The sad effect was a plague of unemployment, bankruptcy, foreclosure, and broken dreams, from Wall Street to main street and beyond. Zelpha Simmons writes about the hardships her family faced during those years. Just a teenager at the time, Simmons took a full-time job as a bookkeeper, earning fifteen dollars a week. The only wage earner for a family of five, her family "made it with a milk cow, garden and chickens and hard work."

A patrician confined to a wheelchair, Franklin Delano Roosevelt won the 1932 Democratic presidential nomination to run against the incumbent, Herbert Hoover, a brilliant engineer who had had a distinguished career in public service and in the private sector before he entered the White House just in time for the calamities that led to the Great Depression.

As FDR was awaiting his inauguration in 1933, Hitler was sworn in as chancellor of the German Republic. In the United States, small and large banks were collapsing. In his inaugural address on March 4, 1933, the new president assured a national radio audience, "The only thing we have to fear is fear itself." Given what was to come, it was an especially bold and inspirational affirmation of the new leadership in the White House.

When President Roosevelt set out to rebuild the American spirit and economy with what he promised was a New Deal, he could not ignore the ominous developments in Europe and Asia. As the 1930s wore on, tensions rose around the globe. The inability of the League of Nations to respond to the Japanese occupation of Manchuria in 1931 weakened the organization. The League ordered Japan to withdraw from Manchuria in 1933; instead, Japan withdrew from the League. In 1933 Germany withdrew from a disarmament conference, then from the League itself. By 1934 Austrian Nazis seemed poised to reconnect Germany and Austria. On July 25 the Austrian prime minister, Engelbert Dollfuss, was assassinated by Austrian Nazis. Italy, not yet a German ally, rushed its troops to the Austrian border, and a show of force prevented the union. In 1935 Hitler began to rebuild the German army, navy, and air force. It was widely known that Germany was violating the arms limitation clauses of the Treaty of Versailles that had ended World War I. Still, German aggression went unchecked. In 1936 Hitler gambled on the Western unwillingness to fight and sent troops into the Rhineland. The French and British did nothing.

Meanwhile, the Italians practiced aggression of their own. A skirmish in the desert in December 1934 served as public pretext for the Italian invasion of Ethiopia in October 1935. The League of Nations responded by prohibiting the sale of war materials to Italy, and while most countries went along with the embargo and it caused some hardship, the war did not stop. Oil, the most important item of all, had been left off the list of embargoed items. Ethiopia was defeated in 1936 and combined with Italian Somaliland and Eritrea into an Italian East African empire.

Spain too proved to be a flash point. In 1936 a group of military men led by Francisco Franco mounted an insurrection against a legally elected republican government, and the country descended into a civil war that would cost more than 500,000 lives.

wounded. Britain: 1 million dead, 2 million wounded. Italy: 600,000 dead, 1 million wounded. United States: 100,000 dead, 200,000 wounded. Russia: 1.7 million dead, 5 million wounded. Losses in a single battle could be appalling: At Verdun (1916), the Germans and the French lost more than 300,000 each; Passchendaele cost the Brtitish more than 250,000.

JAN. 1919

Paris Peace Conference
During the drafting of the Treaty of Versailles, Britain and France both want reparations; France wants reparations large enough to cripple Germany. At the insistence of French and British leaders, President Woodrow Wilson acquiesces to the war-guilt clause, requiring Germany to accept guilt and pay the entire cost of the war.

Austria, Czechoslovakia, Hungary, Poland, and Yugoslavia emerge from the treaty as newly formed or independent countries. The Allies establish a ring of hostile states—Finland, Estonia, Latvia, and Lithuania, all formerly part of the Russian empire—around Bolshevik Russia.

JUNE 28, 1919

Germany signs the Treaty of Versailles.

SEPT. 1919

Adolf Hitler joins the German Workers' Party.

1920

German Workers' Party renames itself National Socialist German Workers' Party, or NSDAP. It will be known to the world as the Nazi Party.

In Great Britain, Winston Churchill, deep in the political wilderness, was increasingly alarmed and characteristically pugnacious in his warnings to the English government. He was ignored.

Then, in a rapid succession of events, the situation deteriorated. During the next three years Hitler took control of the German military and forced Austria to become a part of Germany. He moved on to Czechoslovakia, prompting British Prime Minister Neville Chamberlain to make increasingly desperate attempts at appeasement, ending with the infamously flawed Munich agreement. Czechoslovakia was betrayed, and Chamberlain secured his ignominious place in history by returning to England to proclaim "peace in our time."

Hitler quickly followed with a formal military alliance with his fellow fascist Benito Mussolini of Italy, then startled the West by signing a nonaggression pact with the Soviet Union, pledging not to invade Russia in exchange for Russia promising not to intervene if Germany was attacked by a third party.

Americans would watch these developments in the newsreels when they went to the movies for a little relief from their personal struggles against the ravages of the Depression. Or they would read in the newspapers of Hitler's ruthless ambitions and hear about them on radio, the new medium that became the central nervous system of the country. But the news out of Europe and Asia was not a call to arms for the United States. It remained fiercely isolationist, fighting its own war against the Depression at home.

The United States was determined to remain on the sidelines internationally, bound by the Neutrality Acts of 1935 and 1937. But FDR, who had so skillfully led the nation through the economic crisis with a patchwork of government aid programs, banking reforms, and iconic optimism, was deeply worried about the overseas developments. By the autumn of 1939, in one of his radio fireside chats, the master communicator assured the American people, "This will remain a neutral nation." Then he added, "But I cannot ask that every American remain neutral in thought as well." He was nudging the United States into the fight.

Within a month President Roosevelt was working with Congress to repeal the arms embargo in the Neutrality Act. The repeal, which would permit England and France to buy arms from the United States on a cash-and-carry basis, passed in early November, just eight months before the German invasion of France and the Netherlands.

United States defense preparedness efforts were stepped up. In September 1940 the American government conducted the first peacetime draft in its history. By the end of 1940, with FDR re-elected, Congress had approved $37 billion in military spending. In March 1941 Congress passed the Lend-Lease Bill, which permitted Roosevelt to lend, lease, or in any way dispose of war materials to any country considered vital to American security. Although the initial appropriation was $7 billion, by the end of the war the United States had spent roughly $50 billion on Lend-Lease. It was understood this would provide material assistance to the Allied cause.

As the Battle of the Atlantic raged, Hitler invaded the Soviet Union on June 22. At first few believed the Soviets could survive more than several months. By winter, however, even though Nazi troops were not far from Moscow, it had become clear that the USSR would not collapse. Roosevelt announced that Marines would occupy Iceland as a step in the defense of the Western Hemisphere, and he began military Lend-Lease aid to the Soviet Union in November. By the end of the war, the USSR would receive $11 billion worth of this assistance.

At the same time, American relations with Japan soured. The United States had watched unhappily as Japan seized larger and larger slices of Chinese territory during the 1930s. American power was insufficient to halt Japanese aggression, and anyway, Japan was a larger trading partner than China. Still, Japanese movement in Southeast Asia in 1940 pressured the administration to do something. In July 1940, Roosevelt placed an embargo on aviation fuel and the high-grade scrap iron wanted by Japan. In September 1940 Japan seized northern French Indochina. Five days later came the news that Japan had signed the Tripartite Pact with Germany and Italy. Each nation pledged to aid the others if attacked by a nation not currently involved in the war. Because the Soviet Union was explicitly exempted from the pact, Washington was the clear target. Roosevelt later extended the embargo to all scrap metal. In July 1941, when Japanese troops moved into southern Indochina, the president froze all Japanese funds in the United States, effectively stopping trade with Japan.

The diplomacy of the remainder of 1941 was ineffective. In October a new Japanese government was formed, headed by General

---

NOV. 8, 1932

Franklin Delano Roosevelt wins the U.S. presidential election.

Between the election and the inauguration, the American economy deteriorates badly. By early 1933 almost every bank in the country has stopped paying depositors, and most banks are threatened with bankruptcy.

JAN. 30, 1933

Hitler becomes chancellor of the German Republic.

FEB. 27, 1933

The German Reichstag is set on fire. One Communist is convicted, but the Nazi Party likely had a role.

MAR. 4, 1933

In his inaugural address FDR asserts that "the only thing we have to fear is fear itself."

The Nazi Party gains 43 percent of the German vote and a small majority in the Reichstag.

MAR. 5, 1933

FDR calls Congress into special session and launches the legislative initiatives that will be known as the New Deal. By the end of his first 100 days in office, Congress will have enacted legislation on banking, industry, agriculture, labor, and unemployment relief.

MAR. 10, 1933

The first concentration camp is established near Munich at Dachau.

MAR. 23, 1933

The German Reichstag passes the Enabling Act, which gives Hitler special powers.

JULY 25, 1934

Austrian Nazis assassinate Chancellor Engelbert Dollfuss.

Hideki Tojo, and the next month negotiations began between the two governments, with the Japanese demanding that the United States release their assets and resume normal trade relations. The United States' response was to insist that Japan remove its troops from China and Indochina, and recognize the legitimacy of the Chinese nationalist government headed by Chiang Kai-shek. By the end of November negotiations had effectively broken down. On November 26, the Japanese carrier force that would strike Pearl Harbor, Hawaii, set sail. Without warning, the Japanese attack began on December 7, 1941. Emery Morrison was standing watch on the USS *Raleigh* that morning when enemy planes roared overhead. Within minutes, the *Raleigh's* electrical compartment was hit by a torpedo, and water and oil began gushing into the ship's hull. Morrison describes the crew's frantic efforts to save the badly damaged ship, and finally their long swim to shore through oil-slicked waters, fearing that at any minute the Japanese attackers would return.

By the end of that fateful morning, all the world was at war.

*Bob Cromer (right) with his
mother and brother Earle, 1928.
"This is how we dressed: high button
shoes, long stockings, and
hated garter belts."*

Bob Cromer in 1930, age three.

*Bob Cromer playing with
a homemade toy gun, 1934.
"Tire inner-tubes were all over
the place. We used the rubber
for guns and slingshots."*

*Bob Cromer (center) and childhood
friends, 1935.*

*Bob Cromer with sister Betty
and dog Rinnie in Roundlake, Illinois, 1934.
"We had a summer cottage there with
no running water. We had to walk about
a mile to the pump with buckets."
(All courtesy of Bob Cromer)*

——— • ———

Dear Mr. Brokaw:

I went to war as a replacement, in the 309th Infantry Regiment of the 78th Division. My youth was snatched away from me when, at age eighteen, I went into combat and was forced to grow up overnight. I spent my nineteenth birthday in a small hospital in Vaals Holland, convalescing from my first wound. Combat was terrible and I lost many friends in battle, and yet I think that ours was one of the most fortunate of all generations.

We were privileged to grow up in a time when honor, truth, loyalty, duty and patriotism were real and meant something.

What made the generation great? We were simply a product of our times. Growing up in the Depression was not a great honor, but it was a classroom that taught us to be independent and innovative. We made our own toys out of orange crates and roller skates. We made our kites from newspapers and we melted lead to pour into molds to make soldiers, cowboys and Indians. We made rubber guns from a piece of 2 × 4, a half a clothespin, and a section of inner tube from a car tire. When we played hockey we made makeshift goals and played on the ice on the river, some wearing hockey skates and some wearing racing skates. Whatever games we played we didn't have adults supervising us; we made up our own teams and played by our own rules. I think that this knack for innovation later helped our generation, as soldiers, to devise new and unheard-of ways to overcome unforeseen obstacles in combat.

The Depression was a leveler too. I grew up in what was considered a middle-class family—by today's standards we would be considered poor, but nobody came around to tell us so. Everyone was in the same boat, and extended families helped each other. I wore many clothes that had belonged to one of my cousins or my big brother. Getting some bit of clothing of your own that was new was a big event. There were many people who had much less than we did, but they never let on and we never knew. The community sort of stuck together and family was very important. Parents were role models. I remember getting into a lot of mischief when I was growing up but nothing really bad. In the back of my mind was always the thought, "Don't ever do anything to bring disgrace to your family." I never thought of "me first" or "do your own thing," and neither did anyone else. I am sure that these traits helped us in combat to stick together and look out for each other.

All of these things stayed with us after the war was over (though, really, the war was never over). It changed us all. Somewhere in the deep recesses of the mind there is a little voice that reminds us from time to time, "You survived. You are alive. Don't waste your life. Do something with it."

While I was convalescing once again in a hospital in Paris, after being wounded the second time, I began to think of my future. It was there that I first started to think about becoming a doctor. I wanted to make my life count as one that was worthwhile. But after the atom bomb was dropped (which, incidentally, I believe with all my heart saved me from certain death in the invasion of Japan), for a while I was at loose ends. I thought that perhaps the world would end in a few years, so why not live it up while I could. But that little voice was still there and it said to me, "You must live your life as if the world will go on. You're alive." So, with the help of Public Law 16, I finished college and went on to medical school. I then went to a small rural town where I could be a real doctor. I married, and my wife and I have five children. After 44 years I am still practicing medicine.

I don't know about the "Greatest Generation" stuff. In my mind we were the most fortunate generation, especially in the things that really count. Who could ask for anything more.

Robert Cromer

———— • ————

Dear Tom:

My name is Elias Hellerstein (my friends call me Ellie—a nickname I picked up during the Depression years from my family).

I'll give you a short family background. Both of my parents were born in the 1880s on the East Side of New York. I was the youngest of four children. I was born in 1927 and, growing up, we didn't really want for anything. My father was a bartender who had a steady job in the Depression years. In fact, he worked 50 years as a bartender, right up to the day he passed away in 1959. Of course, things were tight for everybody, even for people who had a steady job. I remember, when I was 8 years old, I used to sell newspapers.

SEPT. 30, 1938
Czechoslovakia is divided without its consent in the Munich agreement. Chamberlain, convinced of a diplomatic victory, calls the agreement "peace in our time." Most of western Europe is wildly enthusiastic.

MAR. 1939
Germany annexes the remainder of Czechoslovakia.
Hitler puts pressure on Poland to adjust the Polish corridor, which separates Germany from parts of Eastern Prussia. Britain and France pledge aid to protect Polish independence.

MAR. 28, 1939
The Spanish Civil War ends with victory by Franco. Spain will remain neutral in the coming European conflict.

APR. 7, 1939
Italy invades Albania.

MAY 22, 1939
Germany and Italy conclude a military alliance.

AUG. 24, 1939
Germany and Russia sign a nonaggression pact, agreeing not to attack each other and to remain neutral if either is attacked by a third power.

AUG. 25, 1939
Hitler demands a free hand against Poland.

AUG. 30, 1939
Poland begins partial mobilization.

SEPT. 1, 1939
Germany attacks Poland, on land and in the air, with an army of approximately 1,500,000. Britain and France mobilize but are willing to negotiate if German forces are withdrawn. Italy remains neutral.

Sept. 3, 1939

Britain and France declare war on Germany.

In a fireside chat, FDR declares that "this nation will remain a neutral nation, but I cannot ask that every American remain neutral in thought as well."

Sept. 8, 1939

FDR declares a limited national emergency.

Sept. 19, 1939

Soviet troops, having invaded Poland from the east, meet German forces near Brest Litovsk.

Sept. 28, 1939

Warsaw surrenders.

Sept. 29, 1939

Germany and the USSR divide Poland.

Oct. 1939

Albert Einstein informs FDR of the possibility of developing an atomic bomb.

Nov. 4, 1939

The U.S. Neutrality Act of 1939 repeals the arms embargo and authorizes cash-and-carry exports of arms and munitions to nations at war.

Nov. 30, 1939

Soviet armies attack Finland.

Dec. 14, 1939

The USSR is expelled from the League of Nations.

Mar. 12, 1940

Finland surrenders to the USSR, losing approximately 16,000 square miles and 25,000 dead.

Apr. 9, 1940

Germany invades Norway and Denmark.

I would buy the papers off the truck (the *Daily News* and *The Daily Mirror*) on 157th St. and Broadway in New York. I would buy 10 of the *News* and 10 of the *Mirrors* off the truck when they came to make their newsstand delivery. I paid a penny apiece, and for 20 cents, I had 20 papers. But I wouldn't sell them for 2 cents, as the newsstands did, because that wasn't enough profit for me—just a penny on each paper. So I would go down to the subway. On the train, I would sell my papers for a nickel apiece. I usually sold every single one of them by the time I got back to 157th St. Pretty good profit in those days. Of course, that was at night. I used to get the papers at 8:30 or 9:00 at night, and by the time I rode downtown a half hour and a half hour back, I was home by 10:00 or a little after. It wasn't that bad. I also sold magazines during the day. I used to sell *Saturday Evening Post* and *Ladies' Home Journal*. I hustled. I was a hustling kid. Right up to now, even in retirement.

Thanks a lot. Bless you.

Elias Hellerstein

———— • ————

Dear Mr. Brokaw:

I also was a member of the greatest generation, born January 25, 1914. I am now 85 years of age. As a small child I remember the end of World War I. Church bells were ringing and guns were being fired in celebration.

Zelpha Simmons standing next to a Ford that she and her husband, Johnny, bought in 1937 for five hundred dollars.
(Courtesy of Zelpha Simmons)

LEFT: *Zelpha Simmons ready for church, 1930s.* RIGHT: *Zelpha Simmons, wearing a dress that she made, around 1940. (Both courtesy of Zelpha Simmons)*

I vividly recall the struggles of the Depression years. I finished Bessemer High School at age 16 in May of 1930 and went to work in the fall at S. H. Kress store in Bessemer, Alabama, for $9.00 a week as a salesclerk, hours 8 a.m. until 6 p.m., on Saturday until 9 p.m. If you had a dime you could buy a box of face powder or a small can of paint. After seven years my salary as bookkeeper was $15.00 a week. I was the sole support of a family of five. We made it with a milk cow, garden and chickens and hard work.

During World War II, the *Birmingham News* daily listed the men who were killed. I read the names of classmates. I wondered will it ever end.

My husband and I did not get higher educations, but we started a business in Bessemer [that lasted] for 40 years. However, our son, John, now has a Ph.D. in mathematics and a Ph.D. in computer science from Indiana University.

May God bless.

Yours truly,
Zelpha P. Simmons

APR. 30, 1940
Norwegian King Haakon VII and his cabinet flee to London.

MAY 10, 1940
Germany invades the Netherlands, Belgium, and Luxembourg. The war in western Europe has begun. Winston Churchill replaces Chamberlain as the British prime minister.

MAY 11, 1940
German forces capture Fort Eben Emael, a key Belgian defense.

MAY 14, 1940
The Netherlands government, headed by Queen Wilhelmina, escapes to London. The army of the Netherlands surrenders.

MAY 16, 1940
FDR asks Congress for $1 billion to modernize the military, including plans to produce 50,000 airplanes a year.

MAY 17, 1940
German mechanized divisions sweep into France.

MAY 28, 1940
With the surrender of Belgium, Allied forces retreat to Dunkirk.

MAY 31–JUNE 4, 1940
The British rescue 200,000 British and 140,000 French troops from the beaches of Dunkirk.

JUNE 4, 1940
Churchill, in a speech before the House of Commons, declares: "We shall not flag or fail. We shall go on to the end. We shall fight in France, we shall fight on the seas and oceans, we shall fight with growing confidence and growing strength in the air, we shall defend our island, whatever the

—— • ——

cost may be. We shall fight on the beaches, we shall fight on the landing grounds, we shall fight in the fields and in the streets, we shall fight in the hills; we shall never surrender."

JUNE 10, 1940
Italy declares war on France and Britain. Italian forces prepare to invade southern France.

JUNE 16, 1940
The World War I hero Marshal Philippe Pétain replaces Paul Reynaud as head of the French government.

JUNE 17, 1940
Soviet forces occupy Lithuania, Latvia, and Estonia.

JUNE 22, 1940
France signs an armistice with Germany at Compiègne. French forces are to be disarmed, and three-fifths of France is to be occupied by Germany.

JUNE 27, 1940
FDR establishes the National Defense Research Committee.

JULY 1940
In London, Charles de Gaulle continues to pledge French opposition to Germany.
FDR appoints Henry Stimson secretary of war and Frank Knox secretary of the Navy, forming a government that includes both Republicans and Democrats.

AUG. 1940
German planes start a bombing offensive to destroy British air strength. The Battle of Britain has begun.

AUG. 17, 1940
Germany declares a total blockade of the British islands.

Dear Mr. Brokaw,

I was eight years of age in 1936, living in Rumford, Maine. My father was a house painter. One day he fell off the old scaffolding, three stories high. The scaffolding fell on him, crushing his leg and ribs. He was laid up for almost a year and in a cast from his toes to his neck, and was unable to work. This was a very hard time as work was very scarce.

This forced the family to go to the town for support. We were 6 children to feed and clothe. The oldest was 14. Every week my mother had to walk to the town hall and sign up; literally beg for food, rent and clothing. Some weeks she would receive a pair of shoes or a check made out to a certain grocery store for food. The town also doled out some flour, cornmeal, turnips or potatoes, but not much of any of these.

I always felt the town manager was a mean old man. He gave my mother such a hard time; she would come out of his office with her eyes red from crying. It made me feel so bad that I couldn't do anything to help.

One say I will always remember, my mother and I were walking home from the town hall with a bag of potatoes and cornmeal on a sled. It was cold, windy and snowing. I told my mother I would find some kind of work so I could give her money each week.

I got a paper route and delivered papers 7 days a week; working from 6 a.m. to finish in time for school. I delivered the "Grit" for 2 cents a week per customer and I had 30 customers; the "Rumford Falls Times" at 3 cents per customer; and on Sunday I received 5 cents per paper and had 50 customers. Everything I earned went to my mother for our family.

There were times we had no electricity because we had no money to pay the bill. We had a couple of kerosene lamps, which were used for light to do our homework for school.

In 1938, we had the best Christmas ever. My Aunt Anna from New Haven sent us a large box of toys and clothes. Also that year, the different clubs of the town of Rumford, Maine, gave our family baskets of food, fruit and nuts. The church, Elks, and VFW helped us through this Christmas season. We usually got a pair of mittens for Christmas and were very proud of them.

When my father had the cast removed and was able to move

Helen Ryan in front of the café where she waited tables for fifty cents a day to earn money for college.

Helen Ryan in 1935.

Helen Ryan in front of her parents' home in Houghton, South Dakota, 1930.

Helen Ryan, senior-year high school photos.

Helen Ryan in 1935, outside her parents' home in Houghton. "There were about five hundred people in that town when I grew up, and I don't even know if it is there anymore."
(All courtesy of Helen Ryan)

Aug. 25, 1940

A lost German bomber drops its load on the center of London. The British will respond by ordering attacks on Berlin.

Sept. 3, 1940

Britain and the United States conclude the destroyers-for-bases deal, in which the British are given fifty obsolete American destroyers in exchange for long-term leases on several naval and air bases in the Western Hemisphere.

Sept. 7, 1940

The Blitz begins as 1,000 German aircraft strike London virtually unopposed.

Sept. 16, 1940

FDR signs the Selective Training and Service Act, the first peacetime draft in American history, providing for registration of all men ages twenty-one through thirty-five.

Sept. 27, 1940

Germany, Italy, and Japan sign the Tripartite Pact, a ten-year military and economic alliance, creating the Axis.

Oct. 7, 1940

German troops enter Romania.

Oct. 28, 1940

Italy invades Greece from Albania.

Oct. 29, 1940

The first draft numbers are selected in the United States.

Nov. 5, 1940

FDR is elected to an unprecedented third term as U.S. president.

around on his own, he couldn't work but he had enough strength to cut rubber tires for fuel to heat the house. My sister and I and our friends would go around to all the garages and bring home the used tires. We would push the tires like hoops to make it fun to do. My father and oldest brother would slice the tires up for the stove. My father would say that the smell of rubber burning was much better than being cold.

In 1936, my oldest brother joined the CCC. This gave my mother some money each month for expenses. We were able to get off the town support. He joined the Army in 1938 and was killed in the Philippines in 1945. I enlisted in the Merchant Marines when I was just 16, so my mother had to sign the papers for me to join. The day I left for the service was the day they held a Mass for my brother.

Sincerely,
Armand J. Beauchesne

———— • ————

Dear Tom:

My husband, Bill, and I lived through the Depression, hoping someday to have a good job when we graduated in 1939 and Bill got in the F.B.I.

My children of eight, now seven, can't believe I worked for $.50 a day to save for college. My parents had all they could do to get $35.00 for tuition. I worked in Citizen Bank for $35.00 and paid my room and board. I went to college with one skirt and sweater and one dress for parties. Today, young ones can't believe it.

I remember the day my mother called and said FDR closed the small bank in Houghton where my father worked. Something like [if] today one goes to work in the morning and by noon he doesn't have a job. My husband went to Inland Steel with Industrial Relations after 11 years in the F.B.I. Steel people are feeling the dumping of steel from other countries. I worry as I have three sons in steel.

Memorial Days are not celebrated like [they were in] days gone by. That was the thing we did on Memorial Day—go to the cemetery.

God bless.

Sincerely,
Helen L. Ryan

Dear Mr. Brokaw,

I have some memories of my parents talking about hard times during the Depression (as I was born in 1935, my childhood memories of outside events really begin with Pearl Harbor—not so oddly, that is still very clear in my memory, as are other WWII memories).

I remember, without being able to put a date on it, my parents arguing about money. At night I could overhear them, as my bedroom was just above the dining room and sound carried extraordinarily well through the heating system vents. I don't remember the details of those arguments—just the tense and, on occasion, raised voices, and the feeling of worry and fear that seemed to fill the air. This was true despite my father being well placed financially (relatively speaking). He had been an aviator in World War I and returned to go to college and then begin teaching at the University of Virginia in the mid-1920s. As a university professor of architecture he was on a state salary, and although there were salary reductions in the mid-30s, I believe, as he told me once, he was never richer after than he was then. On his $2,000 a year or so, he was able to provide for us comfortably, and what's more, to build a new house out in what then were the suburbs, which meant he had a car as well to get to work. He told me that he was able to hire master carpenters, plumbers, and bricklayers for ten cents an hour, and they were overjoyed to get the work.

Not all my parents' friends were so well placed, of course, and I am sure some of the anxiety they felt spread to my family. My mother told me, sadly, of the number of good lawyers who had to keep up the pretense of success (who wants to employ an unsuccessful lawyer?) but if you looked closely you could see how frayed their collars and shirt sleeves had become and how shiny the seats and knees of their dark business suits were. She often would choke up and cry when she would talk about those times: I remember her saying once, "A person shouldn't have to be ashamed to be poor, but we are. All of us are."

Living as we did in a predominantly rural area, with the biggest two businesses being the university and the hospital, the Depression as such had done all sorts of damage to the farmers since the very early 1920s. My father came to Charlottesville from Indiana,

Nov. 11, 1940
British planes destroy or damage half the Italian fleet at Taranto. The attack is seen by some as a model for the Japanese attack at Pearl Harbor.

Dec. 29, 1940
In a fireside chat FDR urges that America become the arsenal of democracy, supplying Britain with the material needed to defeat Hitler.

Jan. 6, 1941
In his State of the Union address, FDR asks Congress to pass the Lend-Lease Bill, allowing him to lend, lease, or in any way dispose of war materials to any country considered vital to American security. The bill will be passed on Mar. 11.

Apr. 6, 1941
German troops invade Yugoslavia and Greece.

Apr. 11, 1941
FDR announces that the United States will extend its security zone farther into the Atlantic Ocean to guard against German submarines.

Apr. 17, 1941
Yugoslavia surrenders to Germany.

Apr. 23, 1941
Greece signs an armistice with Germany.

May 20, 1941
German paratroopers invade Crete.

May 27, 1941
FDR proclaims a state of unlimited national emergency.

June 22, 1941
Germany invades the USSR. Soviet units on the frontier retreat.

JUNE 25, 1941

FDR establishes the Fair Employment Practices Committee to prevent racial discrimination in defense work.

JULY 13, 1941

Britain and the USSR conclude a mutual-aid pact.

AUG. 14, 1941

FDR and Churchill issue the Atlantic Charter, setting forth goals for the world, including denunciation of aggression, right of peoples to choose their own governments, access to raw materials, freedom from want and fear for all nations, freedom of the sea, and disarmament of aggressors.

SEPT. 8, 1941

Germany begins the siege of Leningrad, which will not end until January 1944.

OCT. 17, 1941

The U.S. destroyer Kearny is torpedoed by a German U-boat.

OCT. 31, 1941

The U.S. destroyer Reuben James is sunk by a German U-boat.

NOV. 5, 1941

The Japanese imperial general headquarters issues plans for an offensive against the U.S. fleet at Pearl Harbor, British Malaya, the Philippines, and the Netherlands East Indies.

NOV. 15, 1941

Special Japanese Ambassador Saburo Kurusu arrives in the United States to attempt to reopen trade negotiations.

and he told me how when he first got to Virginia, he was stunned at the terrible damage done to the soil. As he put it, the Blue Ridge Mountains were not blue, they were a dull brown, from having been cut to the bare rock and soil. All the local streams (we called them "creeks") would run a dark reddish brown from eroded soil anytime it rained at all. Once at my grandmother's farm, I saw the red water spread all over the hay fields during a spring flood. I didn't realize then that the water wouldn't have been that color had it not been cutting deep ravines in all the farmland.

Just as the forests had been cut down, the farms had been overworked. According to my mother, it was during this time particularly that many of the smaller farmers lost their farms either to the larger enterprises around them or to money coming in from out of state—or, as my mother phrased it, "Yankee money." And this was the beginning, ironically, of Charlottesville and Albemarle County becoming "fashionable'" as horse country and a place for well-to-do northerners to retire to become gentleman farmers.

All the best
Stan Makielski

———— • ————

Dear Tom:

My name is Steve Kish, born in Duquesne, PA, 1920, August 1. My parents were immigrants from Austria-Hungary. Mom [was] from the Carpathian Mt. Country and my dad's homeland was the Transylvania area. Their native tongue—Hungarian.

Your book brought me back thoughts of my youth, particularly after my father, Louis Kish, died in 1937, at the age of 42 from an illness stemming from typhoid he contracted as a youngster.

I was the oldest at home and had just started my senior year in high school when he passed on in October of 1937. At the time I was employed as a grocery clerk working after school and weekends. $7.00 a week. My mother was going to take me out of school, but the principal and football coach talked her out of that, promising to get me work if she let me graduate.

They were good to their word. I was [one of] four out of ninety students who went to work. I worked steadily until Sept. of 1942, when I was drafted into the service.

When I was called before the Draft Board, they asked me what I contributed to my family's upkeep. My entire paycheck from the factory, I answered. Where do you get your spending money. From a second job at the grocery store.

I was to go in November of 1942. But a young man broke his leg, and they were kind enough to send me in September. All my friends went with me, and I was elated to go. Learned more during the next two and one-half years than I did in twelve years of schooling.

Spent my time as an M.P. until I was injured (bad leg) and received medical discharge at the end of 1944. From then until now [I've] had many forms of employment—steel mills, machine shops, catering company, and finally for seventeen years a bridge estimator.

Publically [I] was a union president, president of Hungarian Social Club, board member of Greek Orthodox Church. My wife is of Greek parentage. Got involved in politics as a councilman and was president of Council for ten years or so.

Steve Kish, age twenty-two, in 1942.
(Courtesy of Steve Kish)

We have a daughter, special ed teacher, and two good grandchildren, one girl and one boy.

Two things make me proud and happy. If I could not help anyone, I would not harm them with words or deed. I am successful because I am going to leave it better than I got it.

With great sincerity,
Steve A. Kish

———— • ————

NOV. 26, 1941

U.S. Secretary of State Cordell Hull says Japan would have to withdraw from Indochina and China, and recognize the Chinese national government. Japan rejects his conditions. The Japanese Pearl Harbor strike force sets sail.

DEC. 3, 1941

Japanese embassies in the United States begin to burn secret documents.

DEC. 7, 1941

Japan attacks the American fleet at Pearl Harbor, Hawaii. Almost 2,400 U.S. soldiers and sailors are killed; 19 U.S. ships, including 8 battleships, are sunk or badly damaged; 188 U.S. aircraft are destroyed. Japanese losses total 29 aircraft and 6 submarines.

DEC. 8, 1941

FDR calls December 7 "a date which will live in infamy." The United States declares war on Japan.

DEC. 11, 1941

Germany and Italy declare war on the United States. The United States ends its neutrality in Europe and declares war on Germany and Italy.

Dear Mr. Brokaw:

My husband was in the Navy at Pearl Harbor when it was bombed. He was 17 years old, and it was, of course, a life-changing experience. Bob retired from the U.S. Navy after 30 years and immediately went to work for the Federal Aviation Administration (FAA). He retired from the FAA after 25 years of service. I have attached a copy of what I said at his retirement party. It gives you some background on Bob and his personality.

I have thought a lot about the kind of man my husband, Bob Barrigan, is. All of the Barrigan men are a little stubborn. But all of them have a great patriotic love for their country. The first time I met Bob's dad, the thing I noticed most about them was how patriotic they were. There were five daughters and four sons, and all four of the sons served in the Navy. During the war years, the Barrigan home in California was a haven for a lot of servicemen. They could always get a meal there or find a place to sleep. Bob was 17 years old, was in the Navy, and was at Pearl Harbor when the Japanese attacked it.

Bob Barrigan at Ford Island Air Station, approximately 4:30 P.M., December 7, 1941. (U.S. Navy Archive photo)

Recently, at the request of the war historian, Bob wrote up his recollections of the events that happened that day. He said he could remember everything as if it were yesterday. Bob was not on his ship at the time of the attack. He and another man had been sent to the island that weekend to pick up some equipment that was needed on the ship. Saturday night Bob had been to a USO dance. He spent the night in a barracks with other servicemen from all branches of the service. That infamous Sunday, of course, there was mass confusion on the island as well as in the barracks. A senior-ranking serviceman rounded up a small band of men, gave them weapons and ammunition, and told them to go to the roof of the barracks and see what they could do. As Bob made his way up to the roof, he noticed firecrackers going off all around him, and when he got to the roof, the firecrackers were going off all around the roof. Of course, it took him a while to realize that it was not firecrackers at all, it was gunfire from the airplanes overhead. The planes were flying in so low to the roof that the men could actually see the faces of the pilots as they came down close to the roof to make their way to the harbor. Late that afternoon, the ranking serviceman told the group of men to go to the mess hall and get themselves something to eat and re-turn to the roof to prepare for a massive attack that everyone thought would take place that night. When they went into the mess hall, there were mounds of cold fried chicken piled on tables and there was also hot orange juice. They looked across the room, and stacked up under tables were bodies. The mess hall had also been turned into a temporary morgue. Of course, none of them could eat at all. To this day, Bob cannot eat cold fried chicken or drink orange juice. At 17 years of age, he grew up in a hurry that day. It changed his life forever—he says for the better. He loved his years in the Navy and credits those years with teaching him about life, compassion, discipline, and how to get a job done.

Bob Barrigan, age twenty, in Washington, D.C., 1943. (Courtesy of Irma Barrigan)

He has also loved his years with the Federal Aviation Administration. He wants the best for his country and for the Federal Aviation Administration. As a lot of you in this room know, if you had an important job to be done in a hurry and it had to be done right, you gave it to Bob Barrigan. He has a way of negotiating and maneuvering the system to get things accomplished that to some people would be impossible tasks. He is always willing to help anyone in need. No matter what the job, he finds a way to get it done. He took on the large jobs, but at the same time there was no job too small or beneath him to do.

Sincerely,
Irma L. Barrigan

———— • ————

Dear Mr. Brokaw:

Having just finished reading *The Greatest Generation,* I need to let you know my feelings about it.

I have intense memories of that time. Born outside of Phoenix, Arizona, in 1924, I fell in love with my husband when we were high school students in Tempe. Two days after his eighteenth birthday, my husband joined the Navy for six years, never dreaming what some of those years would be like. I was seventeen, a freshman in college, when Pearl Harbor was attacked and learned two weeks later (when censored mail finally began to come through) that my husband's ship had been bombed. The men swam ashore through oil-slicked water, but their ship was saved for further duty. During my junior year at Arizona State, my husband came home on ten days leave, and we were married. Later, I moved to Los Angeles, where I could be near whenever the ship docked in Long Beach. After a year of duty in the Pacific, the ship returned, and the ship decommissioned, which meant that my husband was transferred to a newly built ship on the East Coast, where I joined him. With only one year left until college graduation, I continued to follow him until his six years were up and he returned to Los Angeles, but I went to work to support us while he attended Occidental College for a degree in education. That's when I was given a PHT degree: Putting Hubby Through!!

For nearly fifteen years after the end of the war, my husband spoke of it rarely, but then some of his shipmates began to resurface and started some get-togethers. Later on we attended much larger reunions of the ship's members, held in many different states all over the country. There was an unbreakable bond among those ex-Navy men that has lasted all this time, drawing them and their families together in a unique way. When my husband died nearly two years ago, those same shipmates quickly passed the word and called me, wrote to me, and came to see me. After more than fifty years, my husband finally wrote an account of the Pearl Harbor attack, at the request of two people: myself and our 9-year-old grandson, who thought his "Papa" was his hero and knew all about that time in history. Needless to say, I treasure that written account, as well as the short one written by our grandson entitled "My Hero."

Sincerely,
Dovie Morrison

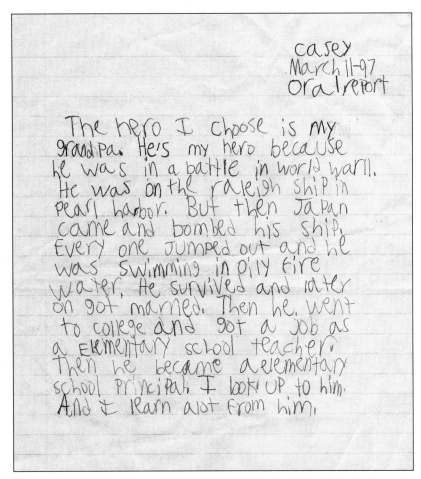

Casey
March 11-97
Oral report

The hero I choose is my grandpa. He's my hero because he was in a battle in world war II. He was on the raleigh ship in Pearl harbor. But then Japan came and bombed his ship. Every one jumped out and he was swimming in oily fire water. He survived and later on got married. Then he went to college and got a job as a elementary school teacher. Then he became a elementary school principal. I look up to him. And I learn alot from him.

School report written by Casey Morrison, age nine, about his grandfather Emery Morrison.
(Courtesy of Kimberly Morrison)

I Remember Pearl Harbor!

Having recently experienced the 50th anniversary of the attack on Pearl Harbor, I have been full of memories of the events in my life that led up to my being present at Pearl on December 7th, 1941. By popular request (two), I have decided to try to put together a loose narrative on what I remember and what I did on that very memorable day. Keep in mind that what I remember happened over fifty years ago, and my memory isn't quite what it used to be.

The morning of December 7th was one more beautiful day in paradise. Clear, blue, warm. I was up early, dressed in the uniform of the day, shorts, T-shirt, cap, white sox, black shoes. I had breakfast and was on my way topside to the radio shack to stand my 8:00–12:00 watch. I was about ten minutes early, so as I climbed the ladder from the main weather deck to the next level, the radio deck, I stopped on the top of the ladder to look over the starboard side of the ship at Ford Island, the navy air base. We were tied up at quay 12 next to Ford Island and directly across the island from battleship row. The *Detroit*, another four-stack cruiser like the *Raleigh*, was tied off our bow; the *Utah*, a battleship converted to a target ship, tied off our stern; the *Curtis*, a seaplane tender, was to port off our stern quarter about a half mile away. As I reached the radio bridge deck, I look over Ford Island to see all of the planes diving in line down to the runways, and I could see the puffs of smoke rising as they dropped something as they took off again. My thought was, what a strange time of day for a drill that realistic; they must be using smoke bombs or flour bombs; they sometimes do. As I stood at the railing midships looking aft, still puzzled, a plane zoomed right over our number one stack, so low I couldn't understand how he cleared our antenna; I could clearly see the pilot, the plane with its large red ball on the side, and the rear gunner, facing aft looking at me as I stared at him. Before it could register that the plane was Japanese, there was a terrific explosion almost under me, and a huge geyser of water shot up by number one stack. I was thrown from the railing where I was standing back against the steel bulkhead of the radio shack about five or six feet. I sat on the deck, back against the shack's bulkhead, dazed, trying to understand what had just happened.

Reality was beginning to register as men on the weather deck and the main deck below began to shout. I got to my feet, walked to the port side to see what had happened. There was nothing to see, but I could feel that we were already beginning to list to port. As I stood there, three more planes roared over the *Utah* behind us, and I saw the third one drop his torpedo. At almost the same moment I saw a huge geyser shoot up midships on the *Utah*, heard an explosion that almost immediately was followed by two more explosions from the *Utah*. She had been hit by three torpedoes, one right after the other. She was started to list immediately and rather fast. As I stood watching, she began to roll over. She started to roll slowly and then increased in speed; our general quarters alarm was sounding, and as I left the bridge deck to go to my battle station on the sound phones inside the radio shack, the *Utah* was totally on its port side and still turning. I entered the radio shack to put on the phones; everything was in total confusion, no one knew what was happening or why. Hawn was the 2nd class radioman and supervisor of the watch. He was pacing the deck, back and forth, shouting, "My time is up, I was to be discharged next week, I was going home and now these God damned Japs have started a war." (This isn't exactly what he said or the way he said it, this is a censored version.)

It seemed like a long time before our guns went into action, but it was really less than five minutes. All of our three-inch guns were under deck awnings and couldn't be elevated. Gunners were cutting the awnings down as fast as they could, and others were trying to get the ready boxes open to get to the shells. Our other 1.1 machine guns soon opened fire, and the "50's" on the bridge and the crow's nest took a little longer as they were farther away from the main deck. Ships all over the harbor were beginning to fire, and the noise was terrific. Antiaircraft bursts were starting to fill the skies, and smoke puffs were appearing all over the sky.

When we were hit with the torpedo, the two forward fire rooms and the forward engine room were destroyed immediately and we had lost all power. We had no steam, hence no electricity, no way to operate radio circuits, no lights, no electric lifts for the ammunition out of the ammunition magazines, and no sound power phones. I stayed on my station with the phones still on to get anything I could, but it was

Dovie and Emery Waln Morrison, 1944.

V-mail from Emery Morrison, sent to his wife from the USS Raleigh, November 1943. (Both courtesy of Dovie Morrison)

No. 1 59 322

To
MISS DOVIE LOU GREEN
RT. 1 BOX 14
TEMPE, ARIZONA

From
E.W.MORRISON RM2/C
(Sender's name)
USS RALEIGH BOX C
(Sender's address)
FLT.P.M. SAN FRANCISCO CALIF.
NOV 5, 1943
(Date)

PASSED BY NAVAL CENSOR
(CENSOR'S STAMP)

CHRISTMAS GREETINGS
to One I Love

My pleasant memories of You
Just seem to have a way
Of adding to the happiness
And joy of Christmas Day—
And so, here's hoping Christmastime
Will lend its magic touch
To make the world a happy place
For One I Love—*So Much!*

V-MAIL

POST OFFICE DEPT. PERMIT NO. 65

pointless so I left the phones and went out onto the radio bridge deck. The *Utah* was upside down, we were listing slowly, oil was seeping out all over the harbor, fires were burning on Ford Island, and over battleship row, the sky was full of smoke and flame. After about twenty minutes there was a lull between waves of planes, but we didn't know that at the time, and most of us thought the attack was all over. Work parties were formed by grabbing anyone available to go below and take anything we could get our hands on from the port side of the ship, take it up on deck and throw it over the side in an effort to stop the listing. Damage Control had already started shifting the ballast, but because of the loss of oil, and water still coming in the torpedo hole, we continued listing. It was spooky down belowdecks. No light, not even some of the battle lights were working. Some men had flashlights but not enough. We took chairs, typewriters, stores, filing cabinets, any and everything we could carry up and over the side. It was pure bedlam because none of this was organized, the up and down ladders were narrow and traffic was trying to go both ways. Try carrying a typewriter up a ship's ladder in total darkness with someone trying to come down the same ladder at the same time. It was a mess, but we did manage to get a lot of material over the side. I didn't think of it at the time but later could imagine what was happening in the ammunition holds as men tried to get three-inch shells up the ladders to the main deck, others trying to carry the machine-gun ammo. But at least these were organized work parties in charge of a petty officer, and they had drilled and practiced on that routine. At the same time others were getting our two planes over the side, the pilots hollering, anxious to get into the air. They didn't have ammunition on board, they were so slow they couldn't have caught a zero if they had tried. The onboard torpedoes were shot out of the tubes on the port side, and as many of us as possible were sent to the catapults to try to move the port catapult far enough over the side to unbalance it, as it was unattached from its base, to dump it over the side too. We were throwing everything we could get our hands on that would move.

This labor was interrupted several times as firing commenced again. There were two more waves of planes that came in and several false alarms that would trigger the whole harbor opening up and firing at anything they thought was in the skies. We were just missed by a second torpedo that passed between our bow and the *Detroit*, just forward of us. We were hit by an aerial bomb that passed just off of the shield of the aft 40-mm gun, down through the carpenter shop, through C Division berthing compartment, past hundreds of gallons of aviation gasoline, through our aft fuel tanks, through the hull of the ship and exploded on the bottom of the harbor. Fuel oil filled our compartment and some of the carpenter shop, and started leaking out the hull. This oil and much more from the *Utah* seeped out and surrounded us. We had been strafed several times, and we had been hit numbers of times by our own shrapnel, so we had dents and nicks all over the ship.

The *Curtis,* a seaplane tender, was tied to a buoy off our aft port quarter about a half mile away, with an open sea-lane between us. Down this sea-lane they spotted a periscope of what we learned later to be a two-man sub. They opened fire with their 40-mm guns trying to hit the sub, but most of their shells were coming directly at us, hitting and skipping out of the water and right over our stacks. Signalmen on lights were frantically calling them to cease firing. I'm still not sure whether they stopped because of the message or because they realized what they were doing and stopped on their own. A destroyer on its way out of the harbor ran over the sub and beached, was able to back off of the beach and leave the harbor.

Our captain felt we were not keeping up with the water that was entering the ship and that we, like the *Utah* behind us, would soon turn over, so he ordered us to make ready to abandon ship. We took what needed to be saved, our codebooks, logs, vital papers, all of the personnel records, and had them all on the starboard side of the ship near the ladder. Everything was loaded into longboats to be taken to the island, about thirty or forty yards away. Those on the guns and the ammunition lockers were told to stay until the very last minute. Swimming in that oil, afraid that at any minute we were going to be strafed, was a scary experience. All of this happened well after the Japanese had left the area, but of course we didn't know that at the time. We thought they might return at any time, as they had three times before. We had only been ashore a short time, less than an hour, when a big tug arrived on our port side with a barge carrying huge steel tanks, almost as large as the barge. They were going to put chains around the hull of the ship, put the tanks into the water, sink them, attach them to the chains, fill them with air and help keep us afloat. It took some time, but they did it and it worked.

While this was going on it had been decided that the ship had stabilized enough to allow what crew had gone ashore to return to the ship. The longboats and whale boats started ferrying us all back to the ship. We were a mess. All we had on that wasn't oil-soaked were our shoes, as we had left them on board, neatly lined up on the uptakes on the weather deck. I guess I got my own back, it didn't seem important at the time.

Through the afternoon we all worked to help secure the ship and to totally stabilize it. We were at such an angle that the gunners on the port three-inch guns were standing in water, some up to their knees, and they were having a bad time trying to elevate the guns enough to do any good. By late afternoon the air tanks had been secured, we were resting at a severe angle but not increasing the angle at all. We all wore kapok life jackets, steel helmets, and our T-shirts, shorts, and sox, all oil-soaked. We had nothing to change into because our lockers were back aft, under the carpenter shop and totally under oil. We were all issued an old WWI 30-cal. rifle and about two clips of ammunition. We were to protect the ship from the Japanese, who were arriving on transports off Barbers Point. Or so we were told. We were dirty, hungry, scared, with no lights, no power, and afraid of the rest of the crew because they were all walking around with rifles in their hands, with none of us really knowing how to load and shoot the things. And all of the time thinking we were to be attacked again at almost any time. As it got dark, anything, and I mean anything, that moved, or that some gunner somewhere in the harbor thought moved, the gunners opened fire, and when one gun went off, they all went off all over the harbor. We had our own planes coming into Ford Island from one of our carriers out at sea. They came in with their lights on, just after dusk; one gunner was convinced it was Japanese so he opens up, and they all open up, including our gunners too. Several of our own planes were downed and pilots killed. It was a spooky night.

[Emery Morrison]

Dear Mr. Brokaw:

On Sunday, December 7, 1941, my mother, my two brothers, my sister and I went to church. We then went to my father's restaurant for lunch. Mom then took us to the movies. I don't remember what was playing, but midway through the movie the film was stopped and the lights went on. The manager came onstage and announced that the Japanese had bombed Pearl Harbor and all members of the Armed Forces should report to their bases immediately. We had never heard of Pearl Harbor. I thought to myself, "We are all too young, this won't change our lives." How wrong I was!! I was 14 years old and in ninth grade.

The next day at school, we were all ushered into the auditorium to listen to President Roosevelt's speech. We were at war.

Tom Lappas, a member of the Ninth Armored Division, March 1942. (Courtesy of Edna Lappas)

My brother was a senior in high school. He graduated in June 1942. By September 1942 he was drafted. We were devastated. He was sent to Camp Polk, Louisiana. I wrote to him every day. He was sent to England and France. When Daddy died in June 1943, my brother was still in Louisiana but came home after the interment. My brother was flown back to the United States because he had a kidney stone and he needed surgery. Just before my brother was scheduled to rejoin his outfit, V-E Day was declared.

I met my husband, Tom Lappas, March 13, 1944. He was home on leave from Camp Polk, LA. He came to visit his uncle, and we were introduced.

He was drafted and went directly to Camp Polk, LA, and then to Kansas, where they mechanized the outfit after a while in the Cavalry. He served in the 89 Ren. Squadron, 9th Armored Division, altogether 3 years and nine months. He went in the Army in Jan. 1942 and was discharged Oct. 1945. He spent Christmas 1944 in a foxhole knee-deep in snow. No relief for 24 hours. When relief came, he cried. His hands were frozen to his gun. He went back to his outfit and fell asleep in a barn. He covered himself with hay, and he would tell us he thought he was at the Waldorf-Astoria.

Tom told many stories to our 3 sons, Constantine, Steve, and John. They were lucky to have had their father in their lives until he passed away November 19, 1998, at age 83.

We attended many reunions with the 89th RCN Squadron. When it came time to leave for home, Tom embraced each one of his buddies, and he felt as though he was saying good-bye to his brothers.

Our son Steve is the head basketball coach at Villanova University. Tom was his biggest fan. He loved going to the games. No father was more proud of his sons than Tom Lappas.

Most sincerely,
Edna Luella
Lappas

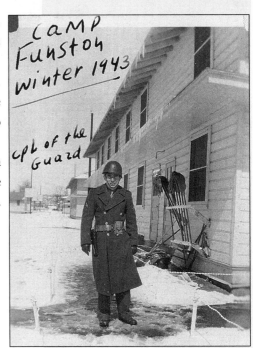

Tom Lappas at Camp Funston, Kansas, 1943.
(Courtesy of Edna Lappas)

———— • ————

Dear Mr. Brokaw:

My personal reflections remind me of how the impact of WWII completely and irreversibly altered the course of my life. It all started on December 7, 1941, that "day of infamy," and climaxed nearly five years hence, when my 10-year marriage became a "casualty of War," shattering hopes and dreams and compromising values. In brief, my story—

Following a business transfer to San Francisco, my then husband and I and our 4-year-old son had just settled into an apartment there. While [we were] preparing breakfast one pleasant but fateful Sunday morning, our attention was drawn to the sight of several uniformed Navy men dashing at a furious pace down the long flight of steps leading from the apartment building to ground level. Shortly thereafter the news broke that there had been a sneak attack on Pearl Harbor by the Japanese. All military personnel had been ordered to report to their stations immediately. Soon radios were ordered off the air with only very short, intermittent announcements coming on now and then. Further information and instruction were relayed to the populace by means of city vehicles, equipped with sirens and loudspeakers, circulating throughout the neighborhoods. Total blackout of the city was ordered. Windows had to be covered. No trace of light, even that from a lighted cigarette, was allowed. Parents were advised to equip their children with I.D. in case of separation. Periodically, dull thuds were noticed coming from the direction of the nearby Presidio, where coast artillery was located. The terror that filled our hearts was indescribable. Swiftly, along with hordes of other women and children, my little one and I evacuated this vulnerable city, boarding a train in Oakland bound for safer ground in Portland, Oregon, where we took refuge at the home of my parents.

Under the circumstances, the pain of separating was great, but within a matter of weeks, we all became united again in Portland, but it wasn't for very long. Having an ROTC Commission as a 2nd Lt. in the Army Reserve, my husband was called to active duty at an eastern-based Army Post. Just a few weeks after [his] reporting there, devastating news arrived that he had sustained an injury on the obstacle course, had been hospitalized with little hope for a quick release. Ultimately, this resulted in his becoming disqualified for overseas service. We tried to comfort ourselves with the thought that perhaps this was a blessing in disguise. At least this would give us the option of camp following, which would enable us to keep our little family together. For the next five years we led the nomadic life during periods of rehabilitation, reassignments and separations. However, we felt lucky to remain together as much as circumstances permitted. And yet, at the end of the line, when return to civilian life was imminent, the unthinkable happened as aforementioned.

I remain eternally grateful to my late parents for their loving support in helping me mend a broken heart, regain my self-esteem and rebuild my shaken confidence at a time when I found myself awed and overwhelmed with the sudden realization of having to face some very heavy lifting in order to carry on as a single mom with a young son to rear and keep happy. Now more than ever I realize he was the "wind beneath my wings" that gave me inspiration and a reason for being which ultimately propelled me to go forward and do what I must . . . and I did!

Brushing up on my long-idle secretarial skills, I tried my wings at becoming a breadwinner by sampling temporary jobs first before accepting full-time employment at a job where I remained 25 years. How comforting it was to know that during my daily absence my young child was receiving the loving care of his grandparents.

Fortunately, being such an obedient, thoughtful, scholarly and goal-oriented child, he was a pleasure to raise. Then and now, he has been my greatest source of pride and joy, the highest pinnacle of which was reached the day he received an M.B.A. degree from Stanford University after a successful climb up some steep and slippery slopes. On Graduation Day, in an outdoor setting on the Stanford campus, in the audience watching this tall, handsome young man in cap and gown receive his diploma were two very proud ladies—his mother accompanied by his lovely bride of one year.

Seven years after my nest had been emptied, my life made a big turnaround! Good fortune shone upon me when a wonderful man came into my life whose life and marriage had also been scarred from the effects of military service in the European Theater. He became my loving husband, an endear[ing] father figure to my grown son as well as, by then, my two wee grandsons, who otherwise would never have had the grandfather experience, both of their biological grandfathers having passed away years before. In May we look forward to observing our 30th anniversary.

Today my husband and I feel very grateful for our life of comfort and peace and companionship, blessed with the health to still remain in our own home with independence.

With sincere appreciation,
Karen Cummins

———— • ————

Mr. Tom Brokaw:

Before the war started, we lived in Indianapolis, IN. I had finally got a job making automobile parts, my husband worked in a bakery and we had bought a home. On December 7, 1941, things changed. My husband enlisted in the Navy, and the factory made war material for Glenn L. Martin bombers. I joined others in Red Cross classes, went through rationing of food, shoes, gasoline, tires and rode the streetcars. The only place to go was church and the shows. I would watch Movietone News and see Pres. Roosevelt either sitting at a table or riding in an open car. I knew he had polio and went to Georgia for treatments, but I did not know he was confined to a wheelchair. I think Roosevelt and Churchill saved the world.

We went from Depression to War and rationing. Made dresses

out of feed sacks. We could not buy a new car until 1950, so things were not available for a long time after the war was over. I am 81 years old, and I think I have lived in the best century of the U.S.

A fan,
Doris Lee

———— • ————

Dear Mr. Brokaw:

I was in the third grade when the Japanese bombed Pearl Harbor. We were out driving with my aunt. My uncle, who was driving behind us, motioned for my aunt to stop and came to the car and told us he had just heard the news over the radio.

Of course, that is all that was talked about in our home that evening, and it made such a great impression on all of us. So when my little brother, who was five years old at the time, woke up the next morning, he asked our mother who won the war! Mother then explained to him she didn't believe the war would be over that soon.

While [I was] growing up, the situation of the war was often discussed in our home. I was one of five children. That was the topic of discussion at our dinner table, and we were always taught to be patriotic. I still get chills and teary-eyed when "The Star-Spangled Banner" is played or the Pledge of Allegiance is recited. I am so proud to be an American and to have had such goodly parents to teach me the proper way to live and to conduct myself.

I remember so well about everything being rationed, such as shoes, meat, etc. My father was a butcher in a grocery store, and my mother stayed home with us. I remember so well that eggs were rationed. One time one of my mother's friends, who was raising chickens, gave her a dozen eggs. We were all so excited the next morning to have

Beverly Moore, age ten, in 1942.
(Courtesy of Beverly Moore)

Beverly Moore with children
Buddy and Laurie, 1977.
(Courtesy of Beverly Moore)

eggs for breakfast. Mother later told us she had to go in the next room so we couldn't see the tears in her eyes over the joy we had in eating eggs for a change.

But you know, Mr. Brokaw, I never remember anyone around me complaining about the shortage of the many items that were rationed. We just understood that it was the patriotic thing to do, that the things that were rationed were needed elsewhere. If we lost the Second World War, what a change it would have made in our society. I shudder to think what would have happened to us. I might not have been alive to be able to bring two children into this world.

Yours very truly,
Beverly C. Moore

ABOVE: *The troops of the Third Armored Division, First U.S. Army, advancing through the ruins of Cologne, Germany. The twin spires of the city's famous cathedral can be seen in the distance.*
(AP/Wide World Photos)

RIGHT: *The first wave of troops of the Sixteenth Regiment of the First Infantry Division making their amphibious landing on Omaha Beach, the Normandy coast, D-Day, June 6, 1944.*
(© Robert Capa/Magnum Photos)

Part Two

·

THE WAR IN EUROPE

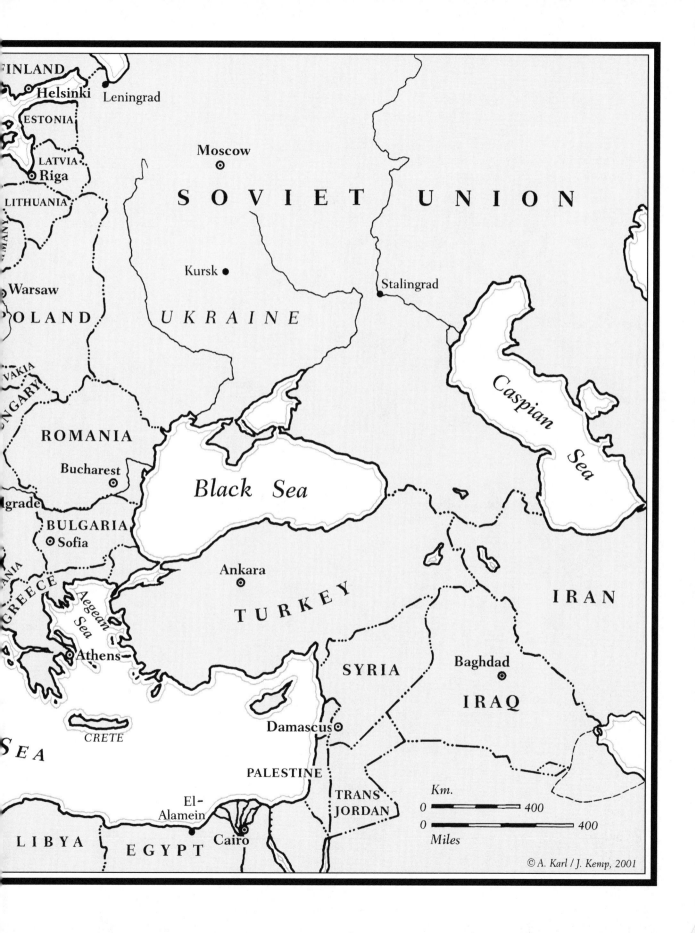

FINLAND

Helsinki ● Leningrad

ESTONIA

LATVIA
◉ Riga

LITHUANIA

● Warsaw

POLAND

Moscow ◉

S O V I E T   U N I O N

Kursk ●

Stalingrad ●

U K R A I N E

Caspian Sea

VAKIA

NGARY

ROMANIA

Bucharest ◉

lgrade

Black Sea

BULGARIA
◉ Sofia

ANIA

GREECE

Aegean Sea

Ankara ◉

T U R K E Y

I R A N

◉ Athens

CRETE

SYRIA

Baghdad ◉

I R A Q

Damascus ◉

S E A

PALESTINE

El-
Alamein

TRANS
JORDAN

Km.

0 ▭▬▭▬▭ 400

0 ▭▬▭▬▭ 400

Miles

LIBYA   EGYPT   Cairo ◉

© A. Karl / J. Kemp, 2001

At THE BEGINNING OF THE TWENTY-FIRST CENTURY, EUROPE IS A stable, economically prosperous continent where the political and financial communities are engaged in historic cooperation. Six decades ago, however, less than an American lifetime, Europe was deeply divided by Fascist ambitions, ruthless military aggression, and fanatical political allegiance. Poland was the first country to fall, prompting Great Britain and France to declare war on Germany but without rushing to Poland's side.

In 1939 and 1940 Finland fell to the Soviets, who needed a buffer against Germany's voracious appetite. Germany in turn invaded Norway and Denmark. British and French troops joined Norwegian troops in a stiff initial fight, but the Allies were forced to withdraw by Hitler's pressures on their own countries.

In the spring of 1940, when Germany was making its lightning strikes into the Netherlands, Belgium, and Luxembourg, the Nazis had 2.2 million troops in uniform, nine motorized divisions, and ten panzer divisions protected by 3,500 combat aircraft. The Allies—France, Great Britain, and the lowland countries—actually had more men in uniform, more tanks, and more than 1,400 combat aircraft. But they had no common defense strategy and no unified political will.

By June 1940 German troops controlled Paris, and France was humiliated into accepting a puppet government. Charles de Gaulle, one of the few senior French officials to flee, went to London, where he declared in a broadcast to the French people: "This war has not been settled by the Battle of France. This war is a world war. . . . Whatever happens the flame of resistance must not and will not be extinguished."

Great Britain, however, was not a safe sanctuary. Shortly after defeating France, Hitler began what came to be known as the Battle of Britain, opening with a bombing campaign designed to so diminish British airpower that an invasion would be possible. By then the British had a new, formidable weapon in their arsenal: the bulldog will and powerful rhetoric of Winston Churchill, who had replaced the pliable Neville Chamberlain as prime minister. As John F. Kennedy said later, Great Britain was alone in the late summer of 1940 in resisting the Führer's thirst for conquest.

The British people had what Churchill would call "their finest hour" in withstanding a withering bombing attack from July to September. The British Royal Air Force was a fierce picket line in the skies against German bombers, and the English people maintained their legendary reserve during the bombing raids that struck at the heart of their capital.

An American in London became the voice of the British people in his daily broadcasts. Edward R. Murrow, a dashing young CBS broadcaster with no traditional journalistic training, brought the war into the homes of Americans by standing on rooftops or recording the hurried footsteps as Londoners filed into Underground—subway—stations during bombing raids. His reports, which began "This is London . . . ," were at once conversational and grave, as if from a troubled friend.

By the fall of 1940 the war had expanded to North Africa, where the Italians had invaded Egypt but were driven out by a much smaller British force. Italy was proving to be an ineffective military ally for Germany, bungling an invasion of Greece as well.

Nonetheless, nothing diminished Hitler's confidence or appetite for conquest, and by early 1941 he had sent his forces into Greece, Yugoslavia, and Romania. His brilliant field commander Erwin Rommel mobilized the Afrika Korps to invade Egypt and head for the Suez Canal. In a series of campaigns that seesawed back and forth across the desert, neither side was able to gain a decisive advantage until July 1942, when the British Eighth Army, under the command of General Bernard Law Montgomery, stopped Rommel's advance at El-Alamein.

In the United States FDR signed the Lend-Lease Act in March 1941, likening Great Britain to a neighbor whose house was on fire. The president was supplying a garden hose without haggling over the price, fully expecting to get it back once the fire was out. It was part of his genius to reduce complicated and controversial matters to homilies understandable by every level of American society. After the Japanese attack on Pearl Harbor, the United States would become much more than a friendly neighbor with a garden hose. It would be fully involved, fighting for its life and values.

In June 1941 Hitler made what would prove to be one of his most hubristic—and flawed—decisions. He invaded the Soviet Union, opening a second major front for Germany. By December Nazi troops were within reach of the Moscow city limits. Other German units lay siege to Leningrad (St. Petersburg), initiating a battle that would continue for two and a half years and cost the Soviets an estimated million and a half lives.

By 1942, while the Germans continued their Soviet offensive,

APR. 9, 1940
Germany invades Norway and Denmark.

MAY 10, 1940
Germany invades the Netherlands, Belgium, and Luxembourg. The war in western Europe has begun. Winston Churchill replaces Neville Chamberlain as the British prime minister.

MAY 11, 1940
German forces capture Fort Eben Emael, a key Belgian defense.

MAY 14, 1940
The Netherlands government, headed by Queen Wilhelmina, escapes to London. The army of the Netherlands surrenders.

MAY 17, 1940
German mechanized divisions sweep into France.

MAY 26, 1940
Evacuation of troops through Dunkirk is ordered. Between May 26 and June 4, 200,000 British and 100,000 French troops will be rescued.

MAY 28, 1940
King Leopold orders the Belgian army to surrender.

JUNE 4, 1940
Churchill, in a speech before the House of Commons, declares: "We shall never surrender."

JUNE 10, 1940
Italy declares war on France and Britain.
Italian forces prepare to invade southern France.

JUNE 14, 1940
German troops enter Paris.

JUNE 16, 1940

The World War I hero Marshal Philippe Pétain replaces Paul Reynaud as head of the French government.

JUNE 22, 1940

France signs an armistice with Germany at Compiègne. French forces are to be disarmed, and three-fifths of France is to be occupied by Germany.

JUNE 24, 1940

France signs an armistice with Italy.

JULY 5, 1940

The parliament of the new French government meets at Vichy.

JULY 10, 1940

The Battle of Britain begins. The German air assault will continue into the summer of 1941.

JULY 16, 1940

Hitler issues orders for the invasion of Great Britain, Operation Sealion.

AUG. 13, 1940

Aldertag (Eagle Day) in the Battle of Britain marks the beginning of an all-out German effort to gain air superiority. The Germans lose 45 planes, the British only 13.

AUG. 17, 1940

Germany declares a total blockade of the British islands.

AUG. 24, 1940

A lost German bomber drops its load on the center of London. The British will respond by ordering attacks on Berlin.

SEPT. 7, 1940

The Blitz begins as a thousand German aircraft strike London virtually unopposed.

the U.S. Eighth Air Force was forming in England. Major General Dwight David Eisenhower took command of the new U.S. European Theater of Operations. British bombers attacked Cologne, Germany, in the first 1,000-plane raid of the war.

By the fall the Allies had invaded North Africa with Operation Torch, the first step in establishing a launching pad for the invasion of Sicily and Italy and Montgomery had begun his counterattack of El-Alamein. At the same time Soviet forces began a counterattack against German troops fighting for Stalingrad. When the Germans surrendered at Stalingrad, they had lost 300,000 troops.

In January 1943 Roosevelt, Churchill, and de Gaulle met in the Moroccan city of Casablanca. Although still on the defensive for the most part, they agreed to seek unconditional surrender from the Axis powers. They also agreed to begin strategic bombing against Germany and, with the North African campaign complete, to commence the invasion of Sicily. But on the larger question of an invasion of Europe across the English Channel, the Allied leaders deferred a decision. Meanwhile, the fighting in the USSR was raging, with both sides committing millions of troops and mammoth armored divisions to epic battles. Slowly the Soviets were turning the Germans back, at great cost to both nations.

By mid-summer the Allies under Eisenhower invaded Sicily. In September the invasion of mainland Italy began with almost no opposition. By then FDR and Churchill had agreed that in 1944 they would launch Operation Overlord, the invasion of Europe across the Channel.

As the fighting in Italy became more intense in the late autumn, German troops replaced Italians, sometimes by imprisoning or extinguishing them. The Italian government had forced Mussolini from power and was secretly negotiating with the Allies. But the Germans were determined to defend their southern flank, and the Italian topography of mountains and rivers was ideal for establishing defensive positions.

In January 1944 the Allies landed 50,000 troops at Anzio to bypass the German Gustav Line and speed the Allied advance to the south. But the operation was overly cautious in the opening days, allowing the Germans to organize an effective counterattack. As a result the Allies were stuck for four months.

By late January 1944 there was good news on the Eastern Front; the Soviets broke the siege of Leningrad after 900 days of hand-to-hand fighting and deprivation, one of the costliest battles in history. By May the Allies were able to begin the offensive that got their forces off Anzio and moving toward Rome. The southern strategy was beginning to work. Mary Ahlstrom's husband, Bill, was one of the infantrymen who fought through the winter rains to help the Allies break through the German stronghold around Anzio beachhead. Ahlstrom, an artillery observer in the 34th "Red Bull" Infantry Divison, was later hit in the leg by German fire at Cassino. Knowing that the Army medics were attending to soldiers more badly wounded than he, Ahlstrom took matters into his own hands, using his belt as a tourniquet to stop the bleeding. Although his leg had to be amputated later, Ahlstrom managed to live through some of the worst fighting in the war.

In June the boldest invasion ever was ready, and on the sixth day of that stormy month it was launched from the ports and airfields of southern England. Operation Overlord, commanded by General Eisenhower, stunned the Germans. By the end of D-Day, 150,000 Allied soldiers had landed and a beachhead had been secured. Archie McDole was among the first wave of troops to land at Normandy. Told that "there was no turning back," McDole jumped from his landing craft into the six-foot-deep water. As he made his way toward shore, McDole wondered if some of the bodies he was crawling over were the same boys he'd been with in the landing craft minutes earlier.

D-Day was the beginning of the end for Hitler, but there were eleven months of bitter fighting ahead. The Germans rallied a counterattack and within a week unleashed a new weapon against Great Britain: the V-I missile. By the end of June a thousand of these unmanned killers had rained down on London and environs.

While D-Day was a hard-won success, the advance off the beaches was stubbornly resisted. Saint-Lô, a small Normandy city just a few miles from Omaha Beach, was not taken by American troops until mid-July.

In East Prussia a plot against Hitler by elite members of the Nazi officer corps failed. The Führer survived the explosion of a bomb planted in his headquarters. Colonel Count Claus von Stauffenberg was tortured and executed for his role. Germany's most popular and effective general, Rommel, was forced to commit suicide because Hitler was convinced he was a principal conspirator.

By August the delayed Allied invasion in the south of France occurred, and on August 25 Paris was liberated by Allied troops

SEPT. 13, 1940
Italy invades Egypt from Libya.

SEPT. 27, 1940
Germany, Italy, and Japan sign the Tripartite Pact, a ten-year military and economic alliance, creating the Axis.

OCT. 7, 1940
German troops enter Romania.

OCT. 12, 1940
Hitler postpones Operation Sealion.

OCT. 28, 1940
Italy invades Greece from Albania.

NOV. 10, 1940
The Luftwaffe attacks Coventry, a British industrial center. Future attacks on British cities will be sporadic.

NOV. 11, 1940
British planes destroy or damage half the Italian fleet at Taranto.

NOV. 20, 1940
Hungary and Romania join the Rome-Berlin-Tokyo Pact.

DEC. 9, 1940
British troops attack Italian positions in the Egyptian desert, beginning a North African offensive.

JAN. 22, 1941
British forces capture Tobruk from the Italians.

FEB. 12, 1941
German Gen. Erwin Rommel arrives in Africa, followed by the first units of what will become the Afrika Korps.

MAR. 1, 1941
Bulgaria joins the Axis.

MAR. 11, 1941
FDR signs the Lend-Lease Act.

and Free French fighters under the command of de Gaulle. On the Eastern Front, Russian forces were on the march into Romania, Bulgaria, and Poland.

In their eagerness to pressure Hitler to concede, the Allies launched Operation Market-Garden, led by General Montgomery. It was a leapfrogging operation designed to seize a series of bridges and open the northern route into Germany. In the end, though, it was too daring. German forces mounted effective counterattacks at Arnhem, the "bridge too far," and resisted so tenaciously at the other bridges that the Allies failed. Even with the tremendous pressures on Germany from the east, west, and south, Hitler was not prepared to surrender, and his military, now including a "home guard" of all able-bodied men between the ages of sixteen and sixty, fought on.

Despite this setback the Allied advance on Germany continued; the inevitability of Hitler's defeat was increasingly clear to his general staff, but he called for a greater effort, predicting the Allies would soon be fighting among themselves.

As the Allies advanced on Germany from the west, Hitler tried one last, desperate scheme: a counterattack to regain Antwerp, the Belgian port that was a vital supply entry point for the Allies. He sent in 400,000 troops led by crack Panzer forces. The Battle of the Bulge was initially successful. Fifteen thousand American troops were taken prisoner during the battle. Bastogne, Belgium, was surrounded, but when a Nazi representative went to Brigadier General Anthony C. McAuliffe to invite a surrender, he was met with a now famous one-word answer: "Nuts."

The standoff went on, with troops dug into deep snow under overcast skies. Finally, in late December the skies began to clear and Allied airpower came into play about the same time that General George Patton's Fourth Armored Division liberated Bastogne. By the time the battle ended in January, there were 75,000 Allied and 100,000 German casualties.

In November 1944, Franklin Roosevelt had been elected to an unprecedented fourth term as president of the United States. He was sixty-two years old, but the Great Depression and World War II had taken a great toll on his health.

In early February the Big Three—Roosevelt, Churchill, and Stalin—met in Yalta in the Crimea to organize the end of the war and decide what should happen after, including establishment of the United Nations. Stalin agreed to enter the war against Japan once

Germany was vanquished. Germany would be divided into four zones of occupation. A failing FDR was later accused of falling into Stalin's trap, which led to the Soviet domination of Eastern Europe.

From February through May the vise of the Allies from the west and Soviets from the east closed steadily on Berlin. As they advanced the troops confronted horrors that had been rumored but never confirmed: the concentration camps of the Holocaust. Sergeant David Hubbard was at the Buchenwald camp shortly after its liberation. It was an indelible experience for the twenty-three-year-old Hubbard, who wrote home to his parents, "Pictures, stories and word of mouth cannot sufficiently tell the story of horrors and beastliness carried on in the concentration camps you've heard about."

By late April the Russians were a few miles from Hitler's bunker in the heart of the German capital. The Führer was in a rage against many of his closest generals, including Göring and Himmler, for attempting to usurp his power or explore prospects for surrender. In a bizarre and appropriately demonic setting, Hitler acquiesced to the wishes of his mistress, Eva Braun, and married her in an early morning ceremony on April 29. The next day he had lunch with his secretarial staff before poisoning his dogs. In mid-afternoon Hitler and Braun retired to their private quarters and committed suicide. She took poison. He used a revolver. Adolf Hitler was fifty-six years old.

On May 7, 1945, Germany surrendered. The war in Europe was over.

SEPT. 3, 1941
Gas chambers are used experimentally for the first time at Auschwitz.

SEPT. 8, 1941
Germany begins the siege of Leningrad, which will not end until Jan. 1944.

SEPT. 19, 1941
Germany takes Kiev.

SEPT. 28, 1941
Nazis murder 33,771 Jews at Kiev.

OCT. 24, 1941
Germany takes Kharkov.

DEC. 6, 1941
Soviets open a counteroffensive against German armies near Moscow. Two days later, Hitler places his armies on the defensive for the winter.

DEC. 19, 1941
Hitler dismisses Walther von Brauchitsch and becomes commander in chief of the German army.

DEC. 22, 1941
British and American Combined Chiefs of Staff agree to give the war against Germany priority.

JAN. 13, 1942
Germany begins a U-boat offensive along the East Coast of the United States.

JAN. 20, 1942
The Wannsee Conference is held near Berlin. Senior SS officials and Nazi party representatives confirm their plans to begin the systematic transportation of all Jews from occupied Europe to concentration camps.

FEB. 1942

The recently formed U.S. Eighth Air Force is moved to England. It will become the nucleus of the American strategic bombing force in Europe.

MAY 30, 1942

British Bomber Command mounts a 1,000-plane raid against Cologne.

JUNE 1942

The United States establishes a European Theater of Operations, commanded by Maj. Gen. Dwight Eisenhower.

A summer German campaign in southern USSR begins. Rostov falls on July 23.

JUNE 21, 1942

Tobruk falls to the Germans. German armies are poised to take Egypt and the Suez Canal.

AUG. 12, 1942

In Moscow, Churchill informs Stalin of the Allies' intention to postpone the invasion of Europe.

SEPT. 1942

German armies penetrate the defense of Stalingrad. The city will become the graveyard for a large portion of the German Sixth Army.

OCT. 23, 1942

British troops under Gen. Bernard Law Montgomery attack German lines at El-Alamein.

NOV. 8, 1942

Operation Torch, the Allied invasion of North Africa, begins, with Eisenhower as commander. This is the other half of the pincer the Allies plan to regain control of North Africa and the Mediterranean.

 •

Dear Mr. Brokaw,

My Uncle Art was born in Manchester, England, in July of 1919. When he was four years old he emigrated to the United States with his parents, Arthur and Clara Nicholls. They settled in the textile mill village of Pontiac in Warwick, Rhode Island. My grandparents later had three more children. Charles, Dorothy, and Gloria were born in this country.

At the start of World War II, both Uncle Art and my father, Charlie, enlisted in the army to serve the country that they so loved. My father went to the Pacific Theater as part of the 183rd Engineers, while Uncle Art dreamed of flying.

After training, Uncle Art became a bombardier on what he considered the finest plane in the world, the B-17 Flying Fortress. His plane was nicknamed "Little Dynamite." He thought the world of his crew and loved the challenge of the classes he took to prepare him for his position.

During the first leave home in February 1942, Uncle Art married his sweetheart, Bettie Maroney. She was the girl of his dreams and he was thrilled that she could accompany him while still in the States. Art and Bettie were so anxious for the war to end so that they could begin a family of their own.

In early 1943, Uncle Art was sent to England and stationed in Bassingbourne. He rarely spoke of his bombing missions, although he participated in raids over Bremen and other German and Dutch cities. Uncle Art was a prolific letter-writer. My Aunt Gloria kept all the letters that he sent home and she gave them to me in 1997. Although I never knew Uncle Art, I now feel that I do. I feel that perhaps the most frightening thing about being in war and in danger of dying is that the person will be forgotten in time. His letters will help his memory to live on.

On May 13, 1943, Uncle Art's plane was shot down by German fighters. He was on a mission to bomb an engine repair factory outside of Amiens, France. Initially, the family was informed that he was missing in action. For five days the family went to church to pray for him. On the fifth day, my grandmother looked at my grandfather and said, "He's gone."

For many years after the war, my family was uncertain as to where Uncle Art's grave was located. A letter was sent to my grandfather asking if the family desired the remains to return to the United States. It was decided that his remains stay in France. The original grave site was temporary, as a permanent military cemetery was being prepared. Uncle Art has the honor of being buried in Normandy American Cemetery overlooking Omaha Beach in France.

In the summer of 2000, my Aunt Gloria, my husband, my daughter and I visited Normandy American Cemetery. Using information sent to us from the American Battle Monuments Commission, we quickly found the grave site. Immediately as we looked upon Uncle Art's grave for the first time, the sky opened up and it began to rain heavily. We took this as a sign from Uncle Art. He knew we had found him at last.

Charlene Nicholls Gamble

Fort Adams, R.I.

January 27, 1942

Dear Mom:

Too bad I don't know the words to the song "Dear Mom" or else I'd put that in. I'm sorry about the way I acted the other nite, I was just kind of peeved about you working, but I guess you're right, it's you that's working and you are your own boss.

Everything down here is just about the same, sleeping, eating and make-believe working. The snow that we had last nite is melting away so I guess we can bank on having some slush now. At the present time I am attending an intelligence school that will last two days. You might think they were giving you something, letting you go to school for all that length of time. Tell Dot and Glo I must be bright as I already told them, because it is called intelligence school.

Now Ma, don't get thick at me because I hate this place down here. I am trying for the Air Corps and this time I intend to go through with it. The requirements aren't as stiff as they were before, and after all it is to better myself. I've already told Bettie and she said that she'd wait for me, so I guess she will. I hope you're not mad at me Ma, but honest this place drives me nuts and the outfit I'm in is too stationary to suit me. It would be a heck of a note after my writing all this if I didn't pass, but I sure hope so. Say a prayer that I do pass and then I know that I will.

Nov. 11, 1942

German forces occupy the remainder of France.

Nov. 19, 1942

Soviet forces move to encircle German troops fighting for Stalingrad.

Jan. 1943

Churchill and FDR meet at Casablanca. They decide to demand unconditional Axis surrender, to make the next campaign against Sicily, and to increase the strategic bombing offensive against Germany.

Feb. 2, 1943

Remaining German troops in Stalingrad surrender. The effort has cost an estimated 200,000 German lives.

Mar. 1943

Soviet forces recapture Kharkov. The Soviets have pushed the Germans back to the start of their 1942 offensive.

Apr. 19, 1943

In the Warsaw Ghetto uprising, several thousand Jews form an armed rebellion against the German army as they resist being deported to camps in Eastern Europe. The uprising lasts until the ghetto is finally overrun on May 16.

May 1943

In Washington, D.C., FDR and Churchill agree in principle on Operation Overlord, the cross-channel invasion of Europe, and set a launch date of May 1, 1944.

July 5, 1943

German armies attack a Soviet salient around Kursk with a million men and 2,700 tanks. By July 12 Soviet victory is clear. This is the end of the last significant German offensive in the east.

I may even be home before you get this letter, so this news might be secondhand.

Good luck and God Bless You.

Art

P.S.   I'm going to show Pa that I'm a better soldier than he thinks I am.

A.

Maxwell Field, Ala.

March 12, 1942

Dear Ma, Dad, Dot & Glo,

I received your letters after I sent you my last letter, and boy I sure was glad to hear from you.

Ma, don't think that I was getting uppity when I addressed you all as folks. I thought that it looked better, but now that I know, they'll all be the same as this one.

I sent two letters to Bettie today. Don't worry about me. I love her very much and I won't do anything to change her mind about me. I get one or two letters from her every day, and it sure is nice to hear from her and everyone else at home.

I got a letter from Charlie today, and if we should get a chance sometime we'll try to see each other. We are only about 250 miles apart, but so far I can only get Wednesday nite off until 12:00.

I don't know whether or not I told you in my last letter, but I was appointed a cadet lieutenant. That kind of stuff is right up my alley—drilling men. I have about eighty men in my platoon, and when I get through with them, I hope they will all be good soldiers. If I treat them right, they may help me when it comes to "book larnin'."

Until I hear from you again—

Good nite, good luck and God Bless You

Art

Remember me to everyone at home.

Santa Ana, California

May 5, 1942

Dear Mom,

I got your package and Dot's letter today. Boy, the cookies were swell, all the boys send their thanks. Not a one of them was crushed either.

You shouldn't bake cookies with tears in your eyes, Mom, you know that it isn't good for you. Charlie and I will be all right, so don't you worry. When we're back in town you'll never even know we were away.

And how are you doing, Dad? You had better watch out when they get you back in the army. I'll admit that they do need a lot of guys *like you* that know their *stuff,* but the army has changed.

See you all later.

Good nite, good luck and God Bless You.

Art

The Biltmore Hotel
Los Angeles

September 6, 1942

Dear Mom and Dad,

Well the big day finally came yesterday, and what a thrill it gave me. Bettie was there and she was the prettiest girl of the lot.

I got my orders to go to Salt Lake City, Utah, so we are both leaving for the place tonight.

I don't know what will come after that, it will probably put me with some tactical unit. I may be sent someplace else within a couple of days, so Bettie is going to stay with me till I get sent away. Would it be all right if she came home to you? Is that the way you meant it in your letter?

I'll write again when I get to my new station. Bettie sends her love.

Your loving son and daughter.

Alamogordo, New Mexico

September 30, 1942

Dear Mom and Dad,

I'm writing this on the train, and if you wonder why the handwriting looks so shaky, that will be the reason.

At present we are somewhere in Texas, and we should reach Alamogordo tonite or tomorrow morning.

Bettie and the other girls left on Sunday nite too, but they should have gotten there sometime this morning because nothing could move as slow as the troop train we're riding on. I don't know just how she is going to like the place, but if it is

Nov. 22–26, 1943

In Cairo, FDR, Churchill, and Chiang Kai-shek discuss plans for Asia. FDR and Churchill will meet again in Cairo in December to discuss the Allied invasion.

Nov. 28–Dec. 1, 1943

At the first Big Three meeting, in Tehran, FDR, Churchill, and Stalin confirm the decision to invade Europe on May 1, 1944.

Nov. 1943–Jan. 1944

Allied troops in Italy attempt to advance against stubborn German resistance between Naples and Rome. The Allies will assault one of these defensive positions, the Gustav Line, for 5 months.

Jan. 20, 1944

The 36th Texas National Guard Division attacks across the Rapido River in one of the strongest parts of the Gustav Line. They are repulsed with heavy losses.

Jan. 22, 1944

In an effort to outflank the Gustav Line, the Allies land 50,000 troops at Anzio. The beachhead will be besieged for four months.

Jan. 27, 1944

Leningrad is relieved after a siege lasting almost 900 days.

Feb. 15, 1944

The Allies bomb the fifteenth-century Benedictine monastery at Monte Cassino. The building had been empty, but the Germans convert the debris into a new stronghold.

very bad, I'm going to send her home. I'll hate to see her go because since she's been out here with me, I've had the happiest time of my life. I know that I got the pick of the lot when I got married, and you should see me, I've changed a lot.

Did you know that this is the longest I've been away from Bettie since she's been out here. That shows you how much we've been seeing each other. We've been married for seven months, two weeks, and four days, and I'm just as much in love now as I was the day we got hitched.

Good nite, good luck and God Bless You All.

Love,
Art

Alamogordo, New Mexico
October 1942
Dear Mom and Dad,

Well I've finally found the time to write to you. Maybe if I ever stop in one place long enough, I'll be able to receive some mail.

This is quite a place. Regardless of where they send me to combat, it can't be any worse than this. I'm not kicking, but I thought I'd give you a general idea of the place.

The field was originally built for the British, and it was so bad that they wouldn't take it. It's ten miles from town, and as soon as you see the place you can't believe it. The better buildings, like the ones we live in, are built in about a day. In the officers' quarters, and it's a damn shame to call them such, there are ten rooms. Each of them is about six feet by ten feet, and they quarter four men to a room. The buildings are all covered with tar paper, and, as we found out yesterday, they leak like a sieve. If we want to wash or take a shower, we have to walk to a building about fifty yards away, and if we should want to visit the toilet, we walk another two hundred yards in the opposite direction. When we go to mess, we have to walk for another half mile. That isn't so bad, but when we are supposed to report to operations, the flight line, or the main part of the camp, that means another mile and a half. Believe me, I've walked more since I've been here than I did all the time I was in the army. It's so bad that you really have to laugh at it.

We work on three eight-hour shifts, and they are called

the Dawn Patrol from 2:00 A.M. until 10:00 A.M., Millionaire's Shift from 10:00 A.M. until 6:00 P.M., and the Graveyard Shift from 6:00 P.M. until 2:00 A.M. I started off on the Dawn Patrol and will be on it for nine days.

We will only be here for 29 days, and in that time we should do a lot of bombing. I hope so anyway. From here we are supposed to go to Topeka, Kansas, for another month and then we go overseas somewhere. If we get sent to Manchester, Connecticut, that means we'll go to England. If we go to West Palm Beach, Florida, we'll go to Egypt. And if we go to Hamilton Field, California, we'll go to Australia or someplace like that. I hope that I go to England, then I'll be in Connecticut for four days and I'll try to get home, or else you can come to see me.

Bettie has a room in town with a very nice lady. She only pays six dollars a week for it, so that isn't too bad.

Good day, good luck and God Bless You.

Love,
Art

November 7, 1942
Dear Mom and Dad,

I received your letter yesterday, and was glad to hear that you had finally heard from Charlie. I sent him a long letter although I hadn't received an answer to my last letter.

Yesterday morning we took off between six and seven o'clock and flew to Tulsa, Oklahoma, and down to Wichita Falls, Texas. There was a ground fog all the way down there and all the way back. Boy that seemed funny, to fly all that way and not even see the ground. It makes good practice for both the pilot and the navigator anyway.

There were about ten crews that were told today to be ready to leave on four hours' notice. Our crew was one of them. If at any time you don't hear from me, you know that I'll be gone. There is no need to worry, I'll be all right. I don't know just where we will go, but I hope that it is England. The battles that are going on now in the Solomons and Libya may be the deciding factors to where we are going. Whatever you do, don't tell anyone else about this or the orders that came out.

At midnight tonite I start a 24-hour pass, so Bettie and I are going to go to communion tomorrow morning. I've been

JULY 25, 1944

Gen. Bradley launches Operation Cobra, the first successful attempt to break out of the Normandy beachhead.

AUG. 1944

Soviet forces advance into Romania.

AUG. 21–OCT. 7, 1944

At Dumbarton Oaks, the United States, Britain, the USSR, and China lay the groundwork for a postwar international organization.

AUG. 25, 1944

Paris falls to American and Free French troops.

SEPT. 1944

Soviet forces advance into Bulgaria.

SEPT. 11–16, 1944

A second conference at Quebec, led by FDR, Churchill, and their staffs, discusses plans for completing the war against Germany and British involvement in the war in the Pacific. The Morgenthau plan for converting postwar Germany from an industrial to an agricultural nation is tentatively approved. FDR will later reject it.

SEPT. 17, 1944

Operation Market-Garden begins. Montgomery parachutes three divisions to take bridges over the Meuse, Waal, and Lower Rhine Rivers, then sends ground troops to meet them. Many of the bridges to the south are taken, but a large portion of the British First Airborne Division is surrounded at Arnhem. Surviving British troops are evacuated Sept. 25–26.

OCT. 9–20, 1944

Churchill and Stalin agree to relative degrees of postwar influence in Balkan nations.

trying to be as faithful to church as I can, that means that
your teachings did me good. Bettie is the same as you are, she
thinks that everything that happens is God's will.

So long for now, folks.

Good nite, good luck and God Bless You All.

Love,
Art

England

February 23, 1943
Dear Mom & Dad

It was a big surprise to all of us when we found out that
we were going to England. I didn't expect it but it didn't make
me mad.

I can't say anything about the trip except that everything
went along well. When we first hit this old coast it looked very
good, and it was something like I pictured it. It seemed funny
to think that I was born here and now after all these years I
was getting my first glimpse of it.

I'm eager as hell to go on the first raid, I've waited so long
for it. It will probably scare the "————" out of me, and I
guess it will be something I'll always remember.

How does it feel to have your daughter-in-law living with
you? Does she like it? She certainly was swell to me and I
hope that she is happy living there. Don't forget to teach her
how to make some of my favorite meals—she knows what
they are.

When you write tell me about everything, about the kids,
etc. There may be times in the near future when I won't be
able to write much, but I'll still be thinking of you.

Good nite, good luck and God Bless You All.

Love,
Art

England

March 1943
Dear Mom & Dad,

Praise the Lord and pass the ammunition, I've finally
been assigned to an operational group and my job is just about
to begin. I'm in a small outfit with a bunch of nice guys, and
I'm sure that your "Artie Pie" will do all right.

I still get a big kick out of all the English, and sometimes I can rattle off a pretty good line of Cockney. When they tell you how to get to a place they say, "You can't miss it." That really tickles me. Most of the people are nice, and I'm waiting for the time when I get a pass long enough for me to go to Salford. I've heard that it was hit pretty hard, so I don't know what I'll find. Nevertheless, I won't stop looking until I find someone that's related to us. I'll feel kind of funny about it though because it might be hard to make conversation. Another thing that I've found out is that the English think all the Americans are filthy rich, and that's one thing they are bitter about. They don't realize that what we pay a pound for here we could get in the States for a dollar. You don't think that every time you pull out a pound note it is four dollars, and at first you are puzzled as to where all your money has gone.

It's funny too, they don't refer to the enemy as Germans. It's always Jerry or the Hun, and every time we use their expressions the guys razz us. Most of the time they say—jolly good show or bloody wizard or really snappy old boy.

They do take everything in stride though, and even the air raids don't worry them anymore. You have to admire their spirit, it hasn't been dampened in the least.

I've got to hang up now, I've got to go to an early meeting in the morning and I must have my beauty sleep.

Remember me to all.

Good nite, good luck and God Bless You All.

Love
Art

England

May 3, 1943

Dear Mom and Dad,

Well folks, here I go again. I'm feeling fine, as I hope you all are.

I'm not in a writing mood tonite, my navigator (Don) was flying with another crew Saturday and didn't come back from the raid. That's the first time it has struck so close to home, and I feel pretty bad about it. Bettie can tell you how close we were. We were roommates since last September. He was well liked by everyone, and he'd go out of his way just to help someone else. It seems wherever I go, or whatever I do, I can

APR. 11, 1945

Allied troops liberate Buchenwald, the first of the major concentration camps reached during their advance through Germany. Although tens of thousands of prisoners are freed, a large proportion of the prisoners had already been subjected to forced marches a few days earlier as the Germans fled the Allied advance.

APR. 12, 1945

FDR dies; Harry Truman becomes president.

APR. 25–JUNE 26, 1945

The United Nations is organized in San Francisco.

APR. 30, 1945

Hitler commits suicide.

MAY 2, 1945

German forces in Italy surrender.

MAY 7, 1945

Germany surrenders, ending the war in Europe; May 8 is declared V-E Day.

JULY 17–AUG. 2, 1945

At Potsdam, Truman, Churchill, and Stalin discuss the future status of Germany. Truman and Churchill tell Stalin of the development of a new and powerful bomb for use against Japan. On July 26 the Potsdam Declaration repeats the demand for unconditional Japanese surrender.

JULY 26, 1945

Clement Atlee becomes prime minister of Britain.

see him and hear him. I even wake up at nite and imagine I hear him talking to me. I guess I'll get over it before long. If I can get away from it, I never want another roommate because it's bad to get attached to anyone like that.

I sent you some flowers for Easter, did you get them?

Good nite, good luck and God Bless You All.

> Your loving son,
> Art

England

May 12, 1943

Dear Dad,

I just received your very interesting letter dated April 26th, thanks a lot. It pleased me when I found out that the flowers arrived. The reason I didn't send any for Mother's Day was because I thought there had been some slipup.

I'm in the best of health, and the last time I weighed myself I was thirteen stone two. That's the way you say it, isn't it? I have a little more weight around the belt, but I feel as if I'm in almost perfect condition. When you fly a lot of high-altitude missions, you have to be okay, or else.

What do you think of the boys in Africa? They did a marvelous job, didn't they? Work like that is appreciated all round, and I hope that we can get at their necks from all sides.

I see by tonite's paper that Churchill is in Washington. What do you think the outcome will be? As you can see, I'm asking you a lot of questions—now you'll have to write again.

That's about all for now, say hello to Mom, Dot and Glo.

Good nite, good luck and God Bless You All.

> Your loving son,
> Art

War Department
Commanding General, Army Air Forces
Washington

June 7, 1943

My dear Mrs. Nicholls:

With profound regret I have learned that your husband, Second Lieutenant Arthur Herbert Nicholls, missing in action on May 13, 1943, has since been reported killed in an engagement on that date in the European Theater of Operations.

It has come to my attention that Lieutenant Nicholls met his problems earnestly and energetically as a cadet in the Advanced Flying School at Victorville, California, and graduated with an outstanding record. Being an able officer and bombardier, who completed his missions with skill and valor, he brought credit to his command and won the admiration of his associates. His friendly personality captured their affectionate regard, and they are saddened by his death.

I hope you will be comforted by the knowledge that your husband gave his best in the service of our Country and made the supreme sacrifice for its cause.

In behalf of General H. H. Arnold, Commanding General, Army Air Forces, who is temporarily away from Headquarters, I offer my heartfelt sympathy to you and to other members of the family.

Very sincerely,
BARNEY M. GILES,
Major General, U.S. Army,
Acting Chief of Air Staff

June 23, 1943
South Pacific
Dear Folks,

I received two letters from you today, dated June 1st and 7th.

The priest said a White Mass for Art here at the company on Monday morning. That was before I knew you had received the cablegrams from the International Red Cross. The priest said it would be better to have a White Mass and hope for the best, rather than a Mass for the Dead. I went to Communion, and a few of the fellows told me they had offered up their Communions for Art. Some others told me they would go Sunday for him. So you can be sure he is well prayed for.

Even if he is dead, we know he died for a good cause. You might think that it is a heck of a way to feel, but it's not—it's something to be proud of. It's not like the Germans dying for Hitler, it's dying so that every person in the U.S. might continue to live the life that they have been. That's something to boast about.

Art wrote and told me he went to Communion before each raid, so you needn't worry about him being in the State of Grace.

Art also told me that I had better write home often, and he lectured me on us having the best Mother and Dad in the world, something I didn't need to be told. I'm sure that Art felt the same as I do about you, and was thankful for all you've done for us. I don't forget, you hardly left the house without us when we were kids. We were always dressed as well as any kid in the village, if not better. Even when times were tough, we had the best of food even when you couldn't afford it. All the other things would take pages to write. When a fellow has parents like that, he's happy to fight for them. I know that's the way Art felt. I only hope when I get married that I will be half the husband my father is, and Eva will be half the wife my mother is.

I received another package from you. That's the third one. I would have told you sooner, but when I heard about Art, I didn't feel like doing much of anything. I've got everything I need for quite a while. The Fannie Farmers sure hit the spot. Thanks a million.

Mom, I'm sending a money order that I wanted to send for Mother's Day, but I didn't have enough. I owe you some anyway for the presents you bought for Pop and Glo.

I wish you would tell me just what the cablegram said. Did they say where it happened or if they found Art? And what did Broley say in his letter?

Your loving son,
Charlie

August 6, 1945

Dear Mr. Nicholls,

It is with regrets that I have to write you this letter because I fear that I can give you very little encouragement. I will tell you briefly what I know of the day we went down.

First we were hit by flak. This knocked us out of formation. We were immediately attacked by fighters. I could not see them coming, but I saw five pass us. Without warning, we went into a steep dive and spin. I could not tell from my position in the tail what was happening up in the plane. Neither Bagwell, Mooney nor I got out until the plane broke up.

The Germans told me that eight of us were dead. They showed me a wedding ring, a watch, and several other things that I recognized as Nick's. I asked what had become of him, and they said that he was dead of a head wound. I asked if I might identify him, but they would not let me. Nor would they give me the ring, which I wanted to give back.

I'd like to tell you that Nick was a friend to me. He was always cheerful and ready to help one at any time. I don't think he knew the meaning of fear.

Please feel free to write me at any time. I will do my best to answer any questions that may arise in the future, or about anything that I may not have made clear here.

In closing, let me say that I feel that Nick was not only a great loss to you but also to all his friends and the Air Corps.

Sincerely,

Edward M. Brummal

HEADQUARTERS, ARMY AIR FORCES
WASHINGTON
AAF 201 - (8015) Nicholls, Arthur H. 0729487

6 June 1954

My dear Mrs. Nicholls:

I am writing to you with reference to your husband, the late Second Lieutenant Arthur H. Nicholls.

Information received in this headquarters indicates that Lieutenant Nicholls was the bombardier of a B-17 (Flying Fortress) bomber which departed from England on a bombardment mission to Méaulte, France, on 15 May 1943. At approximately 4:45 p.m., his bomber was hit by fire from enemy aircraft just after leaving the target area. The aircraft subsequently exploded in midair, and three parachutes were seen descending just after the explosion. Three of the crew members were later reported as prisoners of war of the German Government, and the remainder, including your husband, were reported killed in action.

Enclosed is a list of those who were in the aircraft, together with the names and addresses of their next of kin.

You, and other members of the family, have my deepest sympathy in your sorrow. May the knowledge that your husband served our Country faithfully and played a gallant role in defeating our European enemy give you comfort and consolation in the years to come.

Very sincerely,
N. W. REED
Major, Air Corps
Chief, Notification Branch
Personal Affairs Division
Office of the Asst. Chief of
Air Staff, Personnel

———— • ————

Dear Mr. Brokaw:

December 7, 1941, a bitterly cold Sunday, started quietly. I had made a deal with my brother that he would let me listen to the New York Philharmonic at 2:30 p.m. He would have football at 4:00 p.m. The symphony performance was just beginning when a sudden emergency bulletin announced that the Japanese had attacked Pearl Harbor. We were glued to the radio, realizing that war had begun catastrophically.

The next day at noon we sat in assembly as the radio broadcast Roosevelt's call for a declaration of war. The speech had no sooner ended than the air raid alarms began to blow. The principal told us to go home and prepare to die bravely with our families.

All males had to register on their 18th birthday; mine was March 17, 1943. I filled out the forms and checked that I would not bear arms. Within the week I was called before the Board. The first question I was asked was if I meant it. My *yes* caused a stir. One of the women asked if I meant I wouldn't serve. My *no* answer brought the question of would I be ready to be a combat medic. I replied that I was ready. They seemed relieved, and at the end of April I was told to report for my physical at the Newark Armory.

As the physical ended, the last stop was with a psychologist. These interviews were usually perfunctory, rarely lasting more than five minutes. When my turn came, he glanced at a notebook and began to question me about my attitude toward bearing arms. The interview lasted almost twenty-five minutes, when he suddenly told me there was a long line to be interviewed. He took my hand, shook it, and said, "You're the nicest kid I've ever interviewed." He added, "May God take care of you."

I was on my way to the 106th Evacuation Hospital and later the 28th Field Hospital. The more than 270 enlisted men were a curious combination of teenagers and men who were thirty-five to forty. The military were scratching the bottom of available manpower. My primary job was to prepare the daily casualty lists and prepare bodies for the Grave Registration Bureau, but I also was part of a team that pitched tents, set up hospital facilities, and served as litter-bearers. If needed, we'd add four additional hours to the seven-day, twelve-hour shifts. Basic training at Fort Dix, N.J., and Camp Forrest in Tennessee. Then to England to be part of the hidden 3rd Army, billeted in private homes, and then to Utah Beach on D+27. Then the breakout at St. Lo and across northern France to the Battle of Metz. Then sent to a quiet front for the winter, which proved to be the south side of the Bulge. Finally crossing the Rhine, entering Buchenwald, and war's end in Czechoslovakia. Occupation duty in Austria and finally home in January of 1946. It had been a long journey home, and I was a thousand years older.

Sincerely,
Jim Shenton

———— • ————

Dear Mr. Brokaw:

I enlisted in the U.S. Coast Guard in February of 1941 and spent the entire WWII period on Coast Guard and U.S. Naval ships—save for six months in 1943 when I went thru the OCS School at the USCG Academy and the Fire Control Officer's School at the U.S. Naval Shipyard in Washington D.C.

A small Coast Guard cutter I served aboard was instrumental in the sinking of two U-boats in the spring and summer of 1942. One was brought to the surface by our vessel's depth-charge attacks just after the U-boat had torpedoed and sunk three merchant vessels in the convoy we were escorting. Upon breaking the surface, the submarine was sent to the bottom by two U.S. Navy aircraft that were providing air coverage for the convoy. The other U-boat was sunk in the Straits of Florida after it had attacked and sunk a merchant vessel the previous day. We were a part of a flotilla of Navy and Coast Guard vessels that had combed the straits all night. A Coast Guard cutter on our starboard had made the contact and dropped charges. We also made a depth-charge attack. The U-boat was unable to surface and sank with all hands. I never found out the number of the second U-boat. The first one was the U-576, under the command of Kapitänleutnant Hans-Dieter Heinicke.

I wish I had never known the name of the U-boat captain. When I was going through the U.S. Naval East Coast Fleet Anti-Submarine Warfare School in the fall of 1941, I had occasion to go out to sea in the submarines we trained with. Just for two days, as I recall. They were old subs—WWI vintage. The Navy referred to them as "O" boats, "R" boats, and "S" boats. I can't remember whether the ones I went out in were "S" or "R," but I do remember that one of them had trouble with the diving planes sticking when it came time to surface after the day's exercises were completed. All I could think of was how terrifying it would be if we were unable to surface. And when we were allowed to put on the earphones and listen to the "pinging" of the ASW vessels sound gear, I would visualize what it might be like when the sub's hull was ruptured by depth charges and the seawater poured into the tight compartments of the submarine. It was at that time that I entertained the thought that the bravest of all seamen that fought in a war were, beyond any doubt, the submariners. And, for whatever reason, that included the men who manned the German U-boats. So, knowing the name of the skipper of the U-576 made me reflect on the stark fact that all who give their lives for their country in a war have names, have families, and have loved ones who must stay home and grieve when their son, or husband, or brother fails to return.

Sincerely,
Harold D. Muth

———— • ————

Dear Mr. Brokaw:

I have learned so much about the "Greatest Generation" from my own father, Donald T. Atkinson.

One very interesting part of my dad's life was that he was one of five survivors from a B-17 plane wreck during WWII. On May 7, 1943, Dad was the flight engineer and upper-turret gunner on the B-17 called the Big Moose as they were traveling to Europe to join the 100th Bomb Group. Well into this trip, the crew noticed that they were off course. Later they discovered that the enemy had

Donald Atkinson, the father of Kay Ball, age twenty, on the upper turret of his B-17 nicknamed "The Big Moose."

used tactics to disrupt the locational beams of our American aircraft. Not knowing about this evil diversion, the Big Moose ran out of gas and crashed into the Atlantic Ocean about 150 miles off the coast of Iceland. As the crew was spewed into the dark, freezing, and treacherous waters, Dad assisted those injured to a life raft that was floating upside down. He desperately tried to hold on to two of the badly hurt crewmen, but one unfortunately slipped away with a huge wave and was never seen again. Five of the seven surviving crew members were rescued by a British tanker called *Onslaught*. After 30 days on this tanker, while trying to dodge the ever-present enemy submarines, the crew of the Big Moose was returned to the USA (but only to be reassigned to another plane and hop back over to join in the deadly war games).

Donald Atkinson, age seventy-seven, with a turret gun, in the summer of 1999.
(Both courtesy of Kay Ball)

My father has vivid memories of these times, the emotions, the hopes, the fears, the losses. He stays in close contact with his Army Air Corps buddies and joins them every other year at the 100th Bomb Group reunion. During the reunion conventions, hundreds of veterans gather to reminisce and recognize the heroes of this time.

The purpose of this letter is to tell you about a very unique and extremely interesting event that has taken place since my father's crash into the icy Atlantic Ocean. Over 50 years since that fateful day in

1943, a young Icelandic man was fishing off the coast of Iceland. His deep-sea fishing lines became entangled, and he pulled up a major part of the Big Moose B-17 aircraft with the guns still intact. This find is now on display in a museum in Reykjavik, Iceland. The fisherman tirelessly spent years trying to uncover the names of the crew members who were on board this aircraft. The crew of the Big Moose were finally located and notified of this miraculous event. Needless to say, they all were very elated and intensely surprised. My father has since sent his Mae West flotation device that saved his life on May 7, 1943, over to Iceland to be part of this display.

For my Dad's 77th birthday I plan to surprise him by taking him to visit his retrieved plane at this museum in Reykjavik, Iceland. I can't wait to experience the reunion between Dad and this B-17. I want to relive this adventure and really learn to appreciate what Dad and so many others went through to ensure our freedoms of today.

Kay Atkinson Ball

———•———

Dear Mr. Brokaw:

My mom is 75 years old, cannot see, has arthritis in her hands and fingers, and needs hearing aids to hear. After listening to the audio version of your book, *The Greatest Generation,* she started writing you a letter.

She started on Memorial Day, writing a little bit with a heavy black marker. She recently sent what she wrote to me, asking that, if I could read it, I type it up and send it to you. This is more important to her than I can say.

Dad was one of "The Greatest Generation" men. He died three years ago. She wants you to know about him.

Respectfully,
Mike Ahlstrom

Dear Tom,

I have had a cornea transplant, but both retinas are also deteriorating and I can't read anymore. I have written this to you with a large black marker which I hope my son can read, in order to transcribe and send this to you for me.

Today is Memorial Day, officially declared. Every day is Memorial Day for me and the so many others who have lost one of these gallant men.

This morning as I lay in bed, as I do every morning, I wondered what today would bring. My wonderful, caring daughter-in-law knocked on my door with a tray of poached eggs on toast. She knew today would be a miserable one for me, being Memorial Day.

On this official day of memories, I am compelled to write you my thoughts about you and my late husband, Bill.

My husband was in the Iowa National Guard when we were still high school sweethearts in 1940 and 1941. When I met Bill, I was 16 and he was 18. I think really from that day we knew we would spend all eternity together. He was so tall and handsome, with coal black hair and so beautifully tan. I was a skinny redhead with freckles galore. I think we never changed to each other, even though my red hair got lighter and came from the beauty shop over the years, and he maybe got just a bit bald on top. He was called to go to Camp Clairborne, Louisiana, a month after he graduated in 1941. He was there in training for a year. While home on leave for Christmas, he was ordered to report back to Camp Clairborne because of the December 7, 1941, attack on Pearl Harbor. His 34th Division was almost immediately sent to Fort Dix, New Jersey.

Bill and Mary Ahlstrom at home, October 1941. (Courtesy of Mike Ahlstrom)

I graduated in January 1942, and after many letters and telephone calls, I too went to New Jersey. My mother came with me from Boone, Iowa, because I had never been anywhere alone before. We were married on February 1. I got a job in a candy shop, Bill was sent overseas in April.

The 34th Division went to Northern Ireland first, and then on to England. From there they went on to the invasion of North Africa and fought Rommel. Then it was the invasion of Sicily, and the awful invasion on the Italian mainland at Anzio. Then came Cassino, and on up the boot to Rome and beyond. I'm sure you know of the record of that great 34th Red Bull Division: more [consecutive] days in combat and more casualties suffered [per capita] than any other division in U.S. history.

Bill lost his right leg and a large muscle in his upper left arm at Cassino. He was a forward artillery observer, radioing back information to direct the big guns. He came down from his outpost for supplies and was writing me a letter when German planes flew over dropping bombs. He had no bunker or foxhole there and was hit. When the shrapnel went into his leg and arm, he tied his belt around his leg to stop the spurting blood. There were so many hurt and killed that day he knew it would be a while before aid could get to him. The first "doctor" he was taken to was a dentist. He put his leg in a cast, but three days later gangrene had set in, and they had to amputate several inches above the knee.

He was in hospitals for over a year and finally discharged from the Veterans Hospital in Atlanta in December 1944. He got a leave once during that year of convalescence and rehabilitation, and met his son Michael William for the first time. Mike was 16 months old. When he was home for good, he got a job as the radio and desk clerk for the Boone, Iowa, Police Department. Later he became city treasurer of Boone, the hometown in which we were both born and raised. He started at $98 a month. Forty-one years later, upon retirement, we were thankful his pay had increased many times.

We had a wonderful life together. We lived the American Dream. We had another son and then a daughter. They all went to college and graduated, some with graduate degrees. We were so fortunate that they are all good citizens and all very successful.

Bill met and corresponded with dozens of his 34th Division buddies. I still keep in touch with those men and their wives. They all meet in Amana, Iowa, every year in August. I went with my daughter the year after Bill died. They came from California, Nevada, Minnesota, Illinois, Arizona, Pennsylvania, all over Iowa, and other states, too. It has always been absolutely inspiring to see the endearing feelings they have for each other. Bill always said they were closer than brothers. Now each year there are more and more empty chairs. Many of the boys in Bill's outfit had gone through school together from kindergarten through high school graduation. During the war, it was not uncommon in

Bill Ahlstrom in combat gear at Camp Clairborne, Louisiana, 1941.
(Courtesy of Mike Ahlstrom)

our small town of 12,000 or 13,000 to see Gold Stars in windows. And when our local daily newspaper came out each evening, you were afraid to read who else had answered that dreaded knock on the door. These were lifelong friends, and we would never be seeing them again.

Bill died of a strange lung complication in July 1996. I wish you could have known him. I am most grateful that he chose me to share his life with. Bill was my hero. He never once complained that at age 22 he had lost his leg, part of the use of one arm, had so many surgeries, and was almost always in pain. He was a true patriot. To him, others had made far greater sacrifices. He said he was just doing his job and doing his duty. He even said the German flier who dropped the bombs was doing his duty too, and bore him no malice.

Bill Ahlstrom on leave, 1941: "He was so tall and handsome, with coal black hair."
(Courtesy of Mike Ahlstrom)

One of the most memorable things to me was what happened when Bill and our son Mike went to Italy in the mid-1980s. It hadn't been discussed beforehand, except in the most general terms of seeing some of the areas he had been in during the war as part of the trip, but once there, he said he wanted to go to Anzio and Monte Cassino. During all their years of growing up, he had never talked about the war with the kids. They really didn't know any details. Bill had never forgot, though, after 40 years he had not. He wanted his fallen buddies to know they were not forgotten. Mike told me later that they went to the American Cemetery at Anzio, and that it may be the most beautiful place in the world. Bill asked the office there for the locations of several names we had never heard before. They went to each grave site. Mike gave Bill space to stand alone at each headstone, memories of sights and sounds of another hellish time going through his head. Mike told me he felt like an intruder as his dad stood at each resting place, sometimes crying quietly. When they got to Monte Cassino, Bill was very quiet, Mike said. When they drove up to the top of Monte Cassino, it almost didn't seem real to him. How could you just drive right up there, when thousands died trying to get there.

When they got home, Bill found and called the families of the fallen boys and told them he had visited their graves, and that it was a beautiful and perfectly cared for place, and that they rested in great honor. They were so thankful to know.

Now I am 75 years old, left with all my beautiful memories. It has been difficult without Bill by my side. I don't keep my hair even a faint shade of red anymore. I have no reason to, although if Bill could see me he would think it was. I try to tell our 6 grandchildren and 7 great-grandchildren about this hero of mine, and about his high ideals of how the world should be.

I wouldn't take anything for my memories. It has been so difficult to look ahead without my buddy. He will be in my heart forever . . . this ordinary man . . . my hero . . . who did his best . . . always.

With my most sincere regards, and with thanks for the memories, I am . . .

Mary E. Ahlstrom

Bill and Mary Ahlstrom with their son Mike, all together for the first time, May 1944. (Courtesy of Mike Ahlstrom)

——— • ———

Dear Mr. Brokaw:

I served as a ski trooper and as a platoon leader with the Second Infantry Division in Wisconsin and the U.P. of Michigan. The winter was unbelievable. Rumor had it that we were to invade Norway. The plan was abandoned in favor of hitting the so-called soft underbelly of Italy.

I was sent to North Africa, where I joined the Thirty-fourth Division as a rifle platoon leader. We relieved the Third Division at Salerno. My company took over positions where soldiers were being buried at a makeshift graveyard.

One major engagement with the enemy was at Benevento. Since I was from Vermont, it was assumed that I must have scouting blood and I was invariably sent on patrols or outpost duty. The platoon leaders took turns leading the company in its daily activities. It was a terribly rainy night, as is typical in the Apennines during the fall.

We were to stay overnight, and I was to lead the company the next morning. We got sudden orders to move out. The captain sent a runner to tell me to have my platoon fall into the column wherever we could. We fell into place behind the first platoon.

A huge shell hit the middle of the first platoon, the one it was my turn to lead to our next move had the plans not changed. Thirteen men were killed and twenty-three wounded. The platoon leader lost both legs. We patched wounded all night with only the light from lightning flashes. I did not get a scratch but was knocked over by the bodies thrown at me from the explosion. It still haunts me that by a quirk of fate I wasn't leading the company.

Throughout the Second War the 34th suffered an extraordinary number of casualties. All of us who were platoon leaders knew we would eventually become casualties and wondered how bad it would be.

Since it was my turn to lead the company in the attack on Santa Maria Olivetto, I was the first officer to be wounded. I got a bullet through my left

Tess and George Galo, on their wedding day, June 25, 1942.
(Photo by Bartlett Studios)

shoulder about two hundred feet from the edge of the village. Every officer in the company was killed or wounded in a short time. I watched my company commander die slowly over a period of six hours while waiting to be evacuated from a horse barn that served as an aid station.

May the Infinite bless you and yours with good health, happiness and prosperity.

Respectfully,
George Galo

Tess and George Galo reunited after his discharge from the hospital, in the spring of 1943.
(Courtesy of George Galo)

—— • ——

Dear Mr. Brokaw:

I want to share with you my dad's story.

This was written by my wonderful father, Clyde I. Fitz, in November 1992 and dedicated to his three grandchildren (my children), Courtney, Corey and Caitlyn Mongan. While we were excited when we received this on Christmas Day in 1992, my children and I didn't realize its true significance until my dad passed away on July 19, 1998.

The morning he died my children (now teenagers) and I sat around our dining room table sorting through pictures and mementoes of my dad's that we could use as a memorial to him at his funeral service. When I came across this writing I began to read it out loud, and you can imagine the chills that ran down my spine as I approached the end of the writing and realized that my dad had died on the 53rd anniversary of his discharge from the U.S. Army. Ironic it was that it happened that way, but I really believe my dad held on to the last few days of his life to reach this milestone.

He was remarkable at remembering life events and the dates they had occurred. I told my children that if Pappy were alive that day, he would have reminded us that "53 years ago today I was discharged from the Army." To be perfectly honest, if we had heard that, we would have probably rolled our eyes, laughed and went on with our busy lives.

We now realize how important his life was and how much pride he had in his Country and his wonderful "GOOD BUDDIES." He carried this pride to his grave. Now, we also realize what an impact all of our Veterans have had on our lives down over the generations. They have all been taken for granted (not forgotten though). Where would our Country be without all of them?

Sincerely,
Dawn Lowenhaupt

To My Grandchildren—Courtney, Corey, Caitlyn

This may or may not be of interest to you later in school.

Born November 9, 1918, I was a teenager during the Great Depression. Lots more people were out of work than were working.

At my home we had plenty to eat as we had chickens and hogs. Our meat was mostly chicken and pork. Also, had plenty eggs unless the price of eggs was up. All our vegetables came from our garden. Our fruit we got by picking for other people for it. In the spring the chicken hens would hatch up to 20 chicks. We worked for farmers for pigs, and grain for hog and chicken feed. The money we got for eggs and lard went for sugar, flour and other staples.

The Depression was rough, but a good educator. One could live without money.

On December 7, 1941, the Japanese bombed Pearl Harbor. We were at war.

I always felt my place was in the Army, so I enlisted. I was inducted in Baltimore on December 12, 1941, and was issued dog tags. My ASN (Army Serial Number) was 10343459. I never forgot it.

The night of May 7, 1942, I was on my way to Fort Dix, New Jersey, by rail. Arrived at Fort Dix in the afternoon of May 8. Was assigned to "B" Battery, 91st A.F.A. BN, 1st Armored Division.

On June 17, 1942, we landed in Belfast in Northern Ireland. Seemed everything was different—people, money, buildings, fences and the English language.

I was transferred to "A" Btry, 68th A.F.A. Again I had to learn new names and make new friends. We trained in Ireland until fall, then shipped to Scotland, then to England on October 24, 1942.

We stayed in England until Thanksgiving Day, when we boarded ship at Liverpool and sailed that night. Most parts of that ship were very dirty (which we cleaned). Food was very sorry (which we had to eat).

Some five days later we were told we were going to North Africa. We were briefed on what to expect once there. Most of it was useless as most of the people were friendly. It wasn't hot; we didn't need our new sunglasses (it rained most of the first month). Christmas was just another day that year, C rations and all.

Sunday, January 31, 1943, we moved in daylight to the front. As we were pulling into position the Germans bombed our battery. It was 3 P.M. We remember the time, as a lot of GI watches stopped as well as others. Concussion from bombs broke the balance staffs. Had four more air raids before dark. The last one nearly got me; three bombs too close for comfort.

The place was Station De Sened. Monday, February 1, 8 A.M., over a ridge to our right front, 57 dive-bombers appeared. Out of the bright sun they came right at us, dropped their bombs, behind us they turned and came at us again.

Dawn Lowenhaupt's father, Clyde Fitz, who served with the 1st Armored Division in Europe. (Courtesy of Dawn Lowenhaupt)

This time they strafed us with machine guns. I was hit in the armpit to left upper chest. Our half-track with 105 Howitzer and ammunition and trailer were all on fire and lost.

I was knocked down and dazed, but my head cleared and I was able to warn the others of the fire. I got away from it fast.

I was in a hospital over the next five weeks or so. Eight weeks to the day I joined the 68th.

In April we saw a lot of action. El Guettar was a hot spot

until April 7th. Our forces broke through, a thirty-mile rat race that day. After that we were in the hills SW of and in Mateur itself. The hard rough war of Africa ended about the 9th of May. We made lots of mistakes, had hardships and frightening times. Thank God, we seemed to profit from them all and won.

Late in October we started to move again. This time not all at once. I left November 9 from Oran for Naples, Italy. By the time I got to Italy, they were already getting ready for battle. We could only take a few clothes and personal supplies. On the night of the 30th of November, we moved into firing position. We dug in and camouflaged, then carried ammunition down the muddy slippery paths to our guns, three rounds at a time; total weight 155 pounds.

The night of December 4th we were some of the hundreds of guns to fire on Mt. Camino. Our shells were 75% high explosive and 25% white phosphorus. The phosphorus glowed real bright when it exploded. We on the guns had no time to look, but the mountain seemed to be on fire. By morning it was reported the mountain was ours. But the Germans counterattacked and more firing and hard work [ensued].

Mt. Porchia and the mountain village San Pietro were hard fought but were finally taken. At the Rapido River our infantry ran into all kinds of trouble. The little river was swift. The Germans were defending the north bank. Many were the rounds that we fired there.

About the first of March we shipped from Naples to Anzio beachhead. We sure had to dig in there. Everyone had to sleep underground in holes covered with wood and earth. We pitched a double pup tent over the top. Everything—guns, ammunition and holes—had to be camouflaged. Our 105's were fired nearly every day. We always tried to improve our position and our living conditions. We were in for a long stay.

About the middle of April, I was sent back to Naples with a detachment to guard barracks bags and excess equipment. I felt I was letting my buddies down but was told someone had to do that job—it might as well be me.

It was a gravy job; in the rear, guard duty was a snap. Our workday was easy. We didn't sleep on the cold wet ground anymore. The sounds of war were far away—real peaceful.

With the war over in Italy, I returned to "A" Battery. Many

of my buddies were on their way home or elsewhere. We moved a lot of German POWs some 200 miles. They were starting home also.

Near the end of June we received the orders we were waiting for. We were going home. We went the long way— Northern Italy, North Africa, South Africa, South America and then Florida. Most of all of the way by air—10,500 miles. From Florida we went to Ft. Meade, where I was discharged July 19, 1945.

I learned a lot in the Army. I took orders and carried them out the best I could. I never got in big trouble. I hope I did my bit to help keep this great country the land of the free.

I was with the best of men. Could not have picked better. On the other side one needed FRIENDS. Mine were my GOOD BUDDIES.

May God bless them all.

Clyde I. Fitz

November 1992

———— • ————

Dear Mr. Brokaw:

Much attention has been given to the accomplishments, training and development of the black "Tuskegee" pilots during WWII. The Tuskegee experience was an experiment by the War Department to see if black people could fly military aircraft in combat, and to see if they had the physical and mental capabilities to become Air Force pilots. After years of resistance and debate, the War Department in 1941 announced acceptance of applications from Negroes. Candidates for the "Tuskegee Experiment" were drawn from black universities and colleges and selected enlisted men.

The name of the program comes from the fact that the contract for the original training was with the Tuskegee Institute in Alabama. Tuskegee Army Air Base, located in deeply segregated Alabama, was set up and maintained as an all-Negro airbase, with white instructors. From March 1942 to March 1946, 926 pilots completed training and graduated from the Tuskegee Army Flying School.

The initial unique thing about the program was that for black enlistees, there was a specially designed aptitude/educational-level test, which was used to select only the best candidates. (White enlistees just had to pass the basic physical exams and could have their choice of branches of service.)

The unique quality of these enlistees was that they came from many different subcultures in America. There was much cultural and social diversity within the group, and varying levels of social sophistication. Some came from the same city, neighborhood, or black college, where their social interaction went back for generations; others from inner cities and rural areas where this opportunity was a dream come true.

The Tuskegee airmen in front of a B-18. Robert Lawrence is fifth from the right. (Courtesy of Robert Lawrence)

Atypically, we were given no basic training, but were placed into technical school immediately, in order to learn the requirements for running an airbase. A majority was placed into mechanics school, and the rest were divided into weather, operations, transportation, communications, and all other aspects to make up a functioning unit.

We were housed in old WWI barracks, on the south side of the field, greatly separated from the main portion of the base, which had permanent barracks. Our assignments were to go to school, Monday through Friday. Another element imposed upon this original training group was the importation of a contingent of black draftees from Ft. Benning and Ft. Huachuca, brought in to provide support—the "grunt work," KP, yard duty, transportation, and all necessary maintenance. This was a contingent of black soldiers most of whom were illiterate, and except for a few "old soldiers," they were men who had been drafted, unlike the specially tested "enlisted men." This added another social stratum to be dealt with. They were integrated into the barracks with those of us who were going to school full-time. In spite of the educational differences, a bond was forged between the two groups. They provided the support work during the week, while we were assigned their duties on the weekend. The gap between the two groups was bridged through our writing and answering letters for those who could not, teaching literacy, and generally encouraging upward mobility in the ways of the army. The support group in return expressed pride in their ability to help those of us who were able to take advantage of this technical training.

The unit developed. We were at Chanute Field from March through late October, till classes were completed. Then as a unit we were shipped from Chanute Field to Montgomery, Ala., Maxwell Field, by troop train, to make up the cadre for the base at Tuskegee. As we passed through Cincinnati, the orders came to pull down the shades on all windows. So from Cincinnati to Montgomery we traveled with the window shades down, because the "powers that be" felt it was not a good thing to have a whole trainload of black troops observed being shipped into the South. They wanted to keep it secret, or at least as quiet as possible.

Upon arrival at Maxwell Field, 75 men were assigned to go directly to Tuskegee to form the initial group; the rest of the 150 or so technically trained men were left at Maxwell and assigned maintenance duties, regardless of their technical training, such as street sweeping, garbage detail, laundry, and the building of a rifle range. This was a most humiliating experience, as you can imagine, to have been trained for technical work, and then be put to work doing maintenance for the white troops at Maxwell Field.

I was one of the 75 who were sent directly to Tuskegee to live in the tent city while the base was being built. On the initial trip from Montgomery to Tuskegee, we encountered, some of us for the first time, the attitude of whites toward blacks in the South. We were in a convoy of trucks and a civilian's vehicle got between two trucks and was in a minor accident, hit by the truck behind.

Upon investigation by the Alabama Highway patrol, the Sgt. said that since this was a U.S. Army convoy, they'd have to go through the military personnel in order to conduct the investigation. At this time our Sgt. in charge was told, "This is the Confederacy, and we can do whatever we want. And boy, get back up into that truck." They then proceeded to arrest the drivers of both trucks and took them off to jail—a shocking experience for those of us who were in the South for the first time.

As the men were trained and developed in a combat unit, there was the usual advancement in rank among personnel. This resulted in many becoming noncommissioned and commissioned offers, and some pilots. Because there was only one place where those who were black could go after officer's training in the Army Air Corps, there were not the usual transfers to other bases. Everyone remained in the same community. Even our Commanding Officer, B. O. Davis, went through pilot training alongside the cadets he would later command. This created the situation where many old friends, buddies and classmates had to adjust to the protocol and discipline imposed by rank, and had to maintain the relationship the military required between officers and enlisted men. Many old bonds and relationships were put through unusual tests and stresses.

This was quite a study of human nature and the development of a community. I believe that the accomplishments and contributions of these men in later life to many communities throughout the country were due to lessons learned during their maturation process in the Tuskegee experience.

Robert W. Lawrence

———— • ————

Dear Mr. Brokaw,

Sunday, December 7th, 1941. I was on my way to the nurses' residence at Harlem Hospital after attending a football game. Captain Ulysses Campbell was with me when he turned the radio on and we learned that the Japanese had bombed Pearl Harbor and America was at war. Alarmed and shaken, we parked the car to sit and listen to the news being broadcast over every station. I went back to the nurses' home and Ulie rushed to join his unit.

Graduation was still several months away, and the state board examinations had to be taken and passed for registration. The calls for nurses to volunteer became more numerous. Two of my schoolmates, Mary Richards and Alice Dankley, and I decided to enlist as soon as we were eligible.

At that time in our history, black nurses could choose to go to any military installation where there were black soldiers. We knew a great deal about "the Tuskegee experiment" and we wanted to share our skills, encouragement and support to enable our best, most dedicated and brightest young men to demonstrate their ability to become military pilots.

In March of 1943, the three of us received our orders to be sworn in and to travel to Tuskegee, Alabama. There we were assigned to the base hospital at TAAF as of April 2nd, 1943. I was excited and anxious to leave—my mother was terrified of what I might do or say when faced with "Jim Crow," about which I had heard but had not been exposed to as lawfully practiced in the South.

Memories of the humiliation endured by three young women, patriotic and eager to serve, haunt me to this day. We traveled from New York to Washington, then to Atlanta and then to Chehaw, Alabama. Fortunately the trip from Atlanta to Chehaw was only a four-hour one. However, we were cautioned to wait until the last meal call before going to dine. Even so, we were placed in the end of the car and separated by a curtain pulled across to prevent our being seen by any other diners.

I arrived at Chehaw, where there was a tiny shack for a railroad station. But even as small as it was, it had been divided into (separate but "unequal") facilities labeled "Colored" and "White." We were picked up at Chehaw and taken to TAAF. There we were met by Captain Della Raney, our Chief Nurse. I can't say enough about how welcome Captain Raney made me feel.

After being assigned quarters and meeting the other nurses, I wanted nothing more than to bathe and fall into bed. However, there was a farewell party being given for the 99th Fighter Squadron, which was leaving that night for overseas duty. So I stepped into my spanking new uniform and off we all went to the Officers' Club.

That was the most eventful night of my life. I met Charles Dryden, who was a fellow New Yorker, and within thirty minutes I learned that he loved music, loved to dance, was on the rebound, his parents were Jamaican as was my father, we were the same age and had even been born in the same hospital in New York. It didn't

Irma and Charlie Dryden, November 1943.
(Courtesy of Irma Dryden)

take long to realize that this young man "had come from a good table."

Charlie had the warmest smile and the most honest engaging personality I had ever encountered. It was as though we'd known each other on another plane in another time. I was smitten—convinced that fate had a hand in the timing of the meeting. Had I arrived on April 3rd instead of April 2nd, we would not have met. In October of 1943 Charlie returned home from overseas. On November 16th, 1943, we were married.

TAAF was a wonderful place to be. My pride is boundless as I review this accomplishment. Several nurses married Tuskegee Airmen. They have remained our friends over the years.

Sincerely,

Irma Dryden

———— • ————

Dear Mr. Brokaw:

I thought you may find the enclosed letter interesting. It was written to me by my husband, Alfred F. Birra, in July of 1944.

Needless to say, I'm proud of "my man," as are many other widows of heroes throughout this country.

Sincerely yours,

Barbara A. Birra

(Mrs. Alfred F.)

France—July 12, 1944

Hello, Honey:

This makes the third time I've started this letter, and always something comes up to interfere with its writing. We're on a new front and I've just returned after a rather hectic night with Jerry. It seems we wanted to build a bridge at a certain spot, and Jerry, he didn't like the idea at all.

You may recall a few months ago that I wrote you that the company had been detached from the battalion and was on some special work. At the time I couldn't say with whom, naturally enough, but now I can. For six weeks we attended special training in assault and amphibious work. Upon conclusion of this training we were attached to the Fourth Infantry Division, which, as you probably know, was the first unit to land in France. We became part of what is known in the Army as a Combat Team. A Combat Team is composed roughly of a regiment of Infantry, Engineers, Artillery, and other attached technical units. Our particular team was chosen out of the Division to spearhead the Invasion. Thus we became the first American Troops to land on the coast of France. It was not until two days before we embarked and were issued our maps that we knew for certain that it was the real thing.

We had been aboard ship for three days, living a life of

ease and luxury and formulating our final plans when the General came aboard. He made an address to the troops via the P.A. and left sealed orders with the commander of the troops: These orders contained the information as to D-Day and H-Hour. At about five o'clock on the evening of June 5th, it was announced to us that at 0630 on the following morning we would land on the coast of France. The first platoon and the commanding officer of Co. 6, 237th Engineers, would land with the first assault wave. The remainder would come ashore in succeeding waves. We were charged with breaching a concrete seawall and clearing passageways of obstacles and mines so that the tanks that were landing with us could get off the beach. A very vital point, since without the support of the tanks, with their armor and heavy guns, the Infantry would be too busy protecting its own skin to do any real good. Although we knew most of this, it still came as somewhat of a shock, and we set about making last-minute preparations.

There weren't many men who got much sleep that night of June 5th. For the most part, we sat around, talked, played cards, drank coffee and did the usual things a man does when he is worried and a little scared and doesn't want to show it. At 0230 in the morning breakfast was served, of which most of us partook heartily since we knew it would be, if not our last meal, at least the last for quite a few hours or perhaps days. At 0330 we began the business of debarking. The weatherman had been, as is the wont with that particular breed, very wrong in his prediction. Instead of the smooth, glassy sea he predicted, it was very rough and cold, and the night was inky black so that a man had to feel his way about the ship, stumbling and cursing softly. The small landing craft were loosened from the davits, and each absorbed its crew of men and equipment and was lowered into a black sea, which seemed to reach up with hungry arms to drag the frail craft down. How can I describe the feeling which grips you at this moment. Kent echoed my feeling exactly when he said that this precise moment, when the assault boat was being lowered from the mother ship, was the loneliest time in his life. No one says a word except the man at the cables. As the boat goes down the rail, the ship disappears, and with a slap that jars everyone aboard, the craft hits the water. The cables are cast off, and now you're entirely on your own and alone.

We chugged away, and in a few seconds the large mother ship became just a darker blob in a world of darkness and then disappeared from view entirely. It was now time to start for the rendezvous area, where we would meet the rest of the craft that made up our wave. In just a few minutes the spray from the waves slapping the bow and sides of the boat had us all thoroughly drenched, and the men began to snap out of their lethargy only to find themselves miserably seasick. I can safely say that of the thirty men aboard at least twenty were seasick. I myself didn't have time, nor could I display any form of weakness by getting sick. We were soon at the rendezvous area, and the boats comprising the wave got into their proper positions and began to circle. We were about six miles off-shore at this point. Soon things began to happen that made even the most wretched sit up with interest. The show had started. And it started with the Navy. In the distance on all sides we could see the huge sleek forms of battleships and de-stroyers vomiting flames of fire as their fourteen- and sixteen-inch guns opened fire. The air was filled with deafening roars and the screams of shells. Then the coastal defense batteries opened up and added to the general hubbub. We had no sooner become accustomed to this when over the nose of the battleships we heard the roar of hundreds of motors, the air corps were coming in. And come in they did, literally in waves, and made for shore and their targets. That their bombs were effective was evidenced by the fires that soon lit up the entire black night. That the enemy was striking back was also soon evidenced by the ack-ack that started to crosshatch the sky. The entire picture defies description by my limited senses, and no matter how retentive, I could not possibly have absorbed the entire picture and all of the occurrences. But time to get busy now. Dawn has broken, and dimly in a haze of smoke we can see the beach. Now it's our turn. Men scram-ble to their feet, equipment is adjusted, life belts made more secure, for all around us artillery shells are falling, and al-ready several boats have been hit. Rifles are loaded and the safety taken off. The shore is now right off the bow. The coxswain signals me that we're about to touch down, the ramp is lowered, and the Sgt and I stepped off into four feet of water. I look behind, and the men are already off the boat and scattered for protection against the bullets, which are singing around us but for the most part hitting the water. It was a hell of a feeling. We had about 500 yards of water to cross, we couldn't run cause the water was too deep, we couldn't crouch, we couldn't do anything except just what we did. Wade on into the shore. Finally we made it, we were on the beach and could begin to fight back and to do our work. How well we did it you have read about in the papers, told to you by men more gifted than myself. How well we did it is also evidenced by the citations we've won. One for the entire battalion, and a separate one for C Company and for A Company. Sometime when I can I'll write or, better yet, tell you about more that happened, both humorous and tragic. Like the Colonel who came over to me in the midst of heavy fire and said "Captain, how in the hell do you load this rifle?" or like the time that Kent and I were lying in a ditch. I was getting a light from Kent's cigarette when a shell landed so close the concussion blew us about a foot apart but both of us got up unhurt.

I really must go now, darling.

Al

———•———

Dear Tom:

I, too, came up during the Depression at around the age of fourteen (14). My father told me, "There's the world, make the best of it." When I was eighteen (18) I joined the Navy. Things were a lot better. At least I had clothes after training. I went on an amphibious ship which landed troops on the beaches. My first beach was Normandy. We headed for the beach at 1:00 a.m. We were told there was no turning back. They were throwing everything they had (bullets and artillery). As we were going in we rammed in between two telephone poles and were hung up. We let the ramp down for the soldiers to get off. They jumped into the water at about five or six feet deep. About fifteen minutes later four of us had to jump also. I remember getting so far in and then crawling to keep from being killed. Probably some of these boys that I was crawling over were the ones we had just left off. I finally made it onto the beach crawling, where I found a sandbar to hide under. This is where the nightmare began. I lay there for the next four hours, until daylight. Then I realized there was nothing but bodies as far as I could see, and the water was red with blood. From there I went to Marseilles, France. We landed troops on the beaches there, and then on to Oran, Africa, where we picked up troops and transported them to the Riviera. From there we went back to England and over to the South Pacific.

I could go on and on, but this is the basics of my tour of duty with the United States Navy, which I was proud to serve.

Sincerely,
Archie F. McDole, Sr.

———— • ————

Dear Mr. Brokaw:

In Hartford on July 30, 1942, my twentieth birthday, I received my notice to report for a physical examination for the draft and ten days later was informed I was classified 1A.

James Branch at twenty, in a photo taken in Wisconsin during his basic training. (Courtesy of Moen Photo)

At Camp McCoy, Wisconsin, in the winter of 1942–43, I took thirteen weeks of basic training in snow that was sometimes waist-deep. Temperatures were below zero most nights and only ten degrees by day.

In October 1943 we were shipped to Camp Shanks, New York. Two days later we boarded the USS *Florence Nightingale,* a cargo ship that had been converted into a troop carrier. We set sail with a one-hundred ship convoy for Belfast, Ireland, changing courses every five minutes to avoid German submarines operating in the North Atlantic.

We landed in Belfast, North Ireland, ten days after we had left New York. We boarded a train there and were taken to a little town called Newry, County Down, North Ireland.

We left there April 17th on the USS *Rosa,* a South American passenger liner, and arrived in Swansea, Wales, on April 19th. We left there June 4, 1944, aboard a Danish ship for the trip around the tip of England and up the English Channel on June 6th, only to be delayed in getting off the ship by resistance encountered by the first two divisions to go ashore, the 1st and 29th divisions, [that] the 2nd division was to follow. To say things did not go right for [the] 1st

James Branch's Order to Report for Induction, November 2, 1942.

Prepare in Duplicate

Local Board No. 2A   11
Hartford County   003
   021
1240 (LOCAL BOARD DATE STAMP WITH CODE)
Hartford, Conn.

Nov. 2, 1942.
(Date of mailing)

ORDER TO REPORT FOR INDUCTION

The President of the United States,

To   James   D.   Branch
(First name)   (Middle name)   (Last name)

Order No. 12,095

GREETING:

Having submitted yourself to a local board composed of your neighbors for the purpose of determining your availability for training and service in the armed forces of the United States, you are hereby

notified that you have now been selected for training and service in the _____
(Army, XXXXXXXXXXX)

You will, therefore, report to the local board named above at 555 Asylum St. Hartford, Conn.
(Place of reporting)

at 7:30 a. m., on the 24th day of November, 19 42.
(Hour of reporting)

This local board will furnish transportation to an induction station of the service for which you have been selected. You will there be examined, and, if accepted for training and service, you will then be inducted into the stated branch of the service.

Persons reporting to the induction station in some instances may be rejected for physical or other reasons. It is well to keep this in mind in arranging your affairs, to prevent any undue hardship if you are rejected at the induction station. If you are employed, you should advise your employer of this notice and of the possibility that you may not be accepted at the induction station. Your employer can then be prepared to replace you if you are accepted, or to continue your employment if you are rejected.

Willful failure to report promptly to this local board at the hour and on the day named in this notice is a violation of the Selective Training and Service Act of 1940, as amended, and subjects the violator to fine and imprisonment.

If you are so far removed from your own local board that reporting in compliance with this order will be a serious hardship and you desire to report to a local board in the area of which you are now located, go immediately to that local board and make written request for transfer of your delivery for induction, taking this order with you.

Betty L. Truck
Member or clerk of the local board.

D. S. S. Form 150
(Revised 7-13-42)

U. S. GOVERNMENT PRINTING OFFICE   16—18271-3

James Branch and his friend Ralph Herr at the American staging area in south Wales, 1944.

The foxhole occupied by James Branch (right) in the Ardennes in 1944: "My home away from home."

James Branch in Pilsen, Czechoslovakia, with "Old Faithful #13," the truck he used to haul ammo and explosives. (All courtesy of James Branch)

THE UNITED STATES OF AMERICA

VETERANS' ADMINISTRATION

WASHINGTON, D. C.

National Service Life Insurance

DATE INSURANCE EFFECTIVE _JANUARY 1, 1943_

CERTIFICATE No. N– _7 697 394_

This Certifies That _JAMES D. BRANCH_

has applied for insurance in the amount of $ _5,000._, payable in case of death.

Subject to the payment of the premiums required, this insurance is granted under the authority of The National Service Life Insurance Act of 1940, and subject in all respects to the provisions of such Act, of any amendments thereto, and of all regulations thereunder, now in force or hereafter adopted, all of which, together with the application for this insurance, and the terms and conditions published under authority of the Act, shall constitute the contract.

Frank T. Hines
Administrator of Veterans' Affairs.

Countersigned at Washington, D. C.

February 2, 1943
(Date)

L. D. Yankee
Registrar.

Mrs. Beulah Ethel Branch
635 W. Garland
Paragould, Ark.

Insurance Form 369

A $5,000 life-insurance policy issued to James Branch in 1943.

James Branch's dog tags, which he taped together to keep them from rattling.

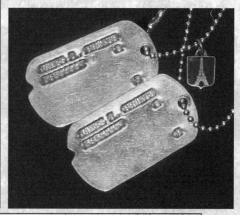

"Somewhere near Aachen / We hang up our stocking": A card sent home to the family, Christmas 1943. (All courtesy of James Branch)

and 2nd waves to hit the beaches is a gross understatement! Incidentally, Omaha Beach had a code name: Easy Red Beach! The only correct part of that turned out to be the adjective Red. The beach was indeed Red, but there was nothing Easy about it!

Finally word came for us to board the landing craft. The famous rope nets had been let down off the ship to enable us to climb down. The navy engineers and others had sunk old ships that had been towed over from England for the purpose of providing a breakwater and shield to protect the landing craft from the withering machine-gun fire from the shore batteries on the chalk bluffs above the beach. By the time we were to leave the ship, word had reached us that the German gunners would try to zero in on landing craft coming in as soon as the ramp let down to unload the soldiers. They would try to put a round into the landing craft full of soldiers. We heard that on at least one occasion they succeeded and killed 99 of the 100 aboard that craft. So as our craft approached the beach, it came to an abrupt stop, and the coxswain, thinking we were in, lowered the ramp.

James Branch next to the memorial to the Second Infantry Division at Saint-Georges-d'Elle, April 1999. (Courtesy of James Branch)

I had positioned myself so that as soon as the ramp went down I went off the side of it into the water, and, having everything I owned either on my back or around my waist, I went in so deep that my knees buckled under the load. I went in over my head, holding my rifle and ammunition high to try to keep them dry as we had been taught to do. We had hit a sandbar and did not go in as far as had been expected, but this probably saved several lives.

Everything was floating in the channel, dead bodies and body parts, tires, backpacks, you name it and if it would float it was there. It was a scene I will never forget. For two days it was doubtful we would be able to stay there, although no one knew or had heard of any contingency plans. As far as we knew, we were there to stay or to die trying!

After the initial shock of battle, of seeing death close up, of not eating for about fifty-six hours, and not getting any sleep, we finally got it all together and became the fighting force that would eventually win the war.

James D. Branch

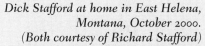

*Dick Stafford and Shirley Jones in
Chicago, November 1943.*

*Dick Stafford at home in East Helena,
Montana, October 2000.
(Both courtesy of Richard Stafford)*

—— • ——

Dear Mr. Brokaw:

I joined the Navy in 1942 at 15 and was promptly kicked out for being too young. I joined again at 16 and was in for the duration. I sustained wounds on Omaha Beach that left me permanently disabled. Unlike a few I know, I was not embittered as a result.

I never went to high school except for a short time, but after the war I took the GED Exam and went on to college. I taught high school and college for more than 30 years. Had it not been for the war, it is most unlikely I would have gotten an education and then gone on to a rewarding career.

While I certainly would not want to repeat my experiences in the war and although I still think of friends who were lost, I am grateful for the experience and for that wonderful G.I. Bill that paid for an excellent education at a Jesuit institution.

Sincerely,
Richard E. Stafford

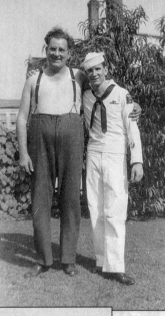

Dick Stafford upon his return from overseas, September 1944.

Dick Stafford on his way back to the Navy after a short leave, November 1943.

Dick Stafford and his father-in-law to be, Chicago, 1944.

Officers and Men

Thanksgivings are manifest of our deepest appreciation for the freedom, liberties and opportunities of this, your land and mine.

In all of the three hundred and twenty-three Thanksgiving Days no other one more plainly demonstrates the blessings of a free America.

Wherever Old Glory stands . . o'er the burning sands of the desert . . . or the frigid Northern climes . . your shipmates and mine will pause for prayer that this Thanksgiving will perpetuate the bounty of our own democracy and bring to the oppressed peoples of other lands . . . a new faith and spirit of freedom . . . such as only you and I and the Pilgrim fathers may claim.

As officer-in-charge, my thanks is to you, the Officers and Men, for your willingness in duty and effectiveness in the performance of the job to be done here at Camp Thomas.

C. T. DICKEMAN
Capt. (CEC) USN

Mixed Fruit

ASPARAGUS SOUP
CROUTONS

CELERY HEARTS - SALTED NUTS - QUEEN OLIVES

ROAST VERMONT TURKEY
GIBLET DRESSING

WHIPPED SWEET POTATOES
MARSHMALLOW SAUCE

BUTTERED GIANT GREEN PEAS

HEAD LETTUCE - FRENCH DRESSING

NEW YORK ROLLS - BUTTER

PUMPKIN CREAM PIE

MIXED NUTS IN THE SHELL

COFFEE   CHOCOLATES

CIGARETTES

Music BY THE CAMP THOMAS DANCE ORCHESTRA

Thanksgiving dinner menu issued to sailors, 1943.
(All courtesy of Richard Stafford)

Dear Mr. Brokaw:

I am 80 years old, my memories are many, both good and bad. My parents were both born in England, lived within 50 miles of each other but never met. Each came to Canada for different reasons, to meet and marry in Victoria, British Columbia. We grew up in San Francisco, California, having come there from Canada on a coastwise steamer in 1922.

My memory took me back to the year of training the Army gave me, sent me to specialized schools, Master gunner, Radio clerk, Code clerk and two colleges for more training. Spent 4 months in signal intelligence at Camp Kohler, near Sacramento. Most of my training gave me a chance to get to know a great bunch of guys.

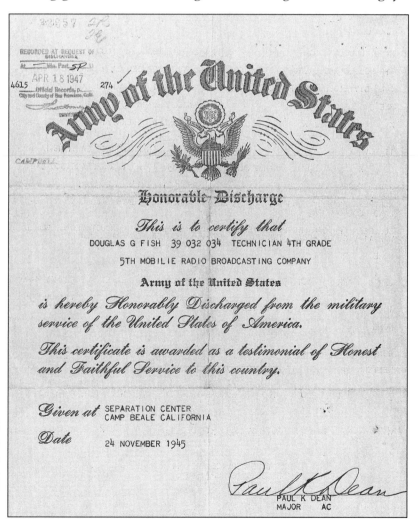

"A testimonial of Honest and Faithful Service to this country": discharge papers issued to Douglas Fish, November 24, 1945. (Courtesy of Douglas Fish)

Also I lost my resentment of being drafted. I began to write to my wife telling her what a privilege it was to be considered an American. Later I realized that I had been chosen to save my adopted country and in a little way contributed to the great effort to preserve the freedom we all enjoy. What a privilege for a foreign-born.

At the end of all my training, I was put in military intelligence, P.W.D. (Psychological Warfare Division). A totally new unit to fight Goebbels's Nazi propaganda. Going to England to prepare for the Normandy Invasion. On that day we were sent to a port of embarkation. For days, it seemed like forever, we waited. We boarded a ship to take us to meet some LSTs, and climbing down the nets in the dark was very scary, some of the guys carried little American flags in their pockets to give to the friends when we waded ashore. So proud of being Americans, but not many lived to fulfill their dream.

I went in the service as a boy and came out a man. I will always believe in the draft because I had an experience that changed my life. We live in such a small world that to be with all different people, race, creeds sure broadened my horizons.

God bless America

Douglas G. Fish, ASN 39032034

PARIS ASSIGNMENT CARD   Nᵒ P 27820

HEADQUARTERS, SEINE SECTION, COM Z
EUROPEAN T OF OPNS, U.S. ARMY

This is to certify that :

Douglas Fish — Name   T/5 — Rank   39032034 — ASN (or Civ)

P.W.D. — Org.   Supreme Hq. AEF — Hq.   is stationed for
duty in Paris.

Brigadier General, A.G.D., U.S.A.
(Brig.) (Maj.) (Lt.) General

Date : 23 November 1944   (Conditions on Reverse)

Paris Assignment Card issued to Douglas Fish, November 1944.
(Courtesy of Douglas Fish)

———— • ————

Dear Mr. Brokaw:

Please let me introduce you to my grandfather. His name is Louis J. Sosa, and he is 78 years old. I call him Papa.

Papa was in the 82nd Airborne during the D-Day invasion. On the day of the invasion, he was riding in a glider (or flying coffin, as he called it) that was supposed to take him into Sainte-Mère-Église, one of the small French towns outside Normandy. As the glider came in for a landing, it crashed into the hedgerows, trapping Papa and everyone else inside. The pilot and copilot were killed, along with many others on board, but Papa managed to crawl past them and escaped through the nose of the glider. He

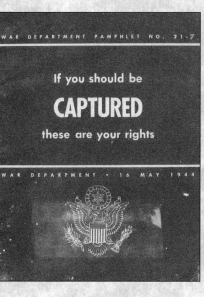

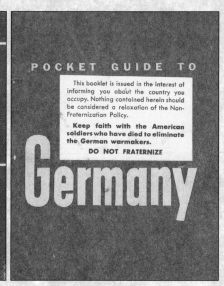

POCKET GUIDE TO

This booklet is issued in the interest of informing you about the country you occupy. Nothing contained herein should be considered a relaxation of the Non-Fraternization Policy.

Keep faith with the American soldiers who have died to eliminate the German warmakers.
DO NOT FRATERNIZE

Germany

FAR LEFT: *The booklet issued to soldiers stationed in Europe to ready them for possible capture. "As a prisoner of war you are in a tough spot, but the Army hasn't forgotten you."*

LEFT: *The Pocket Guide to Germany, issued to soldiers to familiarize them with the country they were invading. "There must be no fraternization. This is absolute!"*

Douglas Fish in Luxembourg, 1944.

Douglas Fish and four friends in Paris, 1944.

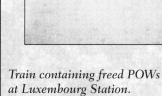

Train containing freed POWs at Luxembourg Station.

Douglas Fish in Paris, 1944.

Peter Robertson, Douglas Fish, and Lieutenant Cronberger, in a photo taken in the Tuileries, Paris, December 1944.
(All courtesy of Douglas Fish)

and the few other survivors managed to find each other and then joined another unit in the fighting.

Papa fought on into Belgium, where he was hit in the leg by shrapnel while serving as a lookout atop an observation tower. The medics wanted to send him to a nearby hospital, but Papa told them "hell no." As he said to me, "we were so close to the German border and we were pushing them back, and there was no way I was turning back then." Papa kept fighting until the Allies crossed the Elbe River, where he shared vodka with the Russians and toasted victory.

Papa used to let me and my sister play with his shoe box of medals from the war when we were kids. Like so many veterans, he never talked about the war. When I became older, I began to realize the magnitude of Papa's wartime experience and decided to pull out the shoe box of medals again. I had the medals framed in the order that they should appear on a uniform and gave them to Papa

Jackie Barron's grandfather Louis Sosa, a member of the 82nd Airborne Division.

for Christmas. It was one of only two times that I've ever seen him cry. The other was on the 50th anniversary of D-Day, when he finally talked about World War II—about the swastika armband in his box of medals, about watching his friends walk beside him one minute and die next to him seconds later, about drinking vodka with the Russians, and even about the wine, women and scenery of Europe.

Lilly and Louis Sosa, 1999.
(Both courtesy of Jackie Barron)

Papa said that he never realized how scared he'd been until near the end of the war, when he was discharged. At the moment when he could finally go home, Papa became convinced that the death he'd avoided during the long years of the war would catch up to him—that his jeep would drive over a land mine, or the plane carrying him home would crash, or that something else "foolish" would happen after all that time spent fighting in the

war. It was on that long journey back to Tampa, Florida, that Papa had what he describes as the first moment when he truly felt that he wouldn't make it . . . the first time he was frightened.

My grandfather is a wonderful man. Despite the atrocities he witnessed, this second-generation American forged ahead and built a family and an honorable life.

Sincerely,
Jackie Barron

———— • ————

Dear Mr. Brokaw,

Way back in the very late 1930s I met a boy. He delivered groceries for my mother, who managed a grocery store. Did it with a wagon for tips alone and saved the money to buy a bicycle. We were good friends, teased each other a lot and laughed and joked around. In 1940, my sister was getting married and he came to my house to wash the windows. This was another way to earn money (in those days receptions were held in the basement with food cooked by friends and neighbors). As I was the maid of honor and in my first formal dress, he took one look at me and decided he liked what he saw. We dated each other quite a bit after that, but we attended different high schools and he was so busy becoming an all-state wrestler and I was so wrapped up in my school affairs that we were still just good buddies.

When he asked me to his senior prom, I realized we could become more than just friends. He was so attentive and sweet. We stayed out all night (a first for both of us). I can still remember the restaurant where we ate breakfast. This was the start of a love affair that has lasted over 50 years.

He graduated from high school in 1941 and went to work for the railroad loading boxcars (to stay in shape, as he put it).

We dated—movies, swimming, long walks—like all the kids did back then. In 1942 I graduated from high school, but by that time our country was at war. Boys in my class were given their diplomas early so they could enlist. He was the right age and certainly the right physical condition, but he supported his family so he was given a deferment. His brother was in the regular army, his dad was disabled, so his mom and little sister depended upon him. On Saturday nights we went to a neighborhood bar and danced and sang old songs. We were the best jitterbuggers you ever saw! We would dance a lot and then relax by singing old songs. To this day, "Heart of My Heart," "My Buddy," and "Oh How I Miss You Tonight" all remind me of those wonderful carefree days and bring tears to my eyes.

Uncle Sam then decided he needed one more good man, so in December of '42 he called him. Things were going better at home, his dad was working supporting the family, and he was anxious to go. So off he went to Camp Walters in Texas. One small furlough after basic training. He loved the army, said he was glad he had kept himself in shape because, to quote from his first letter, "some of the lads are having a tough time of it." In May 1943 he called home and said he'd be shipping out soon. His mother, older sister, and I went to New Jersey to see him. We rode what seemed to be a troop train from Chicago to Camp Kilmer. We arrived early Saturday afternoon and set off for the camp. He got a pass for Saturday night, and we all went to a local bar. I had been up all night on the train and was tired, so he and I left early after making plans for the next day. But the army had its own plans. We got a call at 9:00 a.m. Sunday morning that he was confined to base as they were shipping out that evening. We were allowed on base for a few hours to say goodbye. After a very tender farewell with many promises, kisses and tears, both his and mine, we parted.

"This is Wally Williams and me, taken the day he graduated from high school, 6-29-41. What a waste of strong young boys a war makes."
(Courtesy of Betty Morrill)

He was sent to England and seemed to enjoy it. We wrote regularly, and he sent little gifts, like my Mizpah pin (the Lord watch between me and thee when we are absent from one another), my bracelet made of English coins, and even a 1st Lt. Bar he had found somewhere. He met an English girl who could jitterbug (she and I wrote to each other for years).

Then came June 6, 1944. I knew in my heart he would be in the thick of things, but never once did it dawn on me that anything could happen to him. I followed the news reports each day in the paper, but they did not give division numbers. I received a VJ letter dated July 5, 1944, from somewhere in France. He said he was safe and sound and lonesome. I decided he had come through D-Day unharmed—the rest was a piece of cake.

Walford Williams in uniform, 1943.
(Courtesy of Betty Morrill)

In the middle of August '44 came that dreaded telegram: "missing in action." His brother came home on emergency leave from Fort Collins. We, the family and I, decided he had been cut off from his unit or taken prisoner, but nothing bad could happen to him. He was ours, and we wanted him to be alright!!!!

His brother returned to camp and wrote to me saying that while he was home on leave, he received the second telegram: "killed in action." He didn't know how to tell us, his mom and I, so he put it in a bittersweet letter. I cried for a week, put all my mementos in a scrapbook and went on with my life. His family had his body brought home for burial, had a touching memorial service and moved to California.

I married an army veteran, had two children, and was widowed at 37. I taught school for a while and remarried 5 years later. Again I became a widow. All this time, thru two marriages and deaths, I never forgot him.

So much is told of mothers and wives of GIs who were lost in WWII, but so little is mentioned of the sweethearts that were left behind. We too suffered, but without a gold star to hang in our window, just one to hang in our hearts, to remain there forever, symbolic of a life that might have been.

Sincerely,
Betty J. Morrill

———— • ————

Dear Mr. Brokaw:

Sergeant Ben Large was a housepainter from Springfield, Illinois, who once confided to me in a quiet moment that he had lied only twice in his life. First, he lied to get into the Army in World

Sergeant Ben Large.
(Courtesy of Ben Large)

Corporal Ed Mooney, a squad leader in an ammunition convoy, in France, c. December 1944.
(Courtesy of Ed Mooney)

"The occupational forces are not on a glad-hand mission": Special Orders for American-German Relations.
(Courtesy of Ed Mooney)

SPECIAL ORDERS FOR AMERICAN-GERMAN RELATIONS

1. To remember always that Germany, though conquered, is still a dangerous enemy nation.

a. It is known that an underground organization for the continuation of the Nazi program for world domination is already in existence. This group will take advantage of every relaxation of vigilance on our part to carry on undercover war against us.

b. The occupational forces are not on a glad-hand mission.

2. Never to trust Germans, collectively or individually.

a. For most of the past century, Germany has sought to attain world domination by conquest. This has been the third major attempt in the memory of men still living. To many Germans, this defeat will only be an interlude-a time to prepare for the next war.

b. The Germans have no regrets for the havoc they have wrought in the world, except for loss of life and property they themselves have suffered.

c. The German has been taught that the national goal of domination must be obtained regardless of the depths of treachery, murder and destruction necessary. He has been taught to sacrifice everything—ideals, honor, and even his wife and children for the State. Defeat will not erase that idea.

3. To defeat German efforts to poison my thoughts or influence my attitude.

a. The Nazis fouly practice that the most powerful propaganda weapon is distortion of truth. They have made evil use of it and will re-double their efforts immediately upon our occupation of Germany in order to poison our thinking. There will probably be deliberate, studied and continuous efforts to entice our sympathies and to escape the just consequences of their guilt.

b. You may expect all manner of approach—conversations to be overheard, underground publications to be found; there will be appeals to generosity and fair play; to pity for "victims of devastation;" to racial and cultural similarities; and to sympathy for an allegedly oppressed people.

c. There will be attempts at sowing discord among Allied nations; at undermining Allied determination to enforce the surrender; at inducing a reduction in occupational forces; at lowering morale and efficiency of the occupying forces; at proving that Nazism was never wanted by the "gentle and cultured" German people.

4. To avoid acts of violence, except when required by military necessity.

For you are an American soldier, not a Nazi.

5. To conduct myself at all times so as to command the respect of the German people for myself, for the United States, and for the Allied Cause.

a. The Germans hold all things military in deep respect. That respect must be maintained habitually or the Allied Cause is hurt and the first steps are taken toward World War III. Each soldier must watch every action of himself and of his comrades. The German will be watching constantly, even though you may not see him. Let him see a good American Soldier.

War One when he was a lad of sixteen. He passed as eighteen because, he said, "I bought this sack o' Bull Durham an' let the string tag dangle out o' my shirt pocket." Second, he lied to get into the Army in World War Two when he was 41. He was accepted as advertised, 38, and was assigned as a buck private to our truck company in Fort Custer, Michigan. In time, and deservedly so, Ben was promoted through the ranks to staff sergeant in charge of our second platoon.

Ben had a family of warriors too: three children—one son aboard a carrier based at Pearl, a second son fighting with the Rangers in Italy's mountains, and a daughter nursing for the Navy in the South Pacific.

One day in October 1944, while we were based in Pantin, a blue-collar area northeast of Paris, our newly named company commander, Herb Levy, from Fresno, California, was minding his own business when the bomb was dropped into his lap, namely that Ben's Ranger son had been killed in action in Italy, and it was Levy's task to break the news to the old soldier. "My God!" my onetime CO told me four and a half decades later during one of our unit's biennial reunions, this one in Fort Wayne, Indiana, "here I was a 25-year-old kid, a kid some big shot in the Army had told, 'You are now an officer.' So it was up to me to tell this much older enlisted man whom I respected as I had my father that his cherished son had been killed by the Germans.

"There was nothing to do," he continued, reminiscing, "but bite the bullet and get the job done. So I sent for Ben. He came into the orderly room, unsuspecting, snapped to attention in front of me and saluted. Saluted this runny-nosed kid of an officer! It seemed almost comical at the time, but it was so deadly serious. 'Ben,' I said, 'there's only one way to tell you this and that is to let you have it straight. Your son Jack has been killed in action.' Ben stood stock-still," Herb recalled. "Didn't move for what seemed minutes. Then the tears welled up in his eyes. He brushed his face with his sleeve . . . and he apologized! He apologized, Ed! 'Sorry, sir,' he said. For brushing his tears away!

"It was the most poignant moment of my life," our onetime CO confessed. "'Ben,' I told him, 'you can have anything that is in my power to give you. If you want a leave, if you want to be reassigned, if you want out of the Army, you name it and I'll do my damndest to get it for you.' And you know what that old warrior said to me, Ed? He said 'Sir, just send me on the first convoy to the front.'"

Ben Large did go on an early convoy to the front at age 43, was unaccounted for for several days, and returned without comment to serve with our outfit for the balance of the war.

Cordially,
Ed Mooney

———— • ————

Dear Mr. Brokaw:

I enjoyed reading your book *The Greatest Generation* and can relate with the time and experiences those people lived through. I also am one of those people and vividly remember those days with fondness and sadness.

I am one of the many guys who served in the military during World War 2 who came from Brooklyn.

We finished our basic training in Camp Swift. I was promoted to sergeant, I believe primarily because I could read and write. The entire division was shipped to lovely Louisiana for 3 months of ma-

"For gallantry in action":
Silver Star citation presented
to Sergeant John Pensabene.
(Courtesy of John Pensabene)

35th Infantry Division

Citation for

SILVER STAR MEDAL

TO Sergeant JOHN J. PENSABENE, 32 807 036, Company "C", 320th Infantry

For gallantry in action near Dieding, France, 8 December 1944. Company "C" was engaged in clearing the enemy from Dieding, when it was discovered that an officer was wounded and lay exposed to enemy fire. Sergeant Pensabene and two comrades, all riflemen, volunteered to attempt the evacuation of the officer, but in endeavoring to reach his position while crossing open ground, were subjected to intense direct fire from well-entrenched enemy operating a machine gun augmented by small arms. Realizing that the destruction of the enemy emplacement was a condition precedent to the evacuation of the wounded officer, Sergeant Pensabene, assisted by his comrades, coordinated their fire and movement, and attacked and destroyed the enemy emplacement, killed or captured the enemy personnel, thereby neutralizing an enemy position that hampered the occupation of Dieding. Sergeant Pensabene and his comrades then moved forward to the position of the wounded officer but found him dead. In returning to his company, he and his companions came upon a wounded man and removed him to the aid station. The gallant actions of Sergeant Pensabene are such as to be in accord with the traditions of the military service. Entered Military Service from New York.

GO NO 4
Hq 35th Inf Div
12 Jan 45

PAUL W. BAADE
MAJOR GENERAL U.S.A.
COMMANDING

neuvers. Aside from [the risk of] getting killed, I think combat was easier.

We landed on Omaha Beach. It was the middle of August. I vividly remember climbing that hill and imagining what those guys faced June 6. I finally reached the replacement depot. We had to stay until they called our names for assignment. One day, while we were hanging around, a G.I. who looked like a character from the Bill Mauldin cartoon Willie & Joe, unwashed, uniform a mess, strikes up a conversation with me. "You been in combat yet? You ain't got a chance. The Germans with those 88s [a very accurate artillery weapon]. I'll see you, pal." Somehow, all the propaganda films they showed us about killing the enemy and being a hero quickly faded. We were assembled for assignment. They called my name 3 times before I decided to answer. That guy really shook me up. "You're assigned to the 35th Div." Into an army truck and dropped off somewhere in the woods near Nancy, France, with no ammo, digging tools, etc. I was now a member of Patton's 3rd Army. Shortly, a lieutenant from Tennessee named Bass greeted the new replacements, telling us the unit was being held in reserve. Patton overran his supply lines. We were then offered cognac. Could this be the way the phrase "drink and be merry for tomorrow you may die" started. What a scenario: a buck sergeant from the States in charge of the machine-gun section of guys who have been in combat.

That night the "reserves" started getting shelled to hell. It lasted for hours. I couldn't dig because I had no shovel. I hid behind a tree. I was trying to bore thru the damn thing. You could hear screams. Apparently guys were being wounded or killed. At daylight, we discovered we had no commissioned officers in the unit. They were either wounded or disappeared. The noncoms were running the platoon.

December 8th. For much of the company, a fatal day. For me, a lucky one. We were preparing another attack. I remember the terrain on flat open ground as far as you could see. Beyond this clearing was the woods we had to go into. While we were waiting in a farmhouse to make our move, someone shouted one of the lieutenants from another company was apparently wounded and lying on the open ground about 300 yards away. Whatever possessed me, I thought I should go to his aid. As I was heading in that direction, I noticed a trench about 6 feet deep and the distance of the open ground. I decided to follow the trench. Until today, I still don't know why a freestanding stone wall about 10 feet high and 30 feet long was in back of this trench. I then saw 2 GI's about 50 yards behind me. What possessed me to stay in front of the wall and follow the trench, I don't know. As I approached the end of the wall, I looked into the trench and spotted a machine-gun emplacement. I yelled "get out." They must have thought "what the hell is get out." As they started to move towards their weapons, I fired 8 shots from my Garand rifle. The other 2 GI's now started firing rifle grenades. I figured they were going to kill me instead of the Germans. Suddenly, there was shooting from all directions. I ran around to flank the trench and was kneeling down to see how I could approach it. I reloaded my rifle. Suddenly I felt my right arm go limp. I looked down and saw a hole in my raincoat, blood trickling into my glove. The bullet went thru my arm and missed my body. I'd love to kiss the guy who fired that shot. I yelled to the other guys I was hit and ran like a gazelle to the aid station. Shooting was going on all around. I didn't stay to check it out.

John Pensabene being inducted into the New York City Police Department, February 27, 1948. (Courtesy of the NYPD Photo Gallery)

While I was in the base hospital in France waiting to be shipped to England for surgery, they brought in one of the sergeants from my company. He had casts on his arms and legs and was in pretty tough shape. He told me the Germans were waiting in the woods. Most of the outfit was annihilated.

In August 1945 I was discharged and back in Brooklyn. I went back to my job in the Brooklyn Navy Yard. I received a letter from the War Dept. I was to be awarded the Silver Star. I thought—for getting shot!

My definition of a hero is someone in the wrong place, at the wrong time who in most cases didn't know what the hell he got himself into and was lucky to come out alive.

In 1947, I was appointed to the N.Y.P.D. and a rewarding and pretty exciting career. In 1976 I retired.

It's been a helluva life. I don't think I would want to do it again. If you're in the neighborhood, drop in. If you like Italian cooking.

Sincerely,

John Pensabene

—— • ——

Dear Mr. Brokaw:

Reading your book brought back many memories of events I experienced after the liberation of my hometown, Heerlerheide, situated in the south of the Netherlands, about 12 kilometers from the German border. On that day in 1944, the earth literally shook. Seven armored Sherman tanks rolled over the bridge and the Germans were taken by surprise. They fled with whatever they were able to confiscate (*steal* is a better word)—baby buggies, bicycles without the tires, soap (shaving cream) still on their faces. What a sight and what a difference from the time they invaded our town.

I remember going to the woods behind our home with boys and girls from the neighborhood and sitting amongst the GI's who manned the huge field artillery guns. Guns #1, #2 and #3 were aimed at Geilenkirchen, and here we were. Watching! With our mouths open and arms stretched outwards so we wouldn't jump or hurt our eardrums. We also learned how to catch a baseball or try to hit it. A game we had never heard of.

I remember the early morning of Dec. 16, 1944. It was so quiet! I looked outside and the place was deserted. No ammunition that had lined the streets, no trucks, no army, the 7th Armored Division had been called to the Battle of the Bulge. The night before we had had a sing-along in my aunt's and uncle's home.

I remember the soldier who stood under the eave of the house he was leaning against. Shrapnel had hit his head. His boots and papers were removed from his body and put on top of his folded hands, then covered by a tarp. I don't know his name, but I do remember him. Always will. I remember the black soldiers sleeping in tents pitched in meadows and we kids asking in our school English: "How come they sleep in tents in the mud and the white soldiers are stationed in schools, churches and with civilians?" We learned a lot. Yes. The older I get the more I think about that time in my young life. It was adventurous in a way, but it also could be very very sad. I need to tell you about "Mail Call!" The first time I saw this (in the woods behind our home), I cried. A soldier's voice pierced the air with two words—"Mail Call"—and all of a sudden men (boys really, because most of them were only two or three years older than I) came from tents, foxholes, etc. and swarmed like bees around the mail carrier's jeep. Then it got very quiet because they were reading letters from home, opening packages and sharing them with their buddies and us, a bunch of girls and boys from the neighborhood.

I could go on and on. But I've done enough "rambling" and I hope you don't mind. I just needed to let you know about some people—of the greatest generation—I met.

Sincerely,
Hendrika DeRonde

———— • ————

Dear Mr. Brokaw:

I had to give up my practice of law two years ago, because of disability pertaining to my injuries. After my retirement, I had time to reduce to writing my experiences with the military during WWII. I thought you might find it interesting. I wrote the book primarily for my children and grandchildren.

Yours very truly,
L. J. Varnell, Jr.

The sun rose warm and quickly turned into a hot day on May 29, 1944. We were gathered in front of Bells café, in Spur, Texas, waiting for the 2:00 P.M. bus. My family was present, as well as the families of five other men who had received their notice from the government that Uncle Sam needed us. We were ready to embark on an experience that none of us could conceive. The good-byes had been said, the instructions of my parents had been acknowledged, and the painful parting with my teenage sweetheart had been done the night before.

"Here it comes," someone shouted from the crowd that had gathered to see us off. Black smoke poured from the exhaust of the ancient T.N.M. & O. bus, which slowly pulled around the corner and came to a noisy halt in front of us. As we boarded the bus, the crowd shouted to us: "Give 'em Hell, boys" and "Good luck." The bus slowly pulled away from the crowd, we reintroduced ourselves, and after a few minutes of bantering between us, we fell silent. I had just turned nineteen on April 11 of that year. Most of the men were of similar age. One guy was married and had children. This was the first time that I had ever been away from home except for brief trips or overnight visits. My thoughts were of my family and my girlfriend, who had been by my side when I boarded the bus.

Then the bus arrived in Ardmore, Oklahoma, the home of Ft. Sill Induction Center. Suddenly my homesickness went away, and I was fighting for survival. We were marched, or rather herded, into a big two-story barracks. This was done to calls from grizzly veterans who had served at least 24 hours as members of the military. "You'll be sorr-ry" or "fresh meat." The oath of office was issued to us.

Lester Varnell, age nineteen, in a photo taken in Michigan, 1945. (Courtesy of Lester Varnell)

We were escorted to the barbershop, and each of us came out equal, with the latest style of cut. Shaved. Then to the quartermaster, where we were issued standard gear: underwear, boots, pants, shirts, raincoat and finally an oversize cap. At no time was I asked the size of any garment. The man looked at me, then issued the clothing. I was issued two dog tags on metal chains. They were not to be taken off, even when showering. I inquired "What is the notch for on the end of the dog tag?" I became immediately somber when I was informed that Graves Registrations would drive the tag, with the help of the notch, into my teeth if I was snuffed during battle.

After weeks of training my family came down with my girlfriend Dot. Although young we had discussed the idea of getting married, despite the fact that Dot was still in high school. We both felt that we loved one another to such a point that we wanted to be together for the rest of our lives.

When I came home on a delay in route, everything was set. Dot had arranged for a preacher. My grandparents arranged for us to use their house for our wedding night. Dot, a good friend of ours, and Dot's sister and I went to the preacher's house for our marriage vows. We had no flowers, music or attendants, but we were married as much as if we had all of the extras. But time was short and no one had the money to buy such accessories. Time flew as I knew it would and I had to go. Parting was the most heartrending I ever encountered. I had to physically take Dot's arms from around my neck, aided by Mr. Avara, to get on the bus. I hated buses for many years thereafter, for they represented heartbreak. I returned to Camp Fannin, and about a week later we all received orders to ship out. We were carried by train, which carried us to a pier in Boston, where the biggest ship I ever saw was docked. It was the USS *Amsterdam*.

We hit the North Atlantic on the fourth day out, and it was extremely rough the rest of the way in to Liverpool, England. We marched to the railway station and boarded a troop train. We traveled all night, and the next morning we were in Southampton. We had crossed England in one night, without stopping. We then marched to the docks and were placed on an English cattle boat, which ship stunk to high heaven, and the sailors who ran the boat looked dirty and were a sorry-looking lot. We boarded, and when full it lifted anchor and went to the mouth of the English Channel, there to remain until 3 o'clock in the morning to avoid submarines. The meal that they offered was refused by me. It consisted of mutton that floated on a greasy gravy. It was gray-colored, and I swear that it had wool on it.

A group of us got to talking while waiting for 3:00 A.M. to roll around. We speculated as to what we would encounter in the near future. Everybody was afraid of turning chicken when faced with actual combat. We all agreed that we had just gone through the best training that our country could give us. That we were in the best physical condition we had ever been in during our young lives. We wouldn't take a million dollars for our training, but we wouldn't give a nickel to do it again. I weighed 165 pounds when I entered the army. At the end of basic training, I weighed 200 pounds and there was not an ounce of fat on me, and I had a 30-inch waist. My legs were enormous. Everybody agreed that it was necessary to fight this war and that they wanted to contribute to the downfall of the German government.

My assignment came down. I was assigned to the 79th Infantry Division. I was to go the 314th Infantry Regiment. I met the rest of the squad and was introduced. I didn't like what my eyes told me. The company had seen some hard fighting, and the men were dirty and unshaven. The new recruits and I stood out like a sore thumb. It snowed that night, leaving two or three inches on the ground. It was bitterly cold.

Word came down that we were ready to jump off. I was dressed in winter underwear, had on two pair of woolen pants, shirt, field jacket, overcoat, gloves, jeep cap, helmet and a white denim cloak so we would blend with the snow. On top of this, I carried two bandoliers of loaded magazines and the Browning automatic rifle, which weighs about 20 pounds. I could hardly move, much less walk or run. Everyone was dressed the same way. The big guns began to shoot, and you couldn't hear yourself talk. Orders were given by hand signals. Tanks moved up behind us. About 10 o'clock in the morning we started moving towards Haguenau. Scared!!!! Damn right I was scared, and any person who has faced combat and tells you that he was not scared is lying. The instinct of self-preservation is too strong. I was terrified but went forward because the rest of the company went forward. My apprehension and anxious state almost made me ill. We had gone about ¼ of a mile, and we started receiving incoming shells. This noise, taken with our artillery and tanks, made a din that could not be described. Some Germans could be observed. I started laying down a covering fire so we could advance. A group of Germans broke from the brush and ran to a stone wall. . . . I let off a full magazine of fire, one of the Germans fell. I got sick at my stomach. No one said anything. You can train to do something, but when you are called on to do it, it is not the same. We moved firing and running. As soon as I could, I stopped and pulled off the overcoat. My supply buddies did the same. Suddenly a machine gun opened up. The guy other than my bunk buddy caught a burst of machine-gun fire that ripped his face and almost tore his arm off. He was dead when I got to him. I did not know him well, but I found myself becoming angry to a point that I was consumed with anger. I held him in my arms and cried. I can't even remember his name. I could only think that he wanted to live as bad as the next person.

As I helped strip the ammo belts from him, I became so enraged, I wanted to kill the entire German army. This feeling taken with my training was exactly how the Army had intended for me to react. It had turned me into a person filled with anger and with a desire to get even and destroy anything that got in my way. To demolish the Germans and what they represented.

Word was passed down that a new attack would occur about daylight the next morning. I got very little sleep. I was up at four o'clock in the morning. Got some coffee and double-checked my equipment. About six o'clock the artillery started up, as well as the mortars. Thirty minutes later planes came in, dropping bombs and strafing positions. We got the word to move out about seven o'clock.

The next five or six hours went by like a dream; you can't keep track of the time when every minute you are facing is kill or be killed. The town was close to the German border, and German soldiers were fighting like madmen. Some of my relatives came from Germany, but I had no feeling for them. We cursed the Germans, but to a man we had to admit that they were good soldiers, and some of their equipment was better than ours. The planes fired about 100 yards in front of us. As we advanced, we lay strips of cloth, so our planes could tell where we were located. I fired all the ammunition that I was carrying and most of the extra ammunition that was being carried for me. I recall only bits and pieces of what was going on during the course of the morning. Bodies lay along the route we had traveled, looking like sacks of grain which had been flung at random. The smell of death, blood and cordite filled the air. I was so dirty one could not tell where my pants ended and my jacket began. You were in mud constantly, and every step you made you were looking for cover, be it a wall or shell hole or anything that would give a bit of safety.

We found a building that had not been destroyed and prepared to spend the night there, together with 30 or 40 other guys. Luckily my bunk buddy had gotten through without being hit. My bunk mate and I talked a lot about what we had been through. My sergeant came by and told us that we were not to spend the night in a building as they were expecting a counterattack. We were both beat but managed to dig in the frozen ground. We laid timber and tree limbs over the top.

"Making normal improvement": The postcard concerning Lester Varnell's hospitalization sent to his wife, Doris, on January 24, 1945. (Courtesy of Lester Varnell)

One of the limbs was crooked, leaving a small opening in the top. As it got dark, we went to sleep because we were so exhausted. I didn't give a damn if a German got in the hole with us.

About 10 o'clock in the morning we were in the hole and shelling started again. The first shell hit just to the back of the hole, so close that I remember both of us crying out and clawing at our shoulders as the concussion felt like an electrical shock. A second shell hit just in front of the hole, and the final shell came in the hole. Smoke was so thick that one could not see. When I came to myself and could see, my right leg was lying at an awkward angle, and blood was flowing. As I grabbed my right leg to stop the bleeding, I noticed my right hand was covered with blood. The hole was filled with smoke, heavy with cordite. My bunk buddy got out of the hole, going for help. I noticed that his arm was dangling. I was sitting on the right side of the hole. He was sitting on the left, and I assume that he caught the shell fragment that struck me in the left arm. Shortly thereafter two or three guys came and started to get me out of the hole. As I was being lifted out, my helmet fell off and dropped to the bottom of the hole. It was riddled with shell fragments. I raised my hand to my head; it came back full of blood. My only thought was, "What a hell of a Christmas for my folks, getting notified that I am dead." They put me on a litter and carried me to the Battalion Aid Station. I was notified that they would be unable to give me morphine or any other sedatives because of my head injury. I am sure I was still in shock because I felt little or no pain. They proceeded to clean and bandage my wounds. In addition to my leg and head injuries, I had shrapnel hits on both arms and on my right wrist. They placed my leg in a splint. I asked the doctor, "How bad is it." He replied "Son, your fighting days are over, you have just earned a one-way ticket home."

I was sent to a general hospital well behind the front lines, located at Vittel, France.

The postcard sent to Doris Varnell on March 10, 1945. (Courtesy of Lester Varnell)

The nurses were wonderful and left me with a lifelong respect for the angels of mercy. Major Joe Godfrey was an orthopedic surgeon from Buffalo. He was a soft-spoken man with thinning red hair who I immediately trusted and respected.

On the morning of March 18th, 1945, Major Godfrey came by my bed. He looked sad. "Jake," he said, "I'm going to take you up to the operating room tomorrow, and if your leg is in half as bad a shape as I think it is, I'm going to have to take it." I felt like I had been hit in the stomach. I knew that I might not live, but I never dreamed they would take my leg off. After he left I just stared at the wall. This was what I had feared before Doris and I were married. I just didn't feel that I had the guts to tell her. A goddamn cripple, who would forever be dependent on someone to care for me. As soon as I was able, I wrote to Doris. I was blunt and to the point. I explained that I understood if she wanted to call the whole thing off. I lapsed into a state of depression. I raged at ward boys without cause. I gave the nurses a bad time. I even jumped on the civilian help, most of which couldn't understand English. In two or three weeks I received a letter from Doris. I think everybody in the room was waiting for that letter. I opened it with trembling hands. I don't remember the exact words, but there was no doubt about the contents. She first chastised me for keeping the truth from her, because I had kept the fact that I had been having trouble since January. She then related to me the shock to her and my family that I had lost a leg. She then informed me that she married me because she loved me. She hadn't married my legs. That everything would be alright when I got home. Needless to say I was jubilated. I at least had her until I got back to the States. If at any time she changed her mind, I had made up my mind that I would understand and let her go. I didn't give her enough credit, but every day guys were getting letters from their wives telling them that it was over for some reason or the other. We referred to them as Dear John letters. Far too many guys received those types of letters.

The day I left the 23rd General Hospital was a day of joy

The hospital where Lester Varnell recovered after his surgery, December 1944 to June 1945. (Courtesy of Lester Varnell)

and a day of sorrow. Everybody on the ward was present, even if they were off duty. I was taken to a hospital near Nancy, France.

About three weeks passed, and a group of the doctors making rounds came by my bed. "Varnell, we have decided to ship you home by the quickest available air flight." The next day or two passed quickly. I found myself in an ambulance racing through downtown Paris with all the bells and whistles going full blast. We came to an airfield, and I was carried into a huge hangar where hundreds of other wounded lay on litters. A triage committee came by, and I was tagged out as first available air.

We were due to go into New York, but the weather decided otherwise. We diverted to Wilmington, Delaware. We

Lester Varnell on a family visit to Texas, 1946.
(Courtesy of Lester Varnell)

had a good night's sleep, and the next morning we were welcomed by the chefs from the kitchens and the nurses attached to their local hospital. "What do you want to eat" asked the chefs, and everything that anyone had been dreaming about for months or years suddenly was at our beck and call. Milk was the number-one request, followed by real eggs, bacon, ham, sausage, hotcakes, waffles, bagels and lox, followed by requests for cream gravy and grits. I ate much bacon and eggs, followed with biscuits and gravy and gallons of pure white fresh milk. As soon as we were able to move we were cleaned up, shaved and fresh bed clothing was issued. Then telephone company employees came and started placing calls to our loved ones. My family did not have a telephone, so I had to place the call to a grocery store in the little town of Afton, Texas. I told them that I was back, that we had to go to New York and then be assigned to a hospital near our home. It was wonderful to hear the sound of their voices.

My stay in New York was for a short time only. Three days later I was winging my way toward Texas. Within a day or so my wife, together with my mother and father, arrived. It was a very emotional meeting. I probably weighed about 125 pounds. My wife later told me that I looked like a skeleton.

I told them that I was to be sent to McCluskey General Hospital in Temple in a few days.

The doctors at McCluskey then approached me about consenting to an experimental operation. I thought I had been experimented on enough, but I consented to the procedure they used on me. The idea was to cut around my wound and line the wound with [glass] gauze, which they would pack with regular bandages. Each day they would remove the bandages and repack the glass, after slipping it out a tiny bit. In about 3 weeks they pulled the glass gauze and showed me, by the use of a mirror, the new pink tissue that had formed. The experiment was a success. It had healed from the inside out. I felt for the first time that I was healed.

I was issued my separation papers on the morning of the 6th of December, 1946. It lacked one day being two years that I had spent in the hospitals of the U.S. Army.

The next day, it was dark when the bus left, but daylight came swiftly, and we soon started passing places that were familiar to me. Fields of cotton and grain that fed and clothed the world. I lost myself in deep thought as the bus continued towards Matador, Texas. I had seen a large part of the world in the past two and one-half years. All in all I did not find any-place that I would swap with somebody else. The United States was always a symbol to me, one that I would defend with my life if necessary. I thought of all the men and boys who would not be coming home. I considered myself the luckiest guy in the world.

———— • ————

Dear Mr. Brokaw:

Enclosed is a copy of e-mail I sent to friends about my Christmas during the Battle of the Bulge.

With very best wishes,
I. Harold Storey

A significant number of people (not throngs!) have asked me—during the spreading of the word of my involvement in infantry combat in Europe—to describe some more of conditions in late fall of 1944 and into Northern Europe's worst winter on record up to that time.

Having finally entered and cleared out Metz about November 18, we started to a destination which we passionately dreaded—the German border and the Siegfried Line. Snow was already falling, an enemy in itself because of ease of observation as well as the difficulty of finding a warm enough place to try to sleep some. But the big thing was that we knew that the Germans would defend their border more vigorously than many of the French places during late summer. (I think they thought that their own border just couldn't be breached.)

On December 16 battalion and regimental senior officers came to forward positions to find those of us who were company commanders and tell us personally that our intelligence had discovered German Panzer divisions had been amassed, apparently to attack our front or that of the Soviets. Of course we were all surprised to know they had such capability—and honestly hoped the strike would be to the east!

That very night the Germans launched an attack which would result in the involvement of more than 600,000 American troops, the largest single battle in American history. We were just inside the German border in the Saar Valley, and during the night we got orders to climb on any vehicle headed north, destination somewhere, and see that headlights were turned on, follow the vehicle ahead, bumper to bumper. It was one of Patton's miracles that we arrived in the middle of Luxembourg, 100 miles away, not long after dawn, slipping and sliding in deeper and deeper snow. Rumors were rampant as we were told that Germans had filtered into our ranks in American uniforms, that many of our weapons had been captured and that many atrocities were being committed.

The next few days, cloudy and bitterly cold, were a nightmare of danger in one of the most beautiful places in the world. Casualties from artillery, tanks firing through the trees, and rifle fire, burp guns *and* trench foot kept depleting our ranks as we were trying to push back that part of the "bulge."

It was hard to decide which was the #1 enemy—Germans or weather. Snow and low clouds impeded our movement and had prevented any support from the air. On Christmas Eve, the eighth day of these conditions, the skies became blue, and I stood by a snow-laden fir tree and thanked God that I could hear and eventually see a steady line of planes above! (Patton claimed that this was an answer to his own prayers. I wonder

Harold Storey, in a photo taken in Salisbury, England, where he was hospitalized for four months. He sent the picture to his parents so that they could see he had suffered no facial disfigurement from a neck wound he'd received at the Battle of the Bulge.
(Courtesy of Harold Storey)

how God filters a profane prayer.) The planes kept up the next few days and apparently did enough damage to effectively turn the tide.

Christmas Day—weather beautiful and setting idyllic, with snow on every branch of planted fir trees 10–15 feet all in rows with firebreak avenues every hundred yards or so. I was deeply depressed as I tried to offer some encouragement for these weary folks and we approached the forward slope of the mountain, knowing there would be good observation where the trees played out on the approach to the Sauer River, along which there were many mostly damaged and abandoned bed & breakfasts and small inns. As I stood at the edge of a little road waiting for the rest of my folks to get oriented and catch up using more than one firebreak, Pfc. Castle approached me. He was a replacement medic who had endeared himself to all of us. He wanted to do anything he could—cheerfully—including trudging back a mile or so to bring 5-gallon cans of water when we got messages that water was available. This time he asked my permission to go back to where he had seen two wounded Germans, an officer and an enlisted man, and try to "fix up" their wounds. At first I told him I'd rather he not go alone, that I really should not be there alone (we tried to abide by the rule about getting separated). He indicated the direction, said it wasn't far and that he would hurry. I relented with great appreciation for the compassion of this young kid and felt it appropriate for Christmas. His commitment was to people, not just friends. I became more anxious for us to proceed (mid-afternoon now and darkness came very early), and one of my platoon leaders found me and asked about Castle. I told him what had transpired and said I thought I could find him. After searching down a couple of rows, I did find him. His hand was under the wounded arm of one of the two still alive Germans, and he had died from a bullet through his hel-

Combat Infantryman's Badge, Silver Star, and Purple Heart.

"Daring and courageous actions": the citation for the Silver Star awarded to Harold Storey. (Both courtesy of Harold Storey)

S I L V E R   S T A R

Isaac H. Storey, O 513 520, First Lieutenant

C I T A T I O N

For gallantry in action on 11 September 1944 in the vicinity of ***. Under a relentless barrage of enemy artillery, mortar and small arms fire, the enemy forces attempted three strong counterattacks which were completely repulsed on each attempt. The enemy's repeated offensives proved costly to our forces both in officers and enlisted personnel. Lieutenant STOREY, the lone remaining officer in the company, with utter disregard for personal safety, efficiently and skillfully succeeded in organizing the remaining men in the company and agressively led them to the battalion perimeter which had been pierced by the fierce enemy counterattack. Lieutenant STOREY at all times completely exposed to the intense enemy fire personally went from group to group encouraging his men and spurring them on to greater efforts. Due to the daring and courageous actions of Lieutenant STOREY the company was reorganized and contributed greatly to the establishment of a bridgehead across the ***. Lieutenant STOREY'S bravery and deep devotion to duty, his intrepidity and skillful leadership reflects great credit on himself and is in keeping with the highest traditions of the military service.

met and his head. My emotions nearly tore me apart! Of course I would shoot the squirming and begging men—as they expected. As I cocked my carbine and pointed it at the captain, I still was thinking about the day and my family and the fact there was not much celebration here. Somehow I thought that if I did survive I would never want to remember that I had killed two helpless people on Christmas and would not want my family to know that I had done such a thing. It was really mostly selfish, with some compassion. And I knew it would not be a fitting tribute to the short and beautiful life Castle had lived. (I did not know where he was from and have never been able to find his family since, though just this past July I was able to get his serial number. Difficult for strangers to get family information through army records—rightly so.) We never discovered who had killed him, possibly somebody hiding nearby even as I found him.

By now we thought the war or winter would never end, troops dwindled to weakened strengths. But on January 22nd, it was over for me. A mortar shell hit a tree limb about 18 inches from my head, killed the two artillery people who had come to discuss the situation after we had spotted enemy movement on the next hill. We all were wearing hooded white canvas jackets with white trousers, and though my face felt numb and I realized I couldn't hear with my right ear, I didn't realize what my situation was until blood, delayed by the bitter cold, began dripping from my neck down onto the white clothing as I was crouched down trying to see how badly a fourth friend had been wounded in the face. Soon two people were pulling me up to give me prescribed sulfa tablets and then began dragging me toward a small track in the snow. Shortly a jeep came, I was helped into a seat and we proceeded down a steep hill. The jeep slid off the little road and stuck in the snow. It was about to get dark, and it wasn't long until they got enough people to push and pull and get us on the way down the hill to an aid station at the little Catholic church in Diekirch.

From there to Luxembourg City (a convent) and after a number of days and surgery to Paris in a boxcar with litters stacked three to a side, a woodstove for heat, for more surgery and a few days. The hospital in Luxembourg gave out of pajamas on the day we were taken down to the rail siding to a tent, so I traveled in bandages and very scratchy captured German blankets. (I bet none of my readers has traveled to Paris naked!) All along the way there were gentle and caring chaplains and doctors, many times asking "Are you afraid to die?" I finally learned to say that I wasn't really afraid, but that didn't mean I wanted to!

This is written to partly explain my gratitude for life, for my faith and for the measure of peace that I have experienced. One can readily see why I feel that my blessings have been more than any one person could expect.

I surely want my family and friends to know of my gratitude for them and for life itself. I know God knows it.

———•———

Dear Mr. Brokaw:

We have lived through the Great Depression, the war years, the rebuilding of our great country, from war material to peacetime. The unrest of steel strikes here in our Pittsburgh area, the unrest of all of us servicemen coming home to start over again, but it was not easy. We were not the same boys who left home, some returning very badly wounded, both physically and mentally.

I was a combat infantryman during the war, on the front from Normandy till we met the Russians on the Elbe River.

Bob Eberle on occupation duty in Hirschberg, Germany. (Courtesy of Bob Eberle)

The Battle of the Bulge, we had gone to hell, and some of us returned, many had gone insane, I for one felt many times I too was near it. It was about five months being in combat before we got our first bath and clean clothes, that was in the Ruhr Valley. I was covered with chicken lice after I had crawled in a chicken coop out of the rain.

As for food, it was hard to come by, some days we ate whatever we could find, at times we went three or four with no food, the same was for sleep. I think when we were on the move we went without sleep for four days. At nite or at times when our outfit got too far ahead of the units on either side we dug in, always with the tanks behind us, or nearby, we protected them, but when we got a chance we would crawl over to them and they would give us hot coffee. They had little stoves inside and could have a fire that wouldn't be seen by the enemy. Just to have a tin cup of coffee, how great it was. Then they carried food rations, both the C and the K, on the back of the tanks, if it did not get blown apart from shrapnel.

It has only been in the past five years that I finally was able to open up and tell of my war years. My great-niece was going to spend a summer in Europe for [her] last year in college and was going to follow in my footsteps the places I had gone through in the battles. I drew on maps the routes we took. She came home and gave me a photo album full of pictures of those same places, but many years later.

To this day, every day since May 8th, 1945, is a bonus to me, that I was spared when so many of my close friends died. I feel guilty they died and I lived. Yes, you are so right, we Americans were able to make things work, if first it didn't succeed, you tried again. In the Depression we didn't have the money to go buy the item needed, so we made it.

After the war we had men from every country in the world here to our steel mills, learning how many products were made, from tin plates to nails to pipe and barbed-wire fence, today our wire-making machines are in China, the pipe-making machines are in Korea. What is left of the seven-mile-long steel mill is just weeds, the plant is gone.

Bob Eberle's World War II savings book. (Courtesy of Bob Eberle)

I tried to take advantage of the G.I. Bill for schooling. I tried, but the mind would not let me, there was too much that had happened. I had seen too much death. I was in bad shape like so many others.

It wasn't until I married my wife, Edna, that she was able to bring me back, for there was many a nite that I scared her in my sudden crying out. I was back in the war. I still have sleepless nites, it will always be there. I can still see the boys I left behind. There were times I would be in a foxhole half full of water, with a new man who just came up, maybe share a K ration or ask who he was and from where, then the word to move up, we went into a battle. I heard a voice cry out, looked over and saw my new friend laying badly wounded. I would crawl over to him, hold his head in my lap and listen to him cry out for his mama, "I am afraid," then he was dead. The hot tears would roll down my dirty, muddy, cordite-covered, bearded face, and think will my turn come next and how would I die.

The heroes of the war are the ones that lay beneath the white crosses.

Sincerely,
Bob Eberle

———— • ————

Dear Tom:

My husband, Dick Jones, and I met at a dance in the small town of Unity, Maine, when we were both 17 years old. We immediately fell in love! We had four glorious years going through college at the University of Maine. When he graduated in June 1943

and left for Officer's Candidate School at Fort Benning, Georgia, I went on the accelerated program and, with the soldiers at University of Maine, finished my senior year in December 1943. Then came the moment—to Fort Benning to join Dick while he became a 1st Lt! From there, we lived on several infantry bases in the U.S., where we met many other army couples, lived in rooms with kitchen privileges and watched drills.

In August 1944 we went on leave to our parents in Maine. I suffered some broken ribs in an auto accident while there and could not accompany my husband to Camp Kilmer, New Jersey, at the end of the leave. However, two days later I received a call from him to come to New York City to meet him before he shipped

Dick Jones, nineteen years old, 1943.

out. Broken ribs and all—I took a train to New York! We met at the old Ambassador Hotel. When we said "So long. See you tonight" in our hotel room the next morning, we did not know that it was good-bye.

Dick Jones and Marie Knight, both twenty years old, in front of the ROTC drill grounds at the University of Maine. (Both courtesy of Marie Knight Dion)

I went back home and got a job teaching school. Of course, I had the gas rations, sugar rations, and war bonds to purchase.

Then a telegram arrived in Dec. 1944. I was numb. I knew what it was. He was missing in action in Germany in the Battle of the Bulge. I spent weeks reading the newspapers about the terrible snowstorms in Europe, and the belief that bodies of the dead were left behind and not able to be found. I had nightmares of him laying under the snow.

The next telegram arrived in April 1945, after the thaws of that terrible winter. He was declared killed in action in a Panzer attack in Aachen, Germany, December 18, 1944. He was 21 years old.

His body was escorted home to us that fall by a 1st Lieutenant of the Infantry. That was my good-bye, and even though I went on and changed my profession to medical technology, remarried and had a wonderful son and daughter, deep down my heart remained lonesome for my first love of those bittersweet days.

Lieutenant Richard Jones, age twenty-one, Macon, Georgia. (Courtesy of Marie Knight Dion)

Sincerely,
Marie Knight Dion

———— • ————

Dear Mr. Brokaw:

My father, who was 34 years old(!) when he was drafted in Poughkeepsie, N.Y., in March of 1944, was killed in action during the Battle of the Bulge in Jan. 1945. My last memory of him occurred on a subway platform September 1944. There he stood, so proud and beautiful, smiling sadly and bravely at his 29-year-old wife and her 3 sadly smiling children: me, age 10, my brother, age 8, and baby sister, 3 and ¼.

I can feel it, hear it all these years later. The feeling of unreality is still there, along with pride and, yes, anger at what I felt was his desertion of us (hard to believe isn't it?). After I read your book, I regained most of the feelings of pride and lost a lot of the anger.

My mother told me this story years after he died when she thought I could handle it. When my dad was drafted, my mom had him write a letter to the war dept to say he was the sole support of 5 people and was needed at home. When he had left she found the letter in a suitcoat pocket—he never mailed it!

I guess, being a political idealist (he adored FDR) and a gentle intellectual, he just felt he should answer his country's call. As my mother said, at least he got to live 34 years of his life, and didn't die at 18 or 20, never having known the joys of marriage and children to carry on his proud heritage.

He was such a beautiful, kind man who is buried at the American Servicemen's Cemetery in Luxembourg right near Patton. My dad, who had a talent for writing, [near] Patton, who wrote poetry. Dad would have smiled at that one.

My mom decided to let him lie in peace where he died for his country instead of bringing him home. In 1990 my son, who never knew his grandfather, got to Luxembourg and brought me back some photos.

Sincerely,
Beatrice Wiegand

———— • ————

Dear Mr. Brokaw:

The following story is one of the many experiences that affected me deeply.

Everything taught in flying is geared to safety. Weather, maintenance, procedure, as well as maneuvers like stalling and turning. Not taught was how one should feel when killing. So when I took my pilot training as a cadet in WWII, I was told not how to kill but what maneuvers it took to hit the target.

Monday, January 29, 1945. "Target of opportunity" meant to hit anything that moved across the bomb line, but civilians, if we could tell the difference, were off limits. Although indiscriminate bombing or strafing was not the normal course of business, it was assumed that all traffic carried military personnel or objects of war and would be fair game.

Snow was still on the ground when Joe Wilson and I were returning in our flight of four P-47 Thunderbolts from a mission near Honnef. Since the Battle of the Bulge had recently ended, there wasn't much activity, but we still were hunting for targets of opportunity.

En route back to our base in Belgium at about 2,000 feet, I saw two people working near a rock farmhouse, going about their busi-

Kemal Saied, on a visit to his brother in the infantry, showing off his mustache, Germany, 1945.

Kemal Saied, in flight gear, on the wing of his P-47 Thunderbolt after the plane had been hit in combat, December 1944.

Kemal Saied at his Purple Heart ceremony, 1944.

Kemal Saied, 1945.

Officers in a briefing room in their headquarters, near Saint-Trond, Belgium. (All courtesy of Kemal Saied)

ness of farming. I thought "target of opportunity" and broke away from the flight and dived toward them, adjusting my P-47 to center the targets in my gunsight.

At first they didn't seem afraid of the plane diving toward them, apparently thinking that any civilized human would not harm unarmed people. They were waiting for me to recognize them as farmers, wobble my wings in a salute and pull up without firing, as might have happened to them before.

I continued coming down, hypnotized by the pipper in the gunsight, and they began running when they realized it was my intent to shoot them.

They were getting larger and larger in my gunsight until it seemed that I would ram them instead of shoot them. I squeezed the trigger and let off a one-second burst. In the circle of light in the gunsight, I saw them round the corner of the rock farmhouse, unharmed.

At that instant, I snapped out of my trance and realized what I had just done. Pulling up from the dive, I could feel my whole body flush and felt both hot and cold at the same time. I had never before or since been as ashamed as I was at that moment.

In the years following this, I have thought about it many times and thanked God for my poor marksmanship that day.

Sincerely,
Kemal Saied

———— • ————

Dear Mr. Brokaw:

My husband, John Bolger, is a WWII veteran. I am so very proud of him and what he has done.

I have written a mini-story depicting my husband's life, service time, etc.

Sincerely and most respectfully,
Ebby Bolger

Johnny joined the Army in October 1942. He was eighteen years old. He was shipped overseas on New Year's Day, 1944, on the *Queen Elizabeth*, landing in Gourock, Scotland, then on to Adderberry, England.

In the early spring of 1944, his mother took ill with tuberculosis. She passed away on July 13, 1944. Johnny was nineteen years old, and his youngest brother, Vincent, was 4 years old. It was an extremely hard time for the family; some went into foster care, and others moved in with caring families. Johnny could not be reached overseas to inform him of his mother's passing.

Johnny was an absolutely devoted son to his mother (as all children are), but Johnny always gave special attention and love to his mother. The telegram finally reached him on August 20th, his 20th birthday.

Johnny was a gunner on the 105 Howitzer tank attached to the seventh corp. They saw lots of action. One day in particular, August 27, he saw his young friend hit by mortar shelling but still running; his last word was "Mama."

Johnny served overseas from Jan 1944 to October 1945. He landed on Utah Beach and was also in the Battle of the Bulge. He traveled through Cherbourg, France; Ardennes, Belgium; Malmédy, Belgium; Cologne, Germany; Tuedenlenburg, Germany, towns he never thought he would see in his young life. It would have been a grand experience if there hadn't been a horrific war. He also witnessed the horrors of the concentration camp at Dachau, stating it's something you could never forget.

Johnny returned home in October 1945 but didn't have a home to return to. These years have been quite a sacrifice, but never thought of as such. It was a privilege to have served. Johnny was floundering and returned to the service in July 1946, only to be discharged with family hardship in October 1947.

Johnny married a girl from the neighborhood, Evelyn Likman (Ebby). Johnny and Ebby had four children in as many years—Tommy, Timmy, Colleen and Mary.

He worked hard to support his family, once being a superintendent of a building of 42 apartments (while holding down another job) so his children could afford to go to Catholic school. He

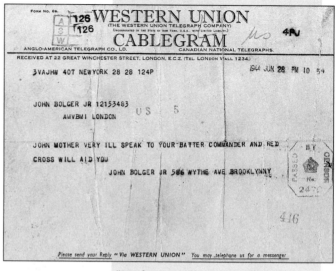

"Mother very ill": Telegram sent to John Bolger, June 1944.

A message from the Red Cross, August 1944.
(Both courtesy of Ebby Bolger)

AMERICAN RED CROSS
August 11, 1944

Commanding Officer   Re: Bolger, John Jr.
Battery B, 87th F.A. Bn.   ASN 12153483
APO 230

Dear Sir:

Our office received a cable several days ago that the above soldier's mother died on July 13th. The cable also advised that the family were writing details. More than likely, the soldier has received a direct message from home and knows about the situation; nevertheless, we are also transmitting this message we received as a double check to make certain that the soldier has been advised.

The family also requested that the Chaplain notify the soldier of the death. Therefore, just as soon as we received the cable we arranged with our division chaplain, Lt. Col. Maurer, to visit your unit and talk to Bolger. He probably has by now. We decided to wait several days before sending you the message in order to give the chaplain a chance to visit you.

We are very sorry that these cable messages cannot be transmitted to us sooner, so that the soldiers can get the news withing two or three days, but it seems that there are a number of bottlenecks in transmission based on censorship and priority.

Please do not hesitate to call on me, either by message center or personally on any matter that needs immediate attention.

Yours,

John Bolger,
December 1946.

John Bolger (center) and two friends, Thomas Rocko
(left) and Thomas Tickner (right), with a captured
Nazi flag, 1945.

John and Ebby Bolger,
Brooklyn, New York, 1943.
(All courtesy of Ebby Bolger)

also worked in construction, then Johnny went to work for the N.Y.C. Transit Authority for 20 years. After retiring, he worked part-time at Shea Stadium, a great job, getting in to see the Mets. He was there when they won the 1986 World Series.

Johnny & Ebby have four grandsons—Brian, John Thomas, Casey and Kevin. John Thomas is currently in the Coast Guard. We are very proud of them all.

Johnny & Ebby finally retired in Cape May, N.J., Camelot, as we call it. On Memorial Day, Johnny doesn't attend the ceremonies. Ebby goes for him and all those other servicemen and servicewomen.

It was a war fought by ordinary, extraordinary young men and women.

—— • ——

Dear Mr. Brokaw:

My father enlisted in the Army Air Corps on November 30, 1942 (5 days after his 18th birthday). He became a fighter pilot, was sent to Europe, and was flying there at age 19–20. He flew 49 combat missions over Germany and was shot down strafing an airfield on April 10, 1945. The story of this last mission and the revelations coming 54 years later are contained in the paper I have enclosed.

Lieutenant Joseph Peterburs, age nineteen, Kingscliff, England, November 1944. (Courtesy of Rick Peterburs)

During a bomber escort mission to Berlin, the bombers were attacked by German Me 262's (twin engine jets). I observed one Me 262 hit two B-17's, and I proceeded to attack it. I had about a 5,000-foot altitude advantage, and with throttle wide open and 50-caliber machine guns blazing, I engaged the jet from the 6 o'clock position and was getting some hits and saw smoke. The jet headed for the deck with me in hot pursuit and Capt. Dick Tracy following close behind me. We chased the jet to an airfield near Berlin that I found out later was Finsterwalde. As we approached, we could see the airfield was loaded with all types of German aircraft. The Me 262 entered a bank of low stratus clouds, and we broke off the chase and

Joseph Peterburs with his training plane.

*Military pass issued to Joseph Peterburs
for flight training.
(Both courtesy of Rick Peterburs)*

started to strafe the airfield. Capt. Tracy was hit on his 2nd or 3rd pass and had to do a quick bailout at about 300 feet. He landed in a river near the airfield and was later captured. I continued to attack the airfield by myself and made about 5 or 6 passes, being hit by intense ground fire on the last two passes. I destroyed at least 5 aircraft, including one FW 190, one Ju 88, two Me 109's and an FW 200. I also damaged several others and inflicted heavy damage on several hangars. With my aircraft severely damaged and burning, I headed back toward friendly lines.

When I was about 15 miles from Magdeburg, I came under attack by an FW 190. Fortunately he missed. However, by this time I had lost a lot of altitude, descending below 1,000 feet, and was unable to keep my aircraft flying, so I bailed out at about 300 feet. I hit the tail of my aircraft with my right knee, pulled the rip cord, chute opened, I swung once and hit the ground. I was captured immediately by local farmers, who were ready to do me in when a Luftwaffe sergeant stationed in the area came to my rescue and took me away from the civilians. He took me to a nearby airfield, where I was placed in solitary confinement and interrogated by the Gestapo for 3 days. While I was there the airfield was bombed every night by the British, and I spent the nights in a bomb shelter with the Germans. I was moved by rail (boxcar) from the airfield to Stalag 11. It was in the process of evacuating because of advancing Allied forces. After 2 days I was put with about 100 British soldiers, and we started our way on foot toward the east. We were on the forced march for about 10 days, during which there were constant attacks by Allied fighters supporting advancing Allied forces.

Ended up at a POW camp at Luckenwalde (Stalag 3), where most of the prisoners were Russian and Scandinavian, as well as Capt. Tracy, who had been there since he was shot down. Within about a week Tracy and I, along with an air force TSgt (who could speak fluent Russian), escaped (security was practically nonexistent) and joined a Russian tank unit. We fought with them from Jüterbog to the Elbe. Sometime during the trek to Wittenberg, Tracy, the sergeant and I got separated. At the Elbe I joined a U.S. Army infantry unit that was meeting with the Russians and doing mop-up operations around Halle. I stayed with the unit for a few days and then took off on my own, eventually ending up in Paris. From Paris I was sent to a POW collection point at Le Havre (Camp Lucky Strike) and returned to the US on a convoy, arriving in New York on the 4th of June 1945.

54 years later I was contacted by Werner Dietrich from Burg, Germany. On 10 April 1945 he was a 13-year-old boy hiding in a ditch and watching the air battles taking place above him. He saw the FW 190 fire its rockets at my aircraft and miss and saw me bail out and get captured. He knew where my aircraft crashed, and in 1996 (after the reunification of Germany) he was able to enlist the aid of a German documentary TV program to help him find and excavate my aircraft. Using the serial number from aircraft parts, he began a long and exhaustive search for the pilot. After searching for 19 months he finally located me. In May 1998 the TV producer contacted me, wanting me to come to Germany for a reunion with Werner. My wife had had a stroke, and I was unwilling to leave her, so the TV program producer made arrangements for Werner and their TV crew to visit me in Colorado Springs and make a follow-up documentary.

The Me 262 pilot was Oberleutnant Walter Schuck, with 206 victories to his credit. He is still alive and has confirmed to Werner the events of this day. He told him he entered a

War Ace With Battle Stars, Scars Adds Heart at Altar

Lt. Peterburs

From a German prison camp to the altar in little more than a month is the latest chapter in the adventures of Lt. Joseph Peterburs, 20, of 245 N. Lovers Lane rd. Wearing the distinguished flying cross, the air medal with five clusters, the Purple Heart and a ETO service ribbon with two battle stars, Lt. Peterburs mustered enough courage at the county clerk's office to apply for a marriage license. He will marry Miss Josephine Heffner, 20, of 2727 W. Highland av., at Holy Assumption church in West Allis at 9 a. m. Wednesday. The couple was employed at St. Joseph's hospital. He enlisted in 1942.

A lot has happened in three years, but the climax came Apr. 10 this year. Lt. Peterburs, flying his P-51 Mustang on a strafing mission over Berlin—it was his fifty-second mission—had his plane knocked out.

He bailed out at 500 feet, his leg struck the tail of the speeding fighter, and he landed with an injured leg and both feet sprained.

He was captured by the German and forced into one of those infamous "marches" to prison camp. Twenty days later he was liberated by the Russians and sent home—an ace with five planes to his credit and two probables and two unconfirmed. After 60 days of leave—and honeymooning—he will report at Miami, Fla., for further assignment.

Lt. Joseph was the fifth member of the Peterburs family to enter military service. His father, William, 60, is a sergeant with an ordnance unit in the Philippines. One brother, Lt. George, 30, has served three years in the infantry in Iceland, France, Belgium and Germany. Another, Lt. William, jr., 2 is stationed with the signal corps at Fort Monmouth, N. J., and expects to go overseas soon. A third brother, Paul, 20, a motor machinist's mate, first class, died when his subchaser was sunk on Aug. 1943.

Happiest of all Saturday, though, was Mrs. Minnie Peterburs, the mother. For her three soldier sons were all home—and she was getting ready for a wedding.

"From a German prison camp to the altar in little more than a month": an article from the Milwaukee Journal, *June 1945. (© 2001* Journal-Sentinal Inc., *reproduced with permission)*

cloud bank at about 3,000 feet to escape my pursuit, but the damage was already done—his engine blew and he bailed out.

My father stayed in the air force after the war. He flew 76 combat missions over North Korea in 1952, being hit in the face by small arms fire on one of the missions. He volunteered to set in the trenches during an atomic bomb detonation in Nevada during the 1954 tests. He ejected from a burning jet in 1955 and in 1967–68 was in Vietnam, where his room was blown apart by a Viet Cong 122-mm rocket during Tet. He commanded the radar command and control system in Central Europe, 1972–78. He retired as a colonel in 1979 with over 36 years of active duty.

Thank you for your attention and I am,

Sincerely,
Rick Peterburs

— • —

Dear Mr. Brokaw:

This letter was written by my husband, James F. Norton, in 1945, when he was a PFC in the Army and 20 years old. When he was wounded (in what turned out to be the Battle of the Bulge) and captured unconscious, he was 19 years old.

Sincerely yours,
Mary Norton

A Beautiful Sunday
April 15, 1945

Dearest Mom and Dad:

This is the second happiest moment of my life, at last a chance to write home. The happiest moment came a few days ago, when the greatest army in the world liberated me.

Things have been happening so fast to me since I've been liberated, my head is still spinning. As much as I've cussed the army, I love it now, and I've never seen a more smooth-working, efficient organization.

Gosh, there's so much to say, I don't even know how to start, and to tell the truth I don't know what I'm allowed to write or not.

I'm back in a huge, beautiful hospital in France, so I guess it won't be very hard for you to guess where I am. I've received nothing but the greatest kindness from everyone, and I never could put it in words what it feels like to be treated as a human being again. I am so happy I don't know whether to laugh or cry. Today we had the meal I've been dreaming about for 4 months—steak and french fries, and how—how I've been eating.

I'll never forget as long as I live when I saw that first Yank. I always said I'd kiss the first one I saw who liberated us, even if it were a 2nd Looie, and you guessed it, he was. He was more surprised than I, and I imagine it's the first time in history an officer has ever been kissed by an enlisted man. Then they gave us chocolate bars and cigarettes and I went wild. From there to here it has been a smooth job of evacuation.

I was shot and taken prisoner on that memorable day—Dec. 16, the first day of the terrific German breakthrough in the Ardennes, when all hell broke loose. The next four months I will tell about when I get home, and will describe them now in two words, Living Hell.

My leg is just about well now, and I'm here more or less to be built up. It will only be a short stay, and I should be back in the States soon, Mom, and when I do get home, I'll probably never get farther than the back porch, as I've had all the excitement and adventure to last me a lifetime.

My biggest concern and something that has always been on my mind is how you two are and how the Missing in Action affected you. But you are both brave, strong parents, so I'm sure everything is all right.

We were all saddened very much yesterday by news of the death of our great leader and a real buddy to every G.I. Joe, President Roosevelt. But it was God's will, and I hope that President Truman can fill his shoes.

Death has faced me many times in the past months, and by the grace of my Lord and Savior I am here today to write this letter. I always considered myself a good Christian until I was captured, and then I learned what a fool I had been and what it really means to have faith and the power of prayer. I prayed day and nite, and these prayers were heard, with the result that today I can really call myself a good Catholic and firm believer in the will of God.

I could fill up pages, but there's so much I'd rather tell than write, and so much more I want to know about you,

Johnny and Bill. This is a poor attempt for my first letter, but I find it much more difficult than I expected. I hope to be in the States before I get an answer. To see your faces again will be the happiest moment of my life. I love you both and thank God every day I have such wonderful parents.

Your loving son,
Jim

———— • ————

Edgar Fergon in uniform, 1943.
(Courtesy of Edgar Fergon)

Dear Tom,

I was a navigator on a B-17 and was shot down July 29, 1943, after bombing Kiel, Germany. I was taken eventually to Stalag Luft III and was marched out in Jan. '45 in a howling blizzard to keep us from falling into the hands of the Russians. We ended up in Moosburg, Stalag 7A. I came home and married JoAnn and we raised 6 kids. We are now retired in Palm Springs. I came home with PTSD (Post Traumatic Stress Disorder) (Shell Shock). It was diagnosed at the Loma Linda VA about 6 years ago. I am 100% disabled.

STANDARD TIME INDICATED / RECEIVED AT

Form 1 F21 F.SD307   S.CC294   C.WC502 (TWO)41 GOVT=PXXWMU

=MRS MARGARET A FERGON=
=1220 B ST SANMATEO CALIF=   1058P=

I REGRET TO INFORM YOUREPORT RECEIVED STATESYOUR SON SECTND
LIEUTENANT EDGAR P FERGONMISSING IN ACTION NEAR KIEL
GERMANY SINCE TWENTY NINE JULYIF FURTHER DETAILS OR OTHER
INFORMATIONOFHIS STATUS ARE RECEIVED YOU WILL BE PROMPTLY
NOTIFIED=

ULIO THE ADJUTANT GENERAL

Telegram informing Ed Fergon's mother that he was missing in action.

Telegram informing Ed Fergon's mother that he was a prisoner of war.

Form 16 F26 F.CB372   C.WC314 (TWO) 33 GOVT=PXXWMU WASHINGTON DC
                                                        20 907P=

=MRS MARGARET A FERGON=
1220 B ST (SENMETO CALIF)

REPORT RECEIVED THROUGH THE INTERNATIONAL RED CROSS STATES
THAT YOUR SON SECONDLIEUTENANT EDGAR P FERGON IS A PRISONER
OF WAR OF THE GERMAN GOVERNMENT LETTER OF INFORMATION
FOLLOWS   FROM PROVOST MARSHAL GENERAL

=ULIOTHE ADGNERAL.

"All is OK": Postcard sent home in January 1943 by POW Ed Fergon.

Kriegsgefangenenlager   Jan 3rd 1944
                         Datum: AUG 8, 43

MOM DARLING PARACHUTES IS FINE ANIMULES.
GEORGE & I GOT OUT OK. WE ARE NOW PRISONER
OF WAR HERE IN GERMANY. ALL IS OK - PLEASE -
DO NOT WORRY. PLEASE WIRE BETTY AND TELL HER.
THIS IS ALL I CAN WRITE AT THE MOMENT. PLEASE
WRITE TO LT. W.C. BISSON AT MY OLD ADDRESS AND HAVE
HIM TAKE CARE OF MY THINGS. FEEL GOOD NEED NOTHING

Stalag Luft 3 official personnel card, as issued to each prisoner upon arrival at the camp. (All courtesy of Edgar Fergon)

| 9 | 10 | 11 | 12 | 13 | 14 | 15 | 16 | 17 | 18 | 19 | 20 | 21 | 22 | 23 | 24 | 25 |

Personalkarte I: Personelle Angaben   *Fergon*

Kriegsgefangenen-Stammlager: **Stalag Luft 3**

Beschriftung der Erkennungsmarke
Nr. 7977
Lager: **STALAG LUFT 3**

Name: FERGON
Vorname: Edgar
Geburtstag und -ort: 7.3.22 Saumateo
Religion: Luth.
Vorname des Vaters:
Familienname der Mutter:

Staatsangehörigkeit: USA U.S.A.
Dienstgrad: 2. Lt.
Truppenteil: USAAF Kom. usw.:
Zivilberuf: Eisenbahnangestellter Berufs-Gr.:
Matrikel Nr. (Stammrolle des Heimatstaates): O-736846
Gefangennahme (Ort und Datum): Kosby B, Süderbraron 29.7.43
Ob gesund, krank, verwundet eingeliefert:

Des Kriegsgefangenen

| Lichtbild | | Nähere Personalbeschreibung |

| Grösse | Haarfarbe | Besondere Kennzeichen: |
| 7.97 | blond | |

Fingerabdruck des rechten 1 Zeigefingers

Name und Anschrift der zu benachrichtigenden Person in der Heimat des Kriegsgefangenen

Mrs. Margaret Fergon
1220 B Street
Saumteo, Calif.

FERGON, E.   Wenden!

CHICKEN CASSEROLE — Raw boned chicken, small new potatoes, white onions, sliced carrots, chopped celery — Line bottom of casserole with strips bacon, alternate layers of chicken & veg. Chicken on top. Smother with cream of mushroom soup & bake — season to taste — (cheese?)

LEFT OVER CASSEROLE — chop left over meat into squares & fry. Add boiled mushrooms, onions & tomato paste, bake

1/4 cup orange juice } boil with 1/2 C sugar
1/4 cup pineapple }
Whip 3 eggs + add 1/4 C brandy. Add to juice (stir well) caramelize 1/3 C sugar & add to above. Cook slowly in double boiler till thick. Pour & cool.

BANANA CUSTARD PUD — alternate layers of sliced banana & vanilla cookies. Pour on custard. Ice box & serve

HAWAIIAN RICE — steamed rice, chopped pineapple & whipped egg white. Form in mould. Pour over sauce of cream, sugar, egg yolk & pineapple juice. Sauce boiled till thick.

STUFFED MEAT LOAF — Fry chopped onion, celery, parsley & pimento. Mix with 1 part ground round, 1 part ground pork & 1/2 pt ground veal. Form in two flat loaves. One bottom of roaster & cover with sliced cheese, sliced hard boiled egg, fresh sliced tomato, strips of bacon, place 2nd loaf on top & smother with tomato sauce. Garnish with small new spuds, onions, carrots & bake. Serve with mint sauce, green peas, muffins & honey.

SHRIMP DELIGHT — boil noodles, add shrimp, white onions & cream of mushroom soup, chopped hard boiled eggs. Sprinkle with grated cheese (add cheese?)

GOULASH — Fry hamburger & onions, add to boiled macaroni and place in casserole — cover with tomato sauce & bake. Serve with grated cheese.

PIGS IN CABBAGE LEAVES — Mix ground round steak with pre-cooked rice (one to one) add garlic, salt & pepper, wrap in cabbage leaves & boil.

DANISH STUFFED SQUASH — half squash stuffed with sausage meat — bake

INDIAN PUDDING — corn meal, molasses, sugar, butter.

BANANA & chopped nuts salad (shredded American cheese?) top with mayonnaise or whipped cream.

EGG BENEDICTINE — boil 1/4 lb butter & 2 C milk, add center cut "ham (whatever)" cook till tender, poach 4 eggs on ham, lift ham & eggs from pan & cover with sauce of 1/4 lb old English cheese, small evaporated milk, 1/2 C mustard, 1 T worcestershire sauce, 2 T sherry wine — cooked in double boiler. When baking ham spread with peanut butter in place of sugar.

EGG NEST — nest of beaten egg white baked on piece of toast, yolks mixed with chopped ham or bacon, fried soft & placed in nest.

HUNTERS PORK CHOP — partly boil chop — place into casserole. Add to cream sauce chopped parsley & green onions, vinegar & worcestershire sauce. Pour over chops & bake till sauce is thick — serve with biscuits.

MILK SPREAD — stir 6 eggs adding flour until fairly thick, add to boiling milk, cook until thick. Season with salt & pepper (can add chopped ham or bacon)

NIBLETS

NUTTY NUGGETS — work together equal parts peanut butter & honey. Add butter, cook until hard, back in water. Roll in marshmellows (to mixture) to desired thickness. Roll in chopped nuts or coconut.

NOTE: FOR PERSONAL TASTE TRY ADDING CHEESE & HARD BOILED EGG TO EVERYTHING

CREOLE CORN CHOWDER — Add to whole kernal corn chopped onion, peppers, pimentos, celery, parsley, okra, diced fried ham, cover with tomato sauce. Bake in casserole.

KRIEGIE CARAMEL PIE — burn one C sugar (with little maple?) till brown, add water till cooked to syrup, add 1 can condensed, 2 T butter. Boil well. — Cool. Beat in klim until thick. Pour into cracker crust.

CHEESE DREAM — soak cream cheese sandwich in beaten eggs — fry. (Var. melted American cheese & ham)

CHICKEN RICE CURRY — Mix steamed rice, chopped chicken, onion, celery, carrots, parsley, curry powder, paprika, olives, bay leaves. Place in casserole, smother with thick sauce of cream, eggs, chopped bacon.

BRUNSWICK STEW — Stew 3 lbs boneless chicken, & 3 lb boned pork. Cook stock & skim off grease. (Grind up meats) to stock add — 3 cans white corn, 3 cans tomatos, 1 can tomato paste. Cook to simmer & add 3 large onions, 2 bell peppers, 1 whole lemon — all chopped. Add meat & continue to boil till thick. Season with red pepper.

SPAGHETTI MEAT LOAF — ground round browned well in oven, cover with 2 box spaghetti — cooked — green peppers, chopped mushrooms & layer of cheese. Cover with butter & one can tomato paste. Bake 1 1/2 hrs.

AMBROSIA — fresh pineapple, oranges, bananas, shredded coconuts, & raisins chopped together. Mix in powdered sugar till thick — chill — serve sprinkled with p. sugar.

SPANISH BREAD — French bread, tomatoes, onions, celery, red pepper, ground round, tomato sauce, chile beans, tabasco, paprika, chile powder. Halve bread & hollow out — toaste shells in oven — fry meat & add beans — add vegetable & seasoning, boil to chili consistency. Pour into shells. Cover with cheese & bacon strips, smother with tomato paste — bake.

CHICKEN BON BONS — add to cooked rice & chopped chicken, form in balls & dip in waffle batter, fry in deep fat.

APPLE GLUM — add corn flakes to sliced apples stewed to almost apple sauce. Mix in sugar & cinnamon. Sprinkle with nutmeg. Serve with whipped cream.

PEANUT BUTTER PIE — 16 oz peanut butter, 2 cans condenso salt, 1 corn starch. Mix & pour in graham cracker crust — bake or chill.

FRIED BANANAS — dip bananas in egg batter, roll in graham cracker crumbs — fry.

STRAWBERRY AIR RAID SPECIAL — chocolate wafer crust, cover bottom with toll house drops, oven long enough to soften — not set. Add crushed strawberries mixed with cream, top with whip cream & chopped nuts — chill.

Menu written by POW Ed Fergon listing the meals he would eat when he returned home.

Ed Fergon (fifth from the right) and his companions in Stalag Luft 3, 1944. (Both courtesy of Edgar Fergon)

It was quite an experience, that WWII, it was horrible, it was mind- and life-changing. (It did mine, I left my life over there.) But it was *glorious* too.

I am extremely proud to have been a part of the greatest time in our history and of the Greatest Generation!

Sincerely,
Ed Fergon

Ed Fergon's POW dog tags. One tag was American; the other was issued by the prison camp. (Courtesy of Edgar Fergon)

———— • ————

Dear Mr. Brokaw:

I met my husband, Dick, in early spring of '43, shortly after joining the Army Nurse Corps at Fort Monmouth, NJ. We were married on Memorial Day '43 and immediately separated by our individual assignments. We did manage to see each other twice before I shipped out in February '44. My husband fretted back in the States. I was sent to Ireland first, then England for training and assigned to the 103rd Evacuation Hospital. We (the 103rd) went to France in July of '44.

We were assigned to the Third Army. We followed close to the lines, did initial debridement of the wounds and shipped the patients back to the rear areas. Our average setup was seven days, then pack up and move forward.

Dick arrived in France in September of '44. He was a combat photographer with the 167th Signal Photo Company. He was on detached service to different divisions. On October 8th, while on assignment with the First Division, he took a sniper bullet in the back of the neck. Miraculously the bullet must have deflected around the spine. He was okay, just a sore neck. If you look carefully at the news photo [taken at the time], you can see the exit wound behind the mastoid process.

He did some fast talking to persuade the medics not to send him home. He'd just gotten there and his wife was there! He wanted to go back to duty. He prevailed.

The enclosed letter was one sent to our parents at the end of the war. He was many miles away from me then, but I saw much of the same thing.

I hope you enjoy this. There is much more to the story, and I have begun to write it down. Hopefully I will finish before I die.

Sincerely,

Jane Sunderbruch

5 May 45

Dear Folks:

Sorry that I've been such a poor correspondent, but my duties have been increased and I've been just too busy to take time out and do any writing. Right now it is midnight, and I have been going ever since 7:30 this morning and still have some work to do. But I did want to get this letter off to let you know that I was still part of the family and hadn't forgotten everyone completely. I'm now a corps photographic officer instead of division and have several units working under me, one of whom is Jimmy Bowne. We have had quite a time up here, and the rat race that has resulted from our latest campaign has brought out so many picture opportunities that we have had a hard time trying to decide which were the most important and which we had to pass by. The German army in this area is finished, and the resulting surrenders and mass movement of humanity have created a chaos that is unparalleled in history. They are beaten and know it, but that does not seem to bother them. They are only interested in getting away from the Russians. When the juncture of our forces with the Russians was imminent, we knew not from our military reports but from the way the German soldiers started to desert and give themselves up. At first a few men, then small units, then larger units. Finally divisions, then corps, then armies came in. They came in with all their equipment and men and officers and surrendered en masse.

You have all undoubtedly seen some of the pictures that have been taken over here. I have seen them too. I saw the ones they wouldn't print. I wasn't fortunate (unfortunate would be a better word for it) enough to get into one of the well-established ones that was set up on a mass production basis with the torture chambers, gas cells and crematoriums. This was just a makeshift setup. It had been a prisoner of war camp, and the SS men moved the POWs out and put these political prisoners in because their other camps had been overrun. I talked with some of them who could talk, and it was a terrible tale. They came to this camp in railroad cars. Railroad cars over here are much smaller than ours in the States, just little jobs with four wheels, but they were loaded into them, 130 men to a car. They were in there 8 days. In that time they had one slice of bread and no water. They have been at this camp just three weeks. Originally there were 3,500; about 10 days ago, 2,300 Jews were added. Since their arrival 300 to 1,000 have died. Not shot or gassed or anything like that, but just starvation. Most of them have been buried in a common grave in back of the camp. But there are still a lot who have not been taken away. I walked into the only washroom in the camp, which is a room about 15 feet wide and 40 feet long. There is a long trough down the center that is filled with water by bringing from a pump outside, the only source of water in the camp. Everyone was supposed to wash in this one trough, but they couldn't get to it. The room was full of bodies. There were at least a hundred. Some of them piled three and four deep and others scattered a little on the floor so that you can walk around the room a little. What a pitiful sight to see those wasted bodies, but not nearly as pitiful as those not yet dead. From there I went into the living quarters. They had new brick buildings. At least the walls are brick and they have a roof, but there is no floor and there are no furnishings. The men sleep on the ground, and there are some bunks made of logs with barbed wire strung between them for the men to sleep on. There are no stoves. If they want warmth or wish to cook (if they had anything to cook) they build a fire on the floor and get the smoke as well as the heat. For food they had a few beets and once in a while were able to get a potato. The filth inside and out was indescribable. There were no latrine or sanitary facilities, and as you walked around the camp it was just like walking around a pigpen. Only these were human beings. The inside was just about as bad. Some were so weak they couldn't get outside. When I went inside they were scattered around in various positions. Some walking around and in pretty good condition, others sitting up and others that could just lie on the ground and look at you. Then others who were still in their blankets and had passed out of their misery but hadn't been moved out of the building yet. I talked with them and heard about the deprivations they had undergone, the beatings they had taken. I talked with the doctor, who was himself a prisoner. He told me about his attempts to keep them alive, he knew not for what.

This camp was just outside a fairly large town. There were barbed-wire fences around it, but no attempt was made to hide it. There is no reason why people in the territory could not have known of its presence. You could even see the bodies in the yard from the highway that went by the camp. So don't let the story that the people didn't know about it take you in.

Let us not forget and relent the way we have in the past. Don't in a few years start circulating the story that these atrocities were the stories of warmongers and Jewish propaganda, that the pictures were posed and retouched. There are too many pictures. Too many people have seen them, people whose veracity cannot be doubted. Read this over and save it for future reference and to show to doubting Thomases. And when I come back I'll have the pictures to back it up.

Love,
Dick

———— • ————

Dear Tom:

I served in two gasoline supply companies in various places across England and early in 1944 served in, and helped shut down, the U.S. Assault Training Center Headquarters in Woolacombe, Devon, England. General Ewart G. Plank was then in the process of establishing Hq. Advance Section Communication Zone in Bristol, England. Since I had learned to type in high school, I was given a desk job with the rank of T/4 (Sgt) in the signal section. Various field units under this command were to be the forward supply echelon for the combat troops. We crossed the channel and disembarked on Utah Beach on July 1, 1944. We followed close behind Patton all the way into Germany. Along the way, we observed (at a safe distance) some of the Battle of the Bulge. Col. Grant and I made a foray into the battle zone, which entitled me to this campaign, along with Normandy, Northern France, Rhineland and Central Europe.

The war's end saw us located in Fulda, Germany, and it was from here that I got to travel to Buchenwald. The horrible spectacle there made me realize just what we were serving for, and the impression has been indelible with me all these years.

Yours very truly,
David R. Hubbard

Dearest Mama, Daddy and all,

It's been 2-½ years since I could write a letter and tell you directly where I was situated. The order came out this afternoon relaxing the censorship regulations. From now on there will be just a spot check by the base censor.

Fulda, Germany, is just a small place about fifty miles northeast of Frankfurt.

Now to get on with the story of my trip yesterday. I know all of you have followed the stories of atrocities committed by these so-called humans in Germany. Pictures, stories and word of mouth cannot sufficiently tell the story of horrors and beastliness carried on in the concentration camps you've heard about such as Limburg, Dachau, Buchenwald and others. I'll try to tell you some of my impressions upon the viewing with my own eyes one of Germany's most notorious camps—Buchenwald. I was there yesterday and still I can't get the sight of those poor souls out of my mind.

There are still several thousand prisoners at Buchenwald, and as soon as our vehicle stopped we had a crowd of them around us. Two of the fellows with me were Jewish, and since most of the prisoners are Jewish it wasn't hard for us to learn all about the place. Two very bright youngsters of about seventeen years offered to guide us, and the first place they took us was the crematorium. This is housed in a neat-looking little white house, and you'd never guess that so many thousands of human bodies had been reduced to ashes inside its walls. We entered through the basement and viewed the chute where the bodies were thrown down into the basement. Not all the victims were lucky enough to be dead upon arrival at this gruesome place and means were provided to kill them there in the basement. Arranged all around the top of the wall, about thirty inches apart, were iron hooks. There were forty of these hooks and up on each one a human was hung just as we'd hang up a coat on the hall rack. The hooks were not designed high enough from the floor so that a jerk of the falling body would break the neck, thereby ending life painlessly, but rather it was a slow, painful death of strangulation. One could still see the marks on the wall made by men in their death throes.

The dead bodies were placed on a modern electric elevator and lifted up to the ground floor, where the roaring blast furnaces awaited them. There were two brick furnaces especially designed for the purpose, each with three openings. Before I forget it, the furnaces had the manufacturer's nameplate on the front as bold as it could be. The steel stretcher was still there, and one of the prisoners demonstrated it for us. Three bodies were placed on this stretcher at a time and shoved in the furnace, and a track contraption outside made it impossible to move the stretcher from one opening to another. Three bodies in each opening made it possible for eighteen bodies to be consumed at a time. The process of turning them into nothing but ashes took thirty minutes, and a trough at the bottom was designed to retain the ashes for removal. A little square wooden box contained the ashes and partly consumed bones of one man. The contents would probably fill a hat.

On rushing days, when the hooks in the basement were inadequate to handle all the victims, a scaffold concern was used out in the yard. It reminds me so much of the old beef rack in the market we used to hang beef on to dry. Piled in another corner of the yard were the plastic and pottery containers which were used to hold the ashes of one body, supposedly for shipment to the victim's people. I have one of them in the room here, and particles of the ashes still remain.

After the crematorium, we visited the living quarters of the remaining prisoners. Such filth, stench and scum I've never seen in my whole life. One poor fellow was laboriously shaving himself with an old broken razor and a blade that looked like a saw blade. I happened to have a pack of blades in my pocket, so I gave him one. His face sure lit up, and I thought to myself how much I dreaded to even shave with a blade but twice.

All the prisoners remarked to us that this camp was the showplace of all the concentration camps in Europe. It was supposed to be the best in existence, and one thought himself lucky to be sent there. I told them that I'd certainly hate to see worse ones.

There was one pitiful looking being of skin and bones only who was actually in the crematorium when he and several others were told to go back to the hospital to put on more weight. The only explanation they could think of was that the SS troops wanted to begin making a better impression because of the close proximity of our troops. This kid is only 16½ years old and nothing but skin and bones after five weeks of liberation and additional food. I have a picture of him, just as I have of other things of interest. Another boy of seventeen, who spoke very good English, told us that he was from Bucharest and that he wanted to return home for a short while and then go to America. This boy was the healthiest specimen I saw in the whole camp and was quite a contrast to the others. Several thousand of the prisoners were evacuated prior to the liberation, and he managed to escape.

I'll end with the statement that, in my opinion, the only good German is a dead German and it's such a pity that so many still remain alive.

Lots of love to all,
David Ray

———•———

Dear Mr. Brokaw:

My name is Klaus Theisen, I was born in 1929 in Düsseldorf, Germany. I would like to try to give you a perspective on life in Germany during those years. Many events were very similar, our young men were drafted, sent to the front and were wounded or killed. Our mothers and wives received the official letter expressing great grief and regret, which read: "We regret to inform you that your son/husband was killed in action for the Führer, Volk and Vaterland." Our beliefs were different since all we knew was the party version of the whole development and conflict. The only information for the public was through newspapers, magazines and movies, all of which were strictly censored and influenced by the Party. We listened to our leadership, and we believed what we heard; the party system influenced us from cradle to grave.

To become a member of the Hitler Youth was the dream of every young boy. The organization offered activities attractive to young men and boys. Of course there was political education, but does a young boy care, or understand what it really means? There was camaraderie, games, special club activities such as motorcycling, sailing, bicycle trips, musical instruments, learning Morse code, sing-alongs around a campfire and so much more. At the time any child anywhere would have jumped at the opportunity to belong to such an organization. My parents were against my joining the Hitler Youth, my pleas did not change my father's position, however a letter from the Party did.

An event of interest was the Kristallnacht. As I went to school that morning I passed several shops in which the windows were smashed, merchandise was thrown on the street and in big letters "JUDE" was written on the wall. Of course in school the subject was discussed by listening to the official party version of what happened and why it was happening. Across the street from us on the second floor lived our family dentist and his practice. All of his equipment was thrown on the street and the sign "JUDE" was written on the wall. I remember asking my parents about this criminal behavior but was quickly told not to talk about it. As far as the dentist was concerned, he was just our dentist. From that time on, all Jews had to wear the Star of David and were not allowed in public places. The official party version of the events was that the Party is encouraging Jews to emigrate to Palestine.

Inevitably, my father was drafted. Since he spoke French, he was part of the army invading France. Not much later the bombing of German cities began. Most houses had basements, but none of them could withstand a direct hit. One night my mother, my two brothers, myself and all the other occupants of our building were in the cellar, terrified, while all around us bombs were exploding. At one point a bomb went directly through my parents' bedroom ceiling and out their bedroom wall and buried itself into the street. It was a time bomb, and it exploded the next morning, when no one was prepared for it. The result was many casualties and much destruction.

The Party started to move women and children to the country, away from the air attacks. I ended up in the Eifel, a poor region where farmers struggled to make a living. The army had confiscated all horses, and there was no fuel available. As an eleven-year-old boy, I was welcomed to the family largely to boost their labor force since all the men had been drafted. I worked long, hard hours, but the food was good and I was safe.

As I completed public school, it was time to enter into an apprenticeship for a trade. Colleges and universities were only available to those who were well-connected or wealthy or extremely intelligent. Considering the times we were in, the only trades available were in the industrial sector. I started on April 1, 1943, and as I turned 14 in June I had to work 12-hour days, six days a week. The Honsel Werke in Meschede was my first employer. It was an industrial giant manufacturing steel and aluminum and of course working for the war effort. The majority of the workers were French, Belgian, Dutch and Polish prisoners of war. We worked side by side and ate the same lousy food. Near the factory ran the main railroad's north-south link, and every morning at about 10:00 a.m. several fighter planes chased a train and while in the neighborhood hit the factory with machine-gun fire.

It was just a matter of time before the factory was the target of a bombing raid. The first major raid missed the factory completely but hit the town very hard. I remember lying in the field pressed to the ground while it shook and lifted with every explosion. You learned how to pray very quickly. After the raid every available body (off shift) worked for two days and nights to free people from bombed-out houses and cellars. There was no water with which to wash, and food and water came from the NSV (party relief organization). There were military police all over, and any loiterers were shot on sight. A human life meant nothing since thousands were lost every day. The second bombing raid shortly after the first hit the factory and once again the city. Again all help was needed. The third bombing raid finished the factory.

With the factory bombed out, I went back to the country, where my mother and two younger brothers were. Three days before Easter 1945, I along with two other boys from the village received the draft order. We had to report to the Volkssturm in Winterberg. The Volkssturm was Germany's last hope, men over sixty years of age and boys under eighteen were now being drafted. It was crazy. The Americans were two days away, but the SS military police all over the country were looking for deserters and draft dodgers. If caught, they would be hung on the nearest lamp pole with a sign around the neck, "I am a deserter." The three of us traveled together to Winterberg to report to the Volkssturm headquarters. We were issued ill-fitting uniforms and assigned to a major traffic intersection where the American army was expected to pass through. Two tiger tanks, one on each side of the intersection, were dug in, since they had no gasoline to retreat further. We had to dig trenches for our own protection and wondered if they would not ultimately become our graves. My friends and I were split up, and we were on opposite sides of the intersection. Morale was low, the tank crews wore top hats (in jest) and were not about to die at this time. As expected, the American army approached the intersection, and shots were exchanged. We were grateful for our trenches. Suddenly civilian authorities appeared and pleaded with the officer in charge and the tank crews to give up and spare the city from artillery and bombardment. No more shots were fired. The tank crew blew up both tanks and disappeared. We, the glorious Volkssturm, didn't know what to do and just sat tight. Before we knew it, American soldiers surrounded us. Needless to say, we were terrified at the prospect of becoming prisoners of war, on the other hand, there was some relief in that the shooting had stopped. Imagine a 15-year-old kid in a uniform way too large, scared stiff, with not a soul to turn to. One American soldier approached me (he could have been my father). He looked at me, signaled to me to put my arms up, and he frisked me. He spoke a lot in a very angry tone, of course I had no idea what he was saying. He then turned me around, kicked me in the butt and told me to go home. That I did understand! I looked at him, he smiled, and I took off, hitting a bush trail back home. At that time I was more worried about the German military police than the American army.

As I came home, I found our village occupied by the American army. I found out that my two friends on the other side of that intersection were not as lucky as I, they became prisoners of war and spent two years in a French coal mine. My father was also a prisoner of war and returned home about a year later.

In 1950 I returned to my hometown and started working in my trade with Mannesmann Röhren Werke. In 1956 the company selected me to move to Canada as part of a team to install and operate a modern seamless tube mill. Of course my wife and I accepted. I retired in 1988. Not happy in retirement, I went to China in 1993 as site representative of a machine manufacturer based in Ohio. We had various projects that kept me in China for the better part of four years. My wife and I have two sons, one lives in Ontario, Canada, and the other is living in Florida. I am now fully retired, spending my summers in Canada and the winters in sunny Florida. My wife and I both struggled through the war years, we had no real youth, by today's standards. But we learned things during those years that have been with us all our lives, namely, appreciate life, health, food, and value the freedom that we are enjoying now.

Thank you, to the Greatest Generation.

Klaus Theisen

———— • ————

Dear Mr. Brokaw:

I am enclosing for your reading a letter my father sent his recently widowed mother, younger sister and fiancée (later to be my mother).

Dad, Maury Robb, went on to become a B-17 pilot, successfully completed 30 missions over Germany and was preparing to go for fighter aircraft training when the war ended. After the war he returned to the University of Pennsylvania, completed a degree in engineering on the G.I. Bill and eventually founded a small plastics company in Philadelphia. Dad became a well-known and highly respected member of the community, donating many hours and years to the Anti-Defamation League of the B'Nai B'rith before his death from cancer in 1986.

In a conversation a few weeks before his death, Dad commented that "aside from you boys and Mom, I think what I am most grateful for was the privilege of flying a B-17 and helping to defeat Nazism."

Best wishes,
Mark Robb

Saturday, March 6, 1943
12:50 P.M.

Dear Mom & Betsy & Bea:

Well, since I wrote last night's letter it has snowed. Last night we had a rather heavy snow which changed to rain this morning—and now there is a slight drizzle.

I got your letter dated Thursday—I noticed that you put the date on—I wish you'd make a habit of so doing. The hangers also arrived—and I lost no time at all putting them to work. There wasn't a hanger in this place when we arrived—

and I'll bet I have more (8 pants & 5 coat) hangers than the rest of the flight combined.

No, Mother, I don't need a scarf—our coat, the standard army coat, is *quite* sufficient. As far as too much money—I haven't as I expect to need some in a week or so. But, as to my switching to another branch, Mother, I am in the army. I enlisted to serve in the Air Corps and I doubt if I'll ever change.

First Lieutenant Maury Robb, B-17 pilot in the Eighth Air Force, in a photo taken in Columbia, South Carolina, 1944. (Courtesy of Mark Robb)

Remember, Mother, some *have* to fly so that peace can be won. Many are not physically or mentally adaptable. To those who are acceptable—and there are very few, as I shall learn—the entire country looks with pride and for a quick victory. The soldiers of the ground forces look with envy and respect upon a flier. But it is not this desire to be among the "Elite" that makes me anxious to graduate and be able to wear a pair of silver wings. It is more than that, it is because of the way Dad brought me up, it is because of the love and respect I hold for Dad that I will never voluntarily ask for a transfer. If this seems confusing, let me explain. You remember how Dad turned down a badly needed line, because he didn't want to take it way from another man— who also needed to make a living? Do you remember how Dad paid rent for 5 or 6 months at 5652 Arlington Street while all around people didn't—and got away with it? Do you remember how Dad trusted some of the houses he represented, even after he was told by you, his wife, that he was being taken over—and that money is still outstanding? It is these things—and a lifetime full of other incidents—perhaps nothing which in itself would be noteworthy—but together they point to one thing—Honor. Honor in more than the everyday way people think of it—Honor in the way the Bible means. To Dad Honor meant more than simply financial integrity—it meant respect for his fellow men, and fair play for everyone.

As Dad once told me—while we were waiting for a red light at 83rd & Market after one of my AZA meetings—he "tried to live by the Golden Rule"—and we and all those who knew Dad agree enthusiastically that he did. To him—and to me—his life was a success—he won the respect and love of everyone who met him—that is success to a great degree.

But what does that have to do with my Army career, you ask? Well, once again it is Honor. Yes, Honor can be defined in many ways—but it cannot be overdone.

Today Honor means Duty. To serve my country—and therefore you, my mother, who has devoted her life to feeding, dressing, training and loving me; to you, Betsy, my sister, to whom I owe a life of freedom and peace in return for the love and respect and fun you have given me; and to you, my Beloved Bea, you I have not been able to promise wealth but only love and respect and a husband who you will be proud of.

And my duty is to serve in the highest position I can fill.

So, my dears, looking at it this way, I really think that you will not want to urge me to switch. In your letter, Mother, you mention my consideration of Bea. I do—I have considered her. I'll admit that it would have been more sensible not to have become engaged—but I am glad I did—even if some might say that it is selfish. She has made me very happy, and I know she has been a great "aide" to you. But as far as switching because of her, I can't. Remember the phrase "I could not love you half as much, if I loved not Honor more." Well, today Honor and Duty and Country are all tied up together.

Thus, I feel that I am doing right and that I am doing what Dad would think right.

Love
Maury

ABOVE: *U.S. Marines moving to positions to attack Japanese forces entrenched on the Matanikou River in Guadalcanal, the Solomon Islands, October 19, 1942.* (AP/Wide World Photos)

RIGHT: *U.S. Marines of the Twenty-eighth Regiment of the Fifth Division raise the American flag atop Mt. Suribachi, Iwo Jima, on February 23, 1945.* (AP/Wide World Photos)

Part Three

·

THE WAR
IN THE
PACIFIC

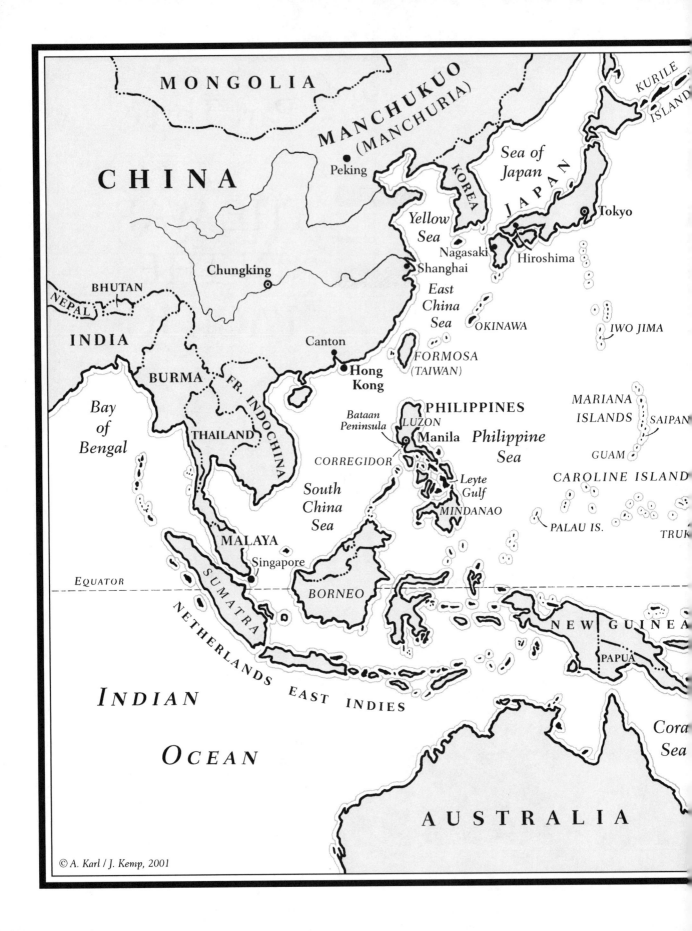

MONGOLIA

MANCHUKUO
(MANCHURIA)

CHINA

Peking

KURILE
ISLAND

Sea of
Japan

JAPAN

KOREA

Yellow
Sea

Tokyo

Chungking

Nagasaki

Hiroshima

Shanghai

East
China
Sea

BHUTAN

NEPAL

INDIA

OKINAWA

IWO JIMA

Canton

FORMOSA
(TAIWAN)

BURMA

Bay
of
Bengal

FR. INDOCHINA

Hong
Kong

PHILIPPINES

MARIANA
ISLANDS

SAIPAN

THAILAND

Bataan
Peninsula

LUZON

Manila

Philippine
Sea

GUAM

CORREGIDOR

CAROLINE ISLAND

South
China
Sea

Leyte
Gulf

MINDANAO

MALAYA

Singapore

PALAU IS.

TRUK

EQUATOR

SUMATRA

BORNEO

NETHERLANDS EAST INDIES

NEW GUINEA

PAPUA

INDIAN

OCEAN

Cora
Sea

AUSTRALIA

© A. Karl / J. Kemp, 2001

NORTH

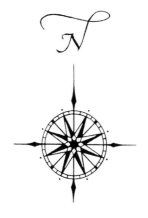

PACIFIC

MIDWAY

HAWAIIAN ISLANDS

Honolulu

Pearl
Harbor

WAKE ISLAND

OCEAN

MARSHALL
ISLANDS

ENIWETOK

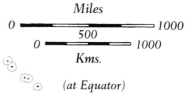

Miles

0   500   1000

0   500   1000

Kms.

(at Equator)

KWAJALEIN

TARAWA

EQUATOR

SOLOMON
ISLANDS

GILBERT
ISLANDS

BOUGAINVILLE

SOUTH   PACIFIC

GUADALCANAL

OCEAN

FIJI
ISLANDS

NEW
HEBRIDES

NEW CALEDONIA

JULY 7, 1937

The Japanese army responds to an incident at the Marco Polo Bridge, near Beijing, with a full-scale invasion of China. Before the month is out Japan will have taken Beijing. This is the beginning of the Sino-Japanese War, which will continue until 1945 and which some historians contend is the real beginning of World War II.

SEPT. 4, 1940

U.S. Secretary of State Cordell Hull warns Japan about aggressive moves against French Indochina.

SEPT. 22, 1940

Japan begins its occupation of Indochina under an agreement signed in Hanoi with Vichy France.

SEPT. 26, 1940

U.S. President Franklin Roosevelt halts exports of iron and steel to Japan as punishment for Japanese activity in Indochina.

SEPT. 27, 1940

Germany, Italy, and Japan sign the Tripartite Pact, a ten-year military and economic alliance, creating the Axis.

OCT. 7, 1940

The Japanese ambassador to the United States says that the U.S. embargo of iron and steel is an unfriendly act against Japan.

APR. 13, 1941

Japan and the USSR conclude a neutrality treaty, allowing the Soviets to protect their rear while Japan protects its northern flank.

JULY 26, 1941

FDR freezes all Japanese assets in the United States.

ASK ANY AMERICAN OF A CERTAIN AGE WHERE HE OR SHE was December 7, 1941, and the likely response will be a clear and vivid account, little diminished by more than a half century of memory. The Japanese surprise attack on Pearl Harbor was an event of such magnitude that it will forever have a fixed place in all accounts of world history. It catapulted the United States into a world war and set in motion events whose consequences could not even be imagined at the time.

The attack on Pearl Harbor was a daring military operation that had the added advantage of complete surprise, a target that was wholly unprepared. American personnel, ships, and planes were compactly arranged in that serene Hawaiian harbor. Just before eight o'clock on a Sunday morning, 360 Japanese aircraft, largely undetected until they dove out of the skies, attacked the U.S. forces. They sank or severely damaged eight battleships, three cruisers, and three destroyers. They destroyed 188 aircraft, most of which didn't get off the ground. American military personnel, scrambling to their posts on that sunny morning, were outgunned and overexposed. When it was all over, in a little more than two hours, more than 2,400 Americans had been killed, another 1,100 wounded.

Within hours of the attack on Pearl Harbor, Japan attacked American positions in the Philippines, began landings on the Malaya Peninsula, and attacked the British base in Hong Kong. These initial strikes were so devastating that the U.S. presence in the Pacific was reduced to a battered force fighting for survival.

The next day, December 8, President Franklin Roosevelt aroused the nation with a radio address that described December 7 as "a date which will live in infamy." The U.S. Congress voted to declare war on Japan. Overnight, isolationists were converted to interventionists. Three days later Japan's allies, Germany and Italy, declared war on the United States, and the U.S. Congress answered with its own declaration of war on the fascist Axis.

At the time the United States was still defined by its European origins; the Pacific and Asia were much less familiar territory. Indeed, when news came of the attack on Pearl Harbor, many Americans had no idea where it was.

They quickly received a painful lesson in the geography of the Far East as Japan captured Guam, overrunning the contingent of 153 Marines and a tiny Insular Force Guard. They watched as reports filtered in of Japanese attacks on places like Hong Kong, Kowloon, and the Gilbert Islands. The Marines on Wake Island held out until December 23, though they sustained 20 percent casualties.

The American defeat in the Philippines had been particularly dramatic and cruel. General Douglas MacArthur, who commanded U.S. forces on that strategically important archipelago, inexplicably, in the hours immediately after Pearl Harbor, failed to disperse American B-17s and fighter planes. When the Japanese attack on the Philippines came on December 8, they were easy targets; more than half were destroyed. Without air cover the U.S. Navy was forced to pull out of the Philippines almost immediately. A Japanese invasion came swiftly.

When the numerically superior Japanese force landed, it began a protracted battle that eventually forced MacArthur's evacuation to Australia, leaving his troops behind, trapped on a rocky outcropping called Corregidor on the outer reaches of Manila Bay. They made a ferociously brave but ultimately futile last stand against a Japanese attack on the ground, from the sea, and in the air.

More than 70,000 American and Filipino troops were captured when the Philippines fell. The prisoners were subjected to the Bataan Death March, a forced march of more than a hundred kilometers through the Philippines jungle with few rations and almost no water. Many of those who made it were shipped back to Japan, jammed into the holds of cargo ships with scant provisions and no medical care. Those who survived that ordeal, and many did not, became slave laborers in Japanese coal mines or shipyards for the duration of the war. Glenn Frazier was among those who endured Bataan, only to face three and a half years of deprivaton and hard labor in a prisoner-of-war camp on the western coast of Japan. Even after the war, he found it difficult to leave behind memories of endless days of eating nothing but watery rice, waking up each morning to shake the prisoner next to him to see if he'd lived through the night, all the while wondering if the girl he'd left at home would still be waiting for him when he returned.

After that ominous beginning, the United States began to recover its equilibrium in the Pacific. From his new base in Australia, MacArthur organized an island-hopping campaign north toward Japan. Admiral Chester Nimitz moved the U.S. naval presence west, preparing to meet the Japanese navy head-on.

AUG. 6, 1941

Japan asks the United States to lift its trade embargo and proposes negotiations.

AUG. 17, 1941

FDR warns Japan that further attempts to dominate Asia will force the U.S. government to take appropriate action.

AUG. 28, 1941

The Japanese ambassador to Washington presents notes in which the Japanese premier insists he wants peaceful relations with the United States.

NOV. 5, 1941

Although negotiations will continue, the Japanese imperial general headquarters issues plans for an offensive against the U.S. fleet at Pearl Harbor, British Malaya, the Philippines, and the Netherlands East Indies.

NOV. 20, 1941

Japan offers new proposals for diffusing tensions with the United States.

NOV. 26, 1941

Secretary of State Hull says Japan would have to withdraw from Indochina and China, and recognize the Chinese national government. This constitutes a rejection of the Japanese proposals of Nov. 20, ending efforts to negotiate a settlement. The Japanese Pearl Harbor strike force sets sail.

DEC. 1, 1941

A council in the presence of the Japanese emperor, Hirohito, votes unanimously to begin hostilities with the United States.

The first important American victory didn't come until May 1942, in the Battle of the Coral Sea off New Guinea. Until then, many in Washington were not sure the United States could prevail in the Pacific. But Japan, despite its head start, was overextended, and American naval forces stopped its southward drive here.

A month after the Coral Sea victory, the Japanese effort to take and hold Midway Island was defeated in four furious days of combat. At the end of the confrontation the Japanese had lost four aircraft carriers and a heavy destroyer, with another heavy cruiser damaged and two destroyers badly damaged. American forces had lost the aircraft carrier *Yorktown,* abandoned and then sunk by an enemy submarine, as well as a destroyer and 147 aircraft. This was the first decisive defeat of the Japanese navy during the Second World War. The string of Japanese victories in the Pacific had been ended.

The counterattack in the Pacific was slow to develop, given the decision reached at the Arcadia Conference to commit the bulk of Allied resources to defeating Germany first. Still, the invasion of Guadalcanal in the eastern Solomon Islands marked a change from a defensive to an offensive posture in the Pacific. The fight for Guadalcanal, begun August 7, 1942, and concluded in February 1943, marked the start of one of the bitterest campaigns in American history. Here the Japanese may have lost as many as 25,000 troops, while the Americans lost approximately 1,600. At the same time, General Douglas MacArthur's forces attacked in New Guinea, taking Buna, Gona, Salamaua, and Lae. Before the end of 1943, American forces had landed on the eastern end of New Britain Island, threatening communications between Rabaul on New Britain's western end and Japanese forces in New Guinea, and preparing the way for the advances of 1944. By April 1944, MacArthur had begun operations along the New Guinea coast, while Admiral William Halsey's forces moved through the Solomon Island chain, with the mutual goal of isolating the Japanese at Rabaul.

In the central Pacific, Marines under the overall command of Admiral Chester Nimitz attacked the Tarawa atoll, in the Gilbert Islands, on November 20, 1943. While the landings went badly at first, by the end of November 23 the island had been secured, at a cost of approximately 1,000 Marine dead and 2,200 wounded. The Japanese had approximately 4,700 dead. In late January 1944, the Marines attacked the Japanese garrison on Kawjalein, in the Marshall Islands. Eniwetok, also in the Marshalls, fell on February 21 after four days of fighting, opening the way to the invasion of the Marianas Islands in June and July 1944. Saipan in the Marianas was declared cleared on July 9. Tinian fell on August 1, and Guam on August 10.

The navy achieved a great victory with the Battle of the Philippine Sea. In two days Japanese carrier strength was cut in half and aircraft strength reduced by two-thirds. American possession of the Marianas Islands made possible air raids on the Japanese home islands by the new American B-29 bombers. Raids began November 24, 1944, and landings on Peleliu began on September 15. Meanwhile, the invasion of the Palau Islands was the costliest of the American Pacific war, with nearly 40 percent of the invading force becoming casualties.

The reconquest of the Philippines was next in American plans; it began on October 20, 1944, with the invasion of Leyte Island by units of the U.S. Sixth Army. A few hours after the initial landings, General MacArthur waded ashore and broadcast to the Philippine people, fulfilling his promise to return to the islands. The Japanese army struggled to defend Leyte, while the Japanese navy maneuvered to destroy the U.S. fleet supporting the invasion. The largest naval battle in history followed, with a decisive victory for the American navy. Fighting would continue in the Philippines until the Japanese surrender in August 1945.

By early 1945 the Japanese empire appeared doomed but still had control of Korea, Indochina, and portions of China, and showed no readiness to surrender. It seemed that an all-out invasion might be necessary.

In preparation for such an assault, the air force needed a fighter base near enough to Japan to allow for the escort of B-29 bombers flying from the Marianas and an emergency landing place for damaged bombers. Iwo Jima, roughly 760 miles south of Tokyo, fit the bill. Landings began on February 19, 1945, with operations continuing until the end of March. Out of 21,000 defending Japanese soldiers, all but 200 were killed. The Marines suffered 6,800 killed and more than 18,000 wounded. For veterans of both landings, Iwo Jima was even more difficult than D-Day had been nine months earlier.

The next American target was Okinawa, in the Ryukyu Islands. It represented a potential staging ground for an invasion of Japan and an air base from which medium-range bombers could attack

JAN. 7, 1942

General Douglas MacArthur, commander in chief of U.S. forces in the Far East, begins the defense of the Bataan peninsula.

FEB. 15, 1942

Sixty-four thousand British, Indian, and Australian defenders surrender in Singapore.

FEB. 24–27, 1942

Battle of the Java Sea
A striking force of 2 Dutch, 1 American, and 2 British cruisers with about 12 destroyers moves to intercept Japanese convoys headed for Java. In three engagements the Japanese navy defeats the Allies with little loss to themselves. This will be the Allies' worst naval defeat of the war.

APR. 18, 1942

Lieutenant Colonel James H. Doolittle launches a strike on Tokyo from the USS Hornet, 800 miles off Japan. The plan is to bomb Tokyo, then fly 1,000 miles to China. Two pilots fall into Japanese hands and are beheaded.

MAY 4–8, 1942

Battle of the Coral Sea
Under U.S. Admiral Chester Nimitz, the American aircraft carriers Lexington and Yorktown, as well as a squadron of American and Australian cruisers, are sent to intercept a Japanese offensive aimed at Port Moresby, New Guinea.
This is the first naval battle in history in which no surface ship on either side sights the enemy. American aircraft find and sink the Japanese aircraft carrier Shoho; the USS Lexington is sunk and the Yorktown

damaged. In return U.S. Navy pilots damage the Japanese carrier Shokaku. *The Japanese suffer their first setback of the war.*

MAY 6, 1942
Allied forces in the Philippines surrender.

JUNE 3–6, 1942
Battle of Midway
In one of the most decisive battles in world history, American aircraft find and destroy the Japanese aircraft carriers Akagi, Kaga, Hiryu, and Soryu, headed for Midway Island. The Japanese sink the USS Yorktown. *Allied forces will shortly go on the offensive in the Pacific.*

AUG. 7, 1942
American landings on Guadalcanal and Tulagi in the Solomon Islands begin, signaling the start of a six-month campaign that will include 7 naval engagements and 10 or more land battles. *This is the first major U.S. assault in the Pacific war.*

AUG. 8–9, 1942
Battle of Savo Island
Japanese forces attack the American navy supporting the Marine invasion off Guadalcanal. In the next 32 minutes the Japanese inflict what one historian has called probably the worst defeat ever on the U.S. Navy in a fair fight. The navy withdraws, having lost 4 heavy cruisers, 1 destroyer, and 1,270 men and leaving 17,000 Marines on Guadalcanal without most of their food, heavy equipment, and ammunition. *The area will henceforth be known as Iron Bottom Sound.*

targets in the home islands. Preliminary bombardments lasted from March 24 to March 31, and on April 1 the invasion began. The fighting was among the most intense the Americans experienced in the Pacific war. The main Japanese force had retreated to a honeycomb of caves at the south end of the island, where it fought a last-stand counterattack for the empire. In the two months the American fleet was stationed off Okinawa, the Japanese flew 1,900 kamikaze missions, sinking thirty-six American ships and damaging four American aircraft carriers. Over the course of the battle, there were approximately 50,000 Allied casualties and 12,000 killed. The Japanese lost 110,000 killed, along with 7,800 aircraft and sixteen ships sunk. Marie Mobley, an Army Nurse with the 75th Field Hospital, treated casualties of Okinawa just five miles from the front lines. Today, she still remembers those young soldiers, and when she shows photographs of the cemeteries where some of them are buried to her grandchildren, she tells them that "each little white cross symbolizes someone's son, husband, father, or loved one."

In the meantime, American planners began to focus on an invasion of the Japanese islands of Kyushu and Honshu. But before the decisive instructions were issued, the strategic bombing campaign against the Japanese mainland entered a new phase. On March 9–10, Tokyo was attacked with approximately 300 aircraft carrying incendiary bombs. The resulting fires destroyed 250,000 buildings, killed at least 89,000, and left 1 million homeless. This bombing campaign would be taken to other Japanese industrial centers over the summer, with similar results.

The U.S. government lost patience with Japan's unwillingness to surrender. On the morning of August 6, 1945, an American B-29 called *Enola Gay* reached its target, Hiroshima, carrying a single bomb weighing 10,000 pounds, with a destructive capacity of 20,000 tons of TNT. In seconds four miles of the city vanished and 80,000 people died. Three days later another bomb was dropped, this time on Nagasaki; 60,000 died instantly. On August 14 the Japanese surrendered. The official documents were signed on September 2, aboard the USS *Missouri* in Tokyo Bay.

Japan had been conquered, but at a terrible price for both sides. On little-known atolls and in deep channels, the bodies of American and Japanese men, airplanes, and ships would become haunting reminders of the war that had raged for three years and eight months following the attack that started it all in Pearl Harbor.

Dear Mr. Brokaw:

My dad, Lt. Robert A. White, USMC, was killed 10/4/45 while attempting to land his Corsair fighter aboard a carrier off Hawaii. We are a Gold Star family. President Kennedy sent a nice letter, which included a Purple Heart lapel pin, when he was in office. My uncle's got Purple Hearts also. Your book opened some old wounds, emotions, which are, sometimes, repressed over the years. But, never, really forgotten. My father entered the Naval Reserve 8/31/42 to 6/1/44, took a commission in USMC 6/2/44, until his death. In his squadron, only his company survived the war. I have included one of his letters.

Bob White
Los Angeles, California

Monday, April 5
Noon

My Dear Wife:

I just finished reading the letter you wrote Friday. Yes I know Richard Wolff. I also know Virginia. See, that is an example of one of the things every one of us faces. We can imagine how bad she feels, but no one who has never gone through that can realize the full extent of her sorrow.

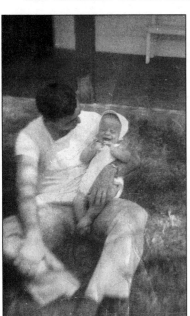

Things like this worry me at times, darling. Not that I am afraid, far from it. But God, we take chances every day, any one of which could put us on the "slab." It isn't the fact that a guy is afraid, but he gets to thinking of his responsibilities to his wife and family and it takes the guts out of him. Of course a married man may have more to fight for, but he still feels guilty about taking the daredevil chances.

Lieutenant Robert White with son Robert White II in 1945. (Courtesy of Robert White II)

NOV. 12–15, 1942

Naval Battle of Guadalcanal Eleven Japanese destroyers and 13,000 troops in transport ships approach Guadalcanal while aircraft carriers north of the Solomons provide air cover. At the same time, 6,000 American troops are on their way. Admiral D. J. Callaghan enters Iron Bottom Sound to await the Japanese. In a wild, confused fight lasting about half an hour, the American cruiser Atlanta *is lost, the* Portland *is wrecked, and the* Juneau *is sunk by submarine. The Japanese lose 2 destroyers, and a battleship is hit more than 50 times. Despite the losses this is a U.S. victory; the Japanese reinforcement effort is turned back and the Japanese garrison on Guadalcanal virtually isolated.*

NOV. 30, 1942

In a major naval battle off Tassafaronga Point, off Guadalcanal, the Japanese sink the U.S. cruiser Northampton *and cripple the cruisers* New Orleans *and* Minneapolis. *This is a major tactical victory for the Japanese, but no Japanese reinforcements are landed.*

JAN. 2, 1943

Buna falls to the Americans, ending the Japanese threat to Australia and clearing the way for MacArthur to drive up the coast of New Guinea while Admiral Halsey moves through the Solomon Islands, creating a two-pronged offensive against the Japanese base at Rabaul, New Britain.

FEB. 9, 1943

American forces on Guadalcanal find that the last Japanese combat troops have left. Winston Churchill will call Guadalcanal "the end of the beginning."

FEB. 21, 1943

American forces land on the Russell Islands in the Solomons.

MAR. 2–4, 1943

Battle of the Bismarck Sea Fighter bombers from the Fifth Air Force spot a 17-ship Japanese convoy attempting to reinforce the Lae-Salamaua area of New Guinea. They sink 8 transports and 4 destroyers. An estimated 3,000 to 5,500 Japanese soldiers drown. American forces lose 2 bombers and 3 fighters.

MAY 11, 1943

American forces invade Attu Island in the Bering Sea. The Japanese garrison fights to the end, then launches a suicide charge ending in a hand-to-hand struggle in the U.S. line. Only 29 Japanese soldiers survive.

JUNE 30, 1943

American forces invade Rendova Island in the Solomons.

JULY 2, 1943

American forces invade New Georgia Island in the Solomons. Resistance will continue until Aug. 25.

AUG. 1943

At the Quadrant Conference in Quebec, the Allies decide to clear northern Burma as soon as possible to reestablish contact with China.

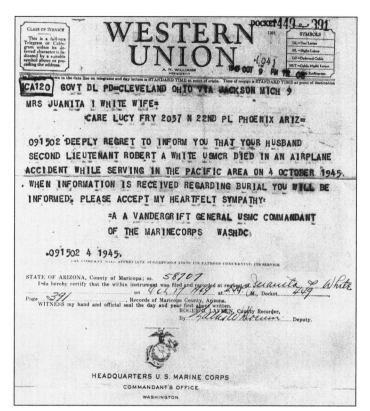

"Deeply regret to inform you": Telegram to Juanita White reporting her husband's death.
(Courtesy of Robert White II)

You are right, darling, I cuss this whole thing at times too, we all do, but God we have to think of what kind of a future we will have if we don't give everything now and win this war. Right now I know of 15 fellows that I knew back home in school, etc., that are dead right now. Not one of them had a chance to live their rightful time. There is no doubt about it, "war is hell." We get that pounded into us every day. They don't mince words either. They never figure out our mathematical chances of living after we start fighting at the front. Even before we finish training, a number of us are going to "get it." But getting it in the Navy Air Corps is no worse than any other outfit. It is just that chance we have to take. Don't worry, though, darling, it is just that chance we'll have to take. We'll make it OK. All we need is faith, and we have that. No matter what happens, just keep up your faith. Don't ever let this thing whip you.

I have been sure of things many times only to have them go to pieces just when I am to reach the goal. That is part of the philosophy of life, Nita. We are in constant competition, and the first time we weaken and give up we are goners. The only thing you can do is keep plugging along, hoping and praying, *but keep going!!*

Lt. Lavoir (coach) gave all the cadets here who are leaving a heart-to-heart talk last Saturday. He told us a lot of things about life, war, etc. But most important we learn—*not to give up*—keep *going*—*don't quit. Die in your tracks before ever giving up.* We have to in life. If we back down every time we are faced with something tough, we are complete failures. Many times since I have been here I have wanted to say—to hell with it. Many times I thought I couldn't get another gasp of breath from my lungs, or couldn't lift my legs for another step, but I kept on, we have to. We can't ever give up.

Life is like that. When the going gets tough, dig in your toes and force yourself to go on, and on, forever.

Everything will work out if we just keep plugging along. In the meantime we'll suffer a lot of heartbreaks, but we are in love—we'll win out! We can't fail.

Will write tonight,
Duffy

———— • ————

Dear Mr. Brokaw:

My brother's name is Billy B. Underwood S 1C. He left the cotton fields of N.E. Arkansas to go to the So. Pacific. He was a navy man. He was in the Amphibious Corp. He was 19 years old when he went into the navy.

My brother was steering an L.C.M. boat, taking supplies to the Islands. He would take sick or wounded youngsters back to the big ship as he went for more supplies. All of this was under terrific fire.

On one occasion, after a direct hit, he recalled using the soft little squares of

Billy Underwood (standing, center) with fellow sailors on Guam in 1944. (Courtesy of Fay Key)

Nov. 20, 1943
Nimitz begins his central Pacific campaign as U.S. forces land at Makin and Tarawa in the Gilbert Islands. Makin, lightly held, falls quickly, but Tarawa is held by more than 5,000 Japanese and surrounded by reefs, on which the landing craft get stuck. Despite these conditions, 5,000 Marines are onshore by the end of the day, with 1,500 men killed or wounded. This is one of the costliest victories, in terms of losses per troops engaged, in U.S. history.

Jan. 31, 1944
Allied forces land on Kwajalein in the Marshall Islands.

Feb. 17, 1944
Allied forces land on Eniwetok in the Marshall Islands.

June 15–20, 1944
Twenty thousand Allied troops land on Saipan on June 15. In a battle sometimes known as the Great Marianas Turkey Shoot, by the end of June 19, 243 Japanese aircraft have been shot down, while the Americans have lost only 29 planes; the Japanese have also lost 2 aircraft carriers, including their largest. On June 20 another Japanese carrier, along with 2 heavy cruisers, goes down. This battle cuts the operational strength of the Japanese carrier force in half and reduces its aircraft strength by two-thirds.

July 9, 1944
Saipan is declared secured by the Allies. Many of the Japanese garrison and civilians have committed suicide.

JULY 21, 1944

Allied forces land on Guam in the Mariana Islands; it will be declared secured on Aug. 11.

JULY 24, 1944

Allied forces land on Tinian in the Marianas; it will be declared secured on Aug. 1.

Guam and Tinian will provide platforms for launching the new American B-29 Superfortress bomber against the Japanese home islands.

SEPT. 15, 1944

Nimitz, aiming at the Palau Islands, lands Allied forces on the southwest coast of Peleliu, garrisoned by 10,000 Japanese troops. Over 7 weeks, Allied Marines and infantry dig the Japanese out of caves, costing the Japanese 13,600 killed and 400 prisoners; American casualties include 1,750 killed.

OCT. 20–26, 1944

Battle of Leyte Gulf

Units of the Sixth Army land on Leyte Island. On Oct. 22, MacArthur wades ashore at Leyte Gulf, pronouncing, "I have returned."

In the following naval battle, Japan loses 4 aircraft carriers, 3 battleships, 10 cruisers, 11 destroyers, a submarine, and 10,000 dead. American losses include 1 light aircraft carrier, an escort carrier, 2 destroyers, 1 destroyer escort, and 200 aircraft.

The land campaign in the Philippines will go on until the end of the war. It will cost the Japanese all their men holding the islands, approximately 350,000, while the Americans will have approximately 62,000 casualties, including 14,000 killed.

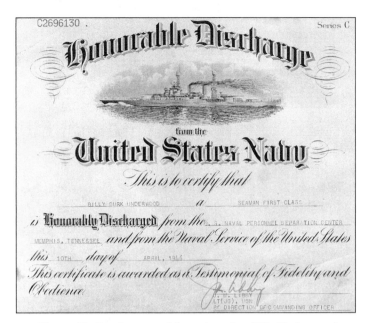

Honorable Discharge certificate issued to Billy Underwood
on April 10, 1946.
(Courtesy of Fay Key)

paper the oranges had been wrapped in to pick up the parts of bodies and tissue to get them out of the boat before he got back to the ship to load up again. It was his crew members'!

This must have had a terrible impact on a simple farmboy who had never seen anything worse than a horse stepping on a chicken. We were brought up in a simpler time. No violence or trouble except the poverty of the Depression and the years following when we worked extremely hard to try to pull ourselves out of our poverty!

I was proud of him, even though he did not return to be a congressman, Sec. of State or even a lawyer. He was just a *good* man. He was a truck driver until '87, when he was found to have cancer. He died in April of '88 and is buried here in Holland, MI.

I still have every letter he ever wrote me from the So. Pacific.

My younger brother was in the navy also during the Korean conflict, but he never was sent overseas. They both did their part, and I am equally proud of them.

Sincerely yours,

Fay I. Key

P.S.   I taught myself to type after I was 75. And I need to teach myself more. Excuse the mistakes and errors!

Dear Mr. Brokaw:

With tears in my eyes I think back to June 1941. I was just out of high school and had enlisted in the U.S. Army Air Corps with three of my buddies.

In a matter of months I went through recruit camp, was assigned and sent to the Philippine Islands. History shows we were thrust into a conflict that we were not ready for; and, as a result we were overrun by the Japanese on Bataan and Corregidor. Those of us at Bataan were force-marched out of Bataan (Bataan Death March) to spend the next 3 and ½ years in prison camps doing hard labor. Finally, when the war was over, those of us that survived came home to America, to pick up our lives. Our help was the GI Bill. It let us go back to school or back to work and start our families.

Harold Hart in 1948, three years after his release from a POW camp.

Blame was not thought of—we were defending our country and its flag. We still are in touch with our buddies and their families. I believe in many cases this friendship is greater than family.

Yours truly,
Harold Hart

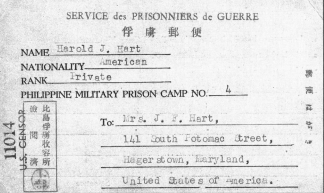

"What I need most of all is food and clothing. Food first."
Card from Harold Hart to his mother, sent from a
POW camp in the Philippines.
(All courtesy of Harold Hart)

Invasion of Iwo Jima

With the air force and navy providing aerial bombardment, the U.S. Fourth and Fifth Marine Divisions assault Iwo Jima, in the Volcano Islands of Japan, where the Japanese have garrisoned 21,000 troops and built extensive defense works. A beachhead is made on the first day, costing 2,400 casualties, including 600 dead. It takes 4 days to reach the summit of Mt. Suribachi, from which a photograph of a squad of U.S. servicemen hoisting the flag will become the basis for the Iwo Jima Memorial in Washington, D.C. The operation will continue to the end of Mar., when the remaining 200 Japanese soldiers surrender; the rest have died. The Marines suffer 6,800 killed, 18,000 wounded; they will receive 27 medals of honor.

MAR. 9–10, 1945

Approximately 300 U.S. B-29 bombers drop 1,667 tons of incendiary bombs on Tokyo, burning a major section of the city. At least 89,000 civilians die.

APR. 1, 1945

Invasion of Okinawa

U.S. forces begin the invasion of Okinawa, in the Ryukyu Islands, held by more than 100,000 Japanese. The campaign is officially ended on July 2. The American forces lose approximately 50,000, the Japanese, 99,000. Perhaps as many as 160,000 Japanese civilians die in the fighting.

Dear Mr. Brokaw:

I have just finished *The Greatest Generation*. Thank you for this tribute to those to whom personal responsibility, honor and duty to God and Country meant so much.

My husband, who is 73, was inducted into the navy when he was 18. After serving many months on an island in the South Pacific, his unit was sent home. On the ship home, he borrowed a razor and shaved for the first time.

We will soon celebrate 49 years of marriage with two children, their spouses and four grandchildren.

Each day we proudly display our flag as a memorial to those who have served our country in the past and a tribute to those who still serve.

Sincerely,
Alice K. Lusby

Floyd Lusby, second from right, in the southwest Pacific, c. 1944–45. (Both courtesy of Alice Lusby)

Floyd Lusby, in white shirt, on the island of New Hebrides (now Vanuatu), c. 1944–45.

Dear Mr. Brokaw:

I was deeply interested in your book *The Greatest Generation* and feel that I would like to give you my personal account even though I couldn't talk about it until about a year ago because of what happened to me in Manila, P.I., on 2/14/45.

After high school, June 1943, I entered the Army as a Medical Dept. and had basic training at Camp Grant, Illinois. I was selected to go to school at Walter Reed General Hospital as a surgical and medical technician graduating in four months. I was then sent overseas on the same Liberty Ship with the same group that I had been with at Camp Grant. We were on the way to Australia to a general hospital, but the Japanese were preparing an attack March 1944 on Bougainville in the Solomons, so after stopping at New Caledonia, we went to Bougainville already in combat. I was assigned to a platoon of infantry—I Company—3rd Battalion—129th Infantry Regiment of the 37th Infantry Division (Ohio National Guard). We had defensive positions all along the perimeter, and after the battle we had patrols to blow up ammo and supply dumps meeting enemy patrols constantly. We were relieved by an Australian division in November 1944. We were in the 1st wave on January 9, 1945, at Lingayen Gulf, Lizon, P.I. We had sporadic firefights on the way to Clark Field & Fort Stolsenberg. The 40th Infantry Division reported these places taken on 1/26/45 as a birthday present for Douglas MacArthur. My regiment—the 129 Inf.—arrived there in trucks 1/28/45 and were met by the Japanese, who gave us a severe fight. On the first day of combat, we had U.S. Marine fighter planes to help us. We had put colored panels and smoke bombs to point where the enemy was. The Jap artillery and mortar and machine guns went quiet, but the planes attacked us and fortunately no one was killed or wounded by our friendly fire. The next day we took a fortified hill with tunnels and Jap tanks. We received casualties from our own artillery fire after we took the hill. We fought there a week before being relieved by the 40th Inf. Division. We guarded the bridges until we received replacements before joining our other 2 Regiments in the Battle for Manila. I earned the Silver Star for saving the lives of two men who were bleeding to death and a Bronze Star for helping the wounded and taking out the dead with a few other soldiers. The Japanese set Manila on fire. MacArthur wouldn't let us use planes or artillery or any heavy weapons. My division asked why when the war was over, and the answer was to save the civilians. My platoon leader, Lt. Sutton, was to lead an attack on a police building where the Japs had fortified and sandbagged the windows and doors. Lt. Sutton told me not to

Two natives of Bougainville, Solomon Islands, 1944. (Courtesy of John Murphy)

Aug. 6, 1945

The Enola Gay, *a B-29 aircraft flying from Tinian, drops an atomic bomb on Hiroshima. Approximately 80,000 people are killed.*

Aug. 8, 1945

The Soviet Union declares war on Japan and the next day will invade Manchuria. The Japanese will be driven back into Korea.

Aug. 9, 1945

An atomic bomb is dropped on Nagasaki. Estimates vary widely, but approximately 60,000 people are killed.

Aug. 14, 1945

Japan accepts terms of unconditional surrender.

Sept. 2, 1945

MacArthur accepts the Japanese surrender on board the USS Missouri *in Tokyo Bay.*

Fred Natale, a friend of John Murphy's and a fellow medic in the 129th Infantry Regiment of the 37th Infantry Division, in Bougainville.

Larry Hay, another friend of Murphy's. (Both courtesy of John Murphy)

go with them and stay with the rest of the platoon. I asked him why they couldn't use covering fire and smoke, and he stated that this was a suicide mission. He was right!! We attacked down an open street crouching all the way. About 100 yards away they opened up with machine guns. I hit the ground at the first sound and could feel and hear the bullets hitting the men. A couple fell on me. I yelled for everyone not to move and stay here on the ground. I could hear gurgling sounds from several of the men and realized that everyone was hit and dying. I was the only one who didn't get hit. It was very hot and humid that Feb day and I could hardly breathe. When no one answered me I realized that they were all dead, so I decided not to move and play dead and to try to get back to my lines hoping that my own men wouldn't shoot me. When the sun sets over there, it goes from light to dark in no time—no twilight. I managed to crawl in spurts, being very careful not to raise up and finally reached our line of departure. When I got close I told them who I was and gave the password.

About two days later one of the medics (I believe it was Sgt. Hogan) asked if I would volunteer to bag and tag the bodies. I agreed, and he said that several infantrymen would use shovels and put them in mattress covers. We had commenced using heavy weapons on the Japs, and they retreated. The Sgt. said that only sniper and mortar fire was being used against us. I directed the men to where the bodies lay in the street and commenced taking their dog tags and marking each one carefully. It was the hardest thing I ever did in my life because I had been with these guys for almost a year and knew them quite well.

We managed to get them all accounted for with the correct tags. Bag and tag is what they called it. After this happened, I could no longer fire my rifle at the enemy because the whole thing to me was senseless.

After Manila we were sent to capture Baguio, the summer capital of Luzon high in the hills, and after that the Cagayan Valley.

I went into the Army a naïve schoolboy and came out feeling that the leaders should do all the fighting while we and the enemy have a few beers, making friends and watching the big shots doing their things. I'm sorry for the sloppy handwriting, but going over this much has really caused me a lot of grief and pain.

Sincerely yours,
John L. Murphy

*Frederick and Frona Tyler in 1943
in Atlanta, Georgia.*

116748

THE SECRETARY OF THE NAVY
WASHINGTON

D-2310

10 December 1945

Mrs. Frona Carroll Tyler
25 Vine Street
New Britain, Connecticut

My dear Mrs. Tyler:

Your husband, Lieutenant Frederick George Tyler, United States Naval Reserve, has been carried on the official records of the Navy Department in the status of missing in action as of 5 November 1944. Your husband's plane, attached to Fighting Squadron EIGHTY, took off from the USS TICONDEROGA to participate in an air strike against enemy shipping in Manila Bay and Harbor, Luzon Island, in the Philippines. Your husband's plane was lost seen in a dive on an enemy destroyer, and it is believed to have been hit by the anti-aircraft fire which was very intense in the area. To date no further information has been received by the Navy Department concerning the fate of your husband.

In view of the strong probability that your husband's plane crashed after being hit by enemy anti-aircraft fire, and that he lost his life as a result there, because no official nor unconfirmed reports have been received that he survived, because his name has not appeared on any lists or reports of personnel liberated from Japanese prisoner of war camps, and in view of the length of time that has elapsed since he was reported to be missing in action, I am reluctantly forced to the conclusion that he is deceased. In compliance with Section 5 of Public Law 490, 77th Congress, as amended, the death of your husband is, for the purposes of termination of pay and allowances, settlement of accounts, and payment of death gratuities, presumed to have occurred on 5 November 1945, which is the day following the expiration of twelve months in the missing status.

I know what little solace the formal and written word can be to help meet the burden of your loss, but in spite of that knowledge, I cannot refrain from saying very simply, that I am sorry. It is hoped that you may find comfort in the thought that your husband gave his life for his country, upholding the highest traditions of the Navy.

Sincerely yours,

James Forrestal

*"What little solace . . ."
Letter sent to Frona Tyler on December 10, 1945,
officially informing her of her husband's death.*

*Carol Tyler Kirk, daugher of Frederick and Frona Tyler,
at the hospital at Long Binh in 1970. "She served two tours
of duty in Vietnam. The second tour, for which she
volunteered, was to honor her father's memory."
(All courtesy of Frona Faulkner)*

——— • ———

Dear Mr. Brokaw:

My husband, Lt. Frederick G. Tyler, was a fighter pilot on the carrier *Ticonderoga* in the Pacific theater. He lost his life on November 5, 1944, while on a mission in the Philippines. I think of him every day. Our daughter, born after her father was lost, became an Army nurse. She served two tours of duty in Vietnam. The second tour, for which she volunteered, was to honor her father's memory.

With appreciation,
Frona C. Faulkner

——— • ———

Dear Mr. Brokaw:

I decided to write and tell you about my husband of 52 years, Odean Sorenson's involvement on Peleliu because it's an interesting story. He grew up in a small town in N. Dak and enlisted in the Marines in 1943. He went in on Sept. 15, 1944, on the very south end of the island, where they were pinned down for several days waiting for the airstrip to be secured. They moved to the upper part of the island and were dug in for 10 to 12 days. The weapons company were called out in early October to secure Bloody Nose Ridge. They were hit with heavy mortars.

Later on October 3rd the tanks and half-tracks were moved up. They were directed to shoot into the caves and anyplace they thought the enemy was located. They ran out of ammo for the 75's and 50's. Lt. Sid Beinke (a favorite of the men) sent Dean back for more ammo and three replacements.

Heading back to the half-track, he was pinned down about 30 yards from it. His orders were to return to their lines. When he finally got to the half-track, their orders were to pull out.

As they were backing out, the front end dropped into a water hole, and as they backed up and went forward the Japanese had their sights on them and they took two direct hits on the base of their 75.

When Dean came to, he didn't think he was out very long be-

"The light that guides our way through life": V-mail sent from Odean Sorenson to Ardelle Sorenson on November 12, 1944.

Odean Sorenson at Mare Island U.S. Navy Hospital, 1945.

Odean Sorenson in uniform at his parents' house in Max, North Dakota, in June 1946. "The picture was taken about a year and a half after Odean's discharge in a full body-brace." (All courtesy of Ardelle Sorenson)

cause of the strong powder smell—he thought his head had been blown off but he hadn't died yet—thought he could make medical history as he could still see, think, hear and smell, etc. He knew something was bad as someone said "Jesus Christ, look at Sorenson!"

When they lifted him up, he could see he was all in one piece and covered with blood—he was paralyzed from the shoulders down.

They flew him briefly to Manus and then to Guadalcanal for about 2 and ½ months, where he had a corpsman named Dalton Driver, who told him recently that he was the worst case of neglect he'd ever seen. He credits Dalton with saving his life.

Dean was sent from Guadalcanal to Mare Island, CA, for a year or so. After much shrapnel being removed, he regained some feeling and could walk with braces (his left hand never came back).

We had 5 children (4 living) and 10 grandchildren. He worked many years and has an attitude you wouldn't believe. He had to take an early retirement as the pain is worsening.

Young people have always gravitated to him because of his personality. For several years he worked as a volunteer with the state staff for Special Olympics.

I'm sure as busy as you are, you must get a lot of letters like this, but I thought someone besides friends and family should know about this wonderful, noncomplaining man—my husband, Odean Sorenson.

Thank you,
Ardelle Sorenson

———— • ————

Dear Mr. Brokaw:

I have read your book *The Greatest Generation* with interest. But there is little or no reference to the Southwest Pacific Theater.

Washington and the Navy (Nimitz) kept MacArthur and the Southwest Pacific Forces on a shoestring for much of the war.

Food and supplies were horrible. During one eight-week period, late 1943, our battalion existed on one-third of the C ration per man per day. When our supply officer, in desperation, wrote directly to Washington, he was put up for court-martial. After an investigation, the court-martial was stopped by General Kneuger, corp. commander, without any punishment.

We sustained casualties but were also reduced in strength by disease. The men were given Atabrine for malaria. Atabrine neither prevented nor cured malaria but suppressed the symptoms enough that the men could continue to fight.

We were exposed to a variety of tropical diseases—schistosomiasis, dengue fever, hepatitis, skin infections (jungle rot), scrub typhus and many others. Most of us brought some of the above home with us, in addition to the physical and mental scars. Two of my friends died of disease contracted in the South Pacific jungles after they returned home.

I am not bitter about the war years but about the treatment differences between the services and the theaters. Many times we knew we were blood relatives of "the Battling Bastards of Bataan, no Father, no Mother, *no Uncle Sam.*"

We cannot walk the beaches in memory à la Normandy. There were too many: Buna, Gona, the Admiralty Islands, Tanamara Bay, Humboldt Bay, Biak, Leyte, Luzon, Mindanao, Mindoro, etc.

Many good men *bled* and *died* in the Southwest Pacific. Most now feel we are new versions of the Unknown Soldiers.

Yours truly,
W. L. Chilcote

———•———

Dear Mr. Brokaw:

I was in the Army five years.

You are so right about most of us avidly shrugging off our war experiences and getting back to a delayed civilian life. Example: When *Saving Private Ryan* came out last year, all six of my children saw the film. A couple of my daughters said, "Dad, you were in the service, weren't you? Were you in the Army or the Navy?"

I suppose that my wife, an Army nurse from a suburb of Philadelphia whom I had met in New Guinea in 1943, had mentioned in those growing-up years that we had been in the Army in WWII. But the kids had forgotten the reference and, after all, there was not the televised Vietnam War to look at daily. Some kids of that era didn't know whether World War II was before, or after, the Civil War!

The night after I started reading your book, Mr. Brokaw, I slept very little. It started me thinking back, back, back . . . remembering. Back in early 1941, a reporter from the Muskegon, MI, *Chronicle,* I had volunteered for the Signal Corps, but the Army assigned me and hundreds of others from Western Michigan to the Medical Dept. After Pearl Harbor and endless training, I volunteered again for a new type of medical unit, one of the first field hospitals designed to serve with the new swift-moving tank and armored units organizing under Gen. George Patton in the Mojave Desert. Patton's troops were sent off to the African invasion and, with typical Army logic, our sun-scorched outfit, the 3rd Field Hospital, was ordered to the jungles of the Southwest Pacific.

Merle Hill at Milne Bay, New Guinea, in 1944: "Cleaning up rotted coconuts to make area for tents. Rained 17 days; muck everywhere."

Reading your book, I started thinking back to the first war casualty our outfit treated in Lae, New Guinea. It was an Australian soldier who had stepped on a Japanese mine. He had been brought part of the way by natives on a makeshift litter of poles and vines.

Merle Hill standing on the wreckage of a Japanese Zero fighter plane at the Lae, New Guinea, airstrip, 1944.
(Both courtesy of Merle Hill)

Then, one after another, more flashbacks. Altogether, our outfit handled 25,000 casualties: burns, trauma, gunshot, disease and shock/mental cases. We served for more than a year with Gen. George Kenney's Fifth Air Force (Army) at Nadzab, New Guinea, then with the 38th Division in the battle to retake Bataan, and finally with the 25th Infantry Division, which was battling Yamashita's ragtag and diseased troops—still vicious fighters—in northern Luzon. The 32nd and 33rd divisions and elements of the third were engaged in that deadly mountain fighting, too. . . .

And then the atom bombs were dropped on Hiroshima and Nagasaki. I can still hear President Truman's voice on Armed Forces Radio warning the Japanese to surrender, or face a bomb of unimaginable force. (Surely Japanese intelligence had learned of the test bomb at Alamogordo!)

To this day I have *never* encountered a veteran of the Pacific end of the war criticizing Truman for dropping the bomb. Because we know full well how many lives it *saved*.

Mr. Brokaw, in 2½ years overseas and about that long in training in the States, I met and served with many of the types of men and women you wrote about in the book. Long overdue that they receive attention and credit.

I was a severely dedicated writer and editor for the *La Crosse Tribune*, for years the slot man in the editing room. And in the Army, nothing heroic at all, just a hard-nosed staff sergeant in charge of the 2nd Platoon of 70 men in the 3rd Field Hospital.

Sincere regards,
Merle J. Hill

——— • ———

Dear Mr. Brokaw:

I know you've heard many stories, but let me tell you about just one more, about a serviceman during World War II.

He was in the Navy amphibious forces serving aboard a P.T. boat, for which he volunteered. He was married on 2-13-43 and in Great Lakes Naval Boot Camp on 2-17-43. After boot camp, diesel school, motor torpedo boat school and Elco Naval Academy school, he got into the war skirmishes at New Guinea in June '44 and many night patrols. His wife was due to have their baby in Oct '44—October 13, 1944, to be exact, the doctor told her. Again he was in many enemy conflicts during his tenure at New Guinea. It's ironic but on October 13, 1944, the skipper of our boat called the crew together for a briefing. He told us to make out our wills and get them back to him and he'd make sure and see to it that the Navy's legal people would process them for us, legal wise. He told us we were going to be involved in something really big, and we'd be told where and what it was when we were under way. At this time we hadn't received any stateside mail and, unbeknownst to us, our mail was not going stateside either.

We left New Guinea on October 13, 1944, headed out to open

Ted Gurzynski, winter of 1939, while in the CCC at Camp Dunbar, Wisconsin.

Ted Gurzynski at Camp Dunbar.

Payday at Camp Dunbar. "That five dollars was for your tobacco, toothpaste, soap and haircut for the month— that was living high on the hog." (All courtesy of Ted Gurzynski)

sea. This was a Friday—sailors' superstition says "It's bad luck to leave a port on a Friday."

We were under way for 6 days and nights, refueling our P.T. boats at sea. On October 19, 1944, we were at our destination, the invasion of the Philippine Islands. The armed forces were landing on Philippines soil to immortalize Gen. MacArthur's famous words "I shall return." Battleships, cruisers and other ships were shelling the shores to help make a beachhead. Planes of all kinds were in the air, ours and Japanese planes were all over the skies, shrapnel fell from the skies like a New York ticker tape parade. The Kamikazes made their appearance here. This was really Hell—I prayed to God I'd go to Heaven—I can't stand Hell—here.

Ted Gurzynski (left) and Richard "Slim" Ciambor on their PT boat off New Guinea in 1944. "We used to get a ration of six beers a week and loads of free cigarettes." (Courtesy of Ted Gurzynski)

It's hard to explain it all, but there was no time to eat, you were handed a sandwich at your gunnery station, you'd eat in a hurry, with your eyes to the skies, bursting blasts of machine-gun fire during and in between bites of your sandwich.

On October 24, 1944, we entered Surigao Strait with our P.T. boats, to guard against any Japanese forces coming through there; our intelligence told us they possibly could come that way to help stem our invasion forces.

They came through all right—nine Japanese warships were spotted on our radar. We radioed back to the higher-ups to send help—"The Japs are coming." The P.T. boats started to engage the enemy in combat with machine guns and torpedoes, to slow the war armada down. The enemy with their searchlights spotted P.T. Boat #493 and proceeded to blast it out of the water with their bigger guns. P.T. #493 was sunk. It was the only P.T. boat lost in the Battle of Surigao Strait on October 25, 1944.

Our dead and wounded were picked up by other P.T. boats. The wounded were taken care of except one man—one crew member refused hospital treatment for his wounds, he felt he wasn't wounded enough, he wanted others to be taken care of first. He felt like he had to lose an arm or leg to be considered wounded—he was only bleeding in a few places. But really he said to his skipper, who was wounded also, that he didn't want his wound treated, because then the War Department would send his wife a telegram that he was wounded in action and she'd probably get hysterical and devastated from the news. He knew she was to have a baby on or about Oct. 13, 1944. But he had not had any stateside news since Sept. '44. This was October 25, 1944. So he didn't know if she had the baby or if she and the baby were healthy and alive. Amidst all the war action and the Kamikaze planes, his thoughts were elsewhere, so he didn't want her to be notified, so the skipper honored his wishes.

Due to the articles of war and U.S. Navy custom, you are entitled to a thirty-day survivor leave if your ship is sunk during enemy engagement in wartime, providing you survive the battle.

So amidst all the Kamikaze attacks, he arrived at San Francisco Naval Base on Dec. 1, 1944, with the same clothing he'd had on his back since Oct. 13, 1944. Finally by mail while in San Francisco, he got in touch with his wife, he found out now in Dec. that his wife gave birth to a baby boy on October 13, 1944, and that they were both healthy and doing fine.

He was discharged in April '45. He was entitled to wear the Purple Heart ribbon—American Campaign, Asiatic Pacific Campaign ribbon with three Bronze Stars, the Philippine Liberation Medal with one Bronze and one Silver Star and the Victory Medal.

Today he is 80 years old, his wife is 78 years old, his son is 55 years old. And they've been married 57 years.

I know this all to be true and factual because I'm the guy.

Ted "Ski" Gurzynski
PT 493
A Survivor

Wendell Ray Frazer.
(Courtesy of Barbara Olson)

Dear Mr. Brokaw:

I am writing to tell you about my father, Wendell Frazer.

My father served in WWII but never talked about it. His entire war experience was reflected only in his refusal to eat pancakes, which he had consumed daily in the Navy. I never knew why he wouldn't talk about it— and I was too scared to probe—so I just chalked it up to his being emotionally distant. I also couldn't figure out why he would give up

Wendell Ray Frazer, father of Barbara Olson, upon his enlistment in the Navy. (Courtesy of Barbara Olson)

rare vacation time to visit his best friend from the Navy.

Now I know.

Thank you for helping me understand my father. He died in 1981 at age 54.

Thanks again,
Barbara Olson

———•———

Dear Mr. Brokaw:

All of us who served in the C.B.I. lived through the Great Depression too. We were shocked by the news of the bombing of Pearl Harbor on December 7, 1941. We volunteered for military service before and after war was declared. And we went where we were sent—ending up in China, India and Burma to aid the British and Chinese in stemming the flow of Japanese aggression in that area.

We flew "the Hump" to and from China, worked on the Burma Road under abysmal conditions, were subject to many tropical diseases, tended the wounded and sick, buried the dead, and lived through monsoons, sandstorms and extreme heat.

And when we returned home we also became lawyers, businessmen, stockbrokers, educators, blue-collar workers, doctors and parents.

Although we called ourselves the Forgotten Theater, we are proud of our contribution to the war effort and keep memories and friendships alive by participating in our very own veterans' association. There are many state groups—which are called bashas after the native huts in Burma—which meet regularly and hold a yearly reunion for all.

WAR DEPARTMENT AAF Form No. 94-F	**U. S. ARMY AIR FORCES** AIR TRANSPORT COMMAND *Passenger Transportation Record*		№ 659824

PRIORITY CLASS (if none, write none) XXXXXX APR-NONE-CRA

DATE OF TRIP	Trip No. (If none, plane No.)	FROM—		TO—
JAN;12	FLT:2	KARACHI		BOMBAY

PASSENGER'S NAME	GRADE OR TITLE	ARM, SERVICE, OR ORGANIZATION	TOTAL BAGGAGE WEIGHT AUTHORIZED INCLUDING EXCESS
CONKLIN, J.E.	LT	US NURSE	55

TRANSPORTATION AUTHORIZED BY	GRADE OR TITLE	ARM, SERVICE, OR ORGANIZATION
WILLIAMS	COL	A.C.

ORDER NO.	PARAGRAPH NO.	STATION ISSUING P. T. R.	DATE P. T. R. ISSUED
V.O.C.O.		KARACHI	JAN: 12

P. T. R. ISSUED BY (signature)	GRADE	ORGANIZATION
	2nd, Lt.	A.T.C.

55/130   *Good for One-Way Passage Between Points Named, Subject to Regulations on Back* *This P. T. R. will be surrendered upon arrival at destination*   16—31768-1

Army Air Forces transportation record for Janet Conklin, first lieutenant in the Army Nurse Corps. (Courtesy of Janet Rodgers)

Janet Conklin upon her return home after serving thirty-one months in India. (Courtesy of Janet Rodgers)

The China-Burma-India Veterans Association is open to those who served in those countries from December 7, 1941, to March 2, 1946.

Thank you for a wonderful book about our generation.

Sincerely,
Janet E. Rodgers
A.N.C. N722843

———— • ————

Dear Mr. Brokaw:

I drove the lead vehicle in the first convoy that traversed the Ledo-Burma Road from Ledo, Assam, India, to Kunming, China. My job was to chauffeur the convoy commander, Col. DeWitt T. Mullett. Although Gen. Pick received most of the glory, he actually traveled with the convoy very little. Gen. Pick was ferried in by air on several occasions to meet with the convoy in bivouac. Col. Mullett was the convoy commander and was with us from start to finish.

With rare exception each of the 113 vehicles was towing a trailer or artillery piece. There was also in the convoy one tractor towing an engineer flatbed trailer on which was a light tank. This tank was our only protection other than each man's rifle. Thank goodness we completed the ordeal without needing either.

When we rolled into Kunming every vehicle was running under its own power except two. One of the wreckers had a deuce-and-a-half (6 × 6 GMC) on the hook, and one motorcycle was hauled in. This was probably the best completion record of all the convoys. The biggest maintenance problem we had was flat tires.

We arrived at the bottom of the Salween Gorge early one morning. It was a very nice day, but the gorge and the suspension bridge we were to cross were still in the shadows of the mountain. There was to be a big picture-taking session by the correspondents, so we had to wait until the light was right for the photographers. Only one vehicle at a time was allowed on the bridge because of the bridge's capacity. At this point the semi hauling the tank and the tank had to be left behind. Individually they were both too heavy to cross the bridge.

This portion of the Burma Road was probably the most treacherous part of the whole trip. The road mileage from rim to rim was some forty miles but by how the crow flies was only about ten

James Garvin on the first convoy along the Ledo-Burma Road, 1945.
(Courtesy of James Garvin)

miles. The steepness of the grades and only one vehicle at a time on the swinging bridge all in first gear consumed some sixteen hours of driving that day.

Upon arriving in Kunming after some 24 days on the road, we bivouacked outside the city. A whole day or so was spent cleaning up our vehicles as well as ourselves for the grand entry into the city. The most disheartening part of the whole trip was to sit on the backseat of my jeep while some Chinese driver drove it into Kunming and received all the glory for the hardships I endured while driving the 1,079 miles. Chinese drivers drove all the other vehicles also.

Thank goodness all the drivers were flown over the Hump back to the Ledo airfield, completing one historical event.

James M. Garvin

— • —

Mr. Tom Brokaw:

I was born in 1925, and the first eleven years of my childhood were spent in abject poverty in the Boston Mountains around Hot Springs, Arkansas. We raised most of our food or gathered it from the mountains around us.

I have two brothers and three sisters. We moved to Southeast Kansas in the spring of 1936. It was here that we got to attend our first full year of school. Needless to say, we were all behind in school. I had to register for the draft during my junior year in high school. I volunteered and was called into the service in July 1943.

Before World War II was over, both of my brothers and one of my sisters had also volunteered. My mother was the oldest child in a very large family. She had six of her brothers who also volunteered. My two brothers were in the Navy, one on a battleship and one on an LST in the Pacific. I was sent to the China-Burma-India Theater, where I took part in the opening of the Ledo-Burma Road in the Namkham Valley. My outfit (armored reconnaissance) fought alongside Merrill's Marauders in the jungles of Burma. We went as far south as Shenweh on the Burma Road. When the war was over in Burma, my outfit was stationed at Mitinyah, Burma, for a short time. We were then sent into China traveling the Ledo-Burma Road, which we had helped to open just a short while before.

All in all we—my six uncles, my two brothers, my sister and I—were very lucky or we had an angel with us. There was only one of the group got wounded, and it was a very minor wound.

I am proud to have served my Country as were all my uncles, my two brothers, and my sister.

None of us came home with a chest full of medals for bravery, but we did come home with a chest full of pride in what we had done.

I am proud to have been a part of the events that shaped our great nation for a major part of the last century.

I came home and went back to high school. I received my diploma in 1946. I worked for Southwestern Bell Telephone Co. for thirty-four and a half years, retiring in 1985.

When I tell anyone about my service in W.W.II, I tell them about "My Incredible Journey." In the two and a half years I was in the service, I circled the globe, landed on three continents, crossed three oceans, crossed the equator and the international date line and drove an army 6 × 6 pulling a generator trailer over one of the most famous roads in history, the Burma Road. I was in Chanyi, China, when the war ended.

Thanks again for telling our story.

Sincerely,
Ernest E. Coffman

— • —

Dear Mr. Brokaw:

I have read your book *The Greatest Generation*. My husband and I are that generation. My husband was a WWII vet. He is 100% disabled from that war.

In all your stories you never once mentioned the 3,000 volunteers Merrill's Marauders, the Forgotten Few. These men, under the command of General Stilwell, endured more suffering than any group of men. They marched from India, through the jungles of Burma, into China with mules carrying their supplies, nearly 800 miles. Their commander, Colonel Hunter, called them "the most put upon, maligned, ill cared for and unrewarded unit of the war."

Many times these men were unable to receive their air drops of supplies and went hungry and naked because uniforms rotted off them. They fought 5 major campaigns and 33 minor from October 1943 to June 1945, and my husband was one of them. My husband, John, did receive a Bronze Star but no others. All of their fighting was behind enemy lines.

I personally believe these brave men should receive far more recognition than they ever have. They truly are the Forgotten Few.

Thank you.

Respectfully,
Madelenne Moyer

— • —

Dear Mr. Tom Brokaw:

In 1940 I married my true love and best friend, John Lingenfelter. We had known each other since childhood. We attended the same church and graduated from the same high school. Our families were friends. After graduating from separate colleges with teaching degrees, we were ready to start our careers.

However, World War II changed our future. From 1943 until the end of the war, John served as a United States naval officer. He served eighteen months in the Pacific as a communications officer.

While he was overseas I lived with my parents. In December 1944 I gave birth to our first daughter, Barbara Anne. He did not see her until she was one year old. During this time we wrote each other every day. Since he couldn't be with us, we tried, in this way, to share this experience of our daughter's growth. One day, in early 1945, a letter came from Pearl Harbor addressed to our daughter, Barbara, instead of me.

I am enclosing a copy of this letter, which I would like to share with you and your readers. Hopefully, anyone reading it will feel his warmth and love for his family.

John arrived home in December 1945.

Several years later our second daughter, Lois Eileen, was born and, thankfully, this time he was present for her birth and infancy. How happy we were!

With deepest regards and appreciation for the stories you have shared,

Dorothy Lingenfelter

My baby,

This is your daddy's first letter to you, and if you have any trouble reading this, just ask Mother to help you—you see, she has had to read a lot of my letters—even way back before you were born.

We have not yet had a chance to see each other, but I've seen a lot of your pictures and they fill my heart with pride and joy that the Good Lord has let me be your father.

If everything goes alright, I expect to see you in the early part of next March, and I know it will be one of the happiest days of my life. Mother tells me that you sometimes don't like the men, but I know we will get along fine.

Your little letters to me always give me so much happiness, my Barbara, and I hope you will sometimes find time in your busy days to say hello to me.

Mother says you have been a very good girl for her, and I know it's because you want to please her who loves you so much every minute of the day. God couldn't have given you a more wonderful mother—I know. You see I, too, love her very much, and I know that you and she and I will always be rich in our love for each other.

Now that the doctor lets you eat ice cream, I know you and Grandpa will be as thick as two thieves. You will soon find out that ice cream is his weakness, and when I come back we will all enjoy it together.

I'm not used to writing to little girls, but I enjoy writing to you a lot.

I hope you will think of me often and lovingly, dear—just as I do about you and your mother. I'll be back with you and Mother as soon as I can. Until then be a good girl—and miss me a little, please.

Daddy

——— • ———

Dear Mr. Brokaw:

A few days ago we celebrated the anniversary of Iwo Jima, and it is because of that celebration that I am writing to you. On May 25, 1943, at Camp Breckinridge, Kentucky, the 38th Field Hospital was activated. As far as I can remember, it was to be experimental, directly under Washington and the only field hospital in the Pacific in W.W.2. It was made up of 24 officers, of which 16 were doctors and dentists, 203 enlisted men, and I was one of those enlisted men.

Our base of operations was Coco Head, Oahu, Hawaii. The 38th was separated into three units and attached, one each, to the 150th, 106th and 165th Regimental Combat Teams of the 27th Infantry Division as we readied for the Saipan campaign. Our group was to be held in reserve for Guam. However, when the Marines were being overcome because the amount of the enemy had been underestimated, we were loaded into L.S.T.'s and ended up on Saipan. I do not wish to go into all of the gory details, which I am sure you have heard before. When Saipan was secured and the Marines turned their attention to the island of Tinian, they asked that the 38th Field Hospital be officially attached to them and dropped from the 27th Division. There were more than sixteen thousand casualties, of which nearly four thousand dead; [that] was the price we paid. Thousands of the wounded were treated in our hospital, where doctors, and everyone else, often worked 19 hours with little rest.

We returned to Oahu, where we spent Christmas 1944, and before mid-January we were informed that the Marines had asked for us to go into combat with them under a garrison status under A.P.O. 86. The combat phase was again under the direction of the Fifth Amphibious Corps, with the Third, Fourth and Fifth Marine Divisions scheduled to do the fighting. We went ashore from D-Day until D-Day plus seven and spent a great deal of time trying

Edward Herold (left) and a friend at an Okinawan tomb where they had sheltered during a 1945 hurricane.

Edward Herold (standing, second from left) with his tentmates on Iwo Jima, 1945.

Edward Herold on Iwo Jima, 1945. (All courtesy of Edward Herold)

to get off the beach, while at the same time attempting to care for the wounded, who were everywhere. We did see, firsthand, that famous raising of the American flag on Mount Suribachi.

When Iwo was secured, we probably had more points than anyone there to go home, but it didn't work out that way. We were ordered to Okinawa, where we started to get ready to invade the Japanese mainland. I can't even imagine what that would have been like, but the bomb was dropped and we felt sure that we would go home. Again, we were wrong, we were to be some of the first occupational troops into Japan. Finally on November 17, 1945, we ended up on Japan's most southern island near the city of Mitsuhama. At this time the "higher headquarters" decided to place the 38th Field Hospital on inoperative status. Since the entire personnel were eligible for discharge, we were placed on a unit deactivation list.

Now, Mr. Brokaw, may I share with you one of the most meaningful experiences that I had in the whole war. Since we had little to do, we spent much of our time in Mitsuhama and some of the smaller villages. Another G.I. and I passed a house and heard an organ playing an American song. We knocked on the door and were greeted by a little girl about eight or nine years old. We were invited into the home and, using our Japanese-American book, learned that one of the pedals on the small portable organ would not work. We fixed the pedal and were invited back. The other G.I. did not go back again, but I spent many happy hours with this family. There was the mother, a very young baby, the little girl and an older sister. If I remember correctly, they had lost some of the men in her family, yet there was no anger, just a feeling of sorrow that people were killed on both sides.

The little girl became my shadow, and I could go nowhere in the town without her holding my hand. Her name was Keiko Nuhara, and she was a beautiful little girl. She came with me shopping and often spoke with anger when she thought I was being charged too much. I couldn't understand all she said, but I could tell that they understood very well! When I informed the family that we would be leaving, they had a very special supper for me. They were all dressed up in their best, and when it was time for me to leave, the mother said that Keiko had something for me. The little girl went into the next room and came out with a beautiful Japanese doll in a handmade glass case. The mother told me it was Keiko's most valuable possession. I tried to think of some way

I could refuse the gift but knew that I had to accept it. Keiko was trying to hide the tears in her eyes, and I had tears in mine. Back at camp I was able to take the glass out, break down the frame and ship the doll home, and, amazingly, it arrived in one piece, and all these years later it graces our guest bedroom. Keiko came to me, put her arms up, and I held her as tears ran down her face. Her mother said she loves you and wants to go with you. If there had been some way, she would have come home with me, and I tried to tell her so. I told Keiko that I loved her, and finally her mother had to come and loose her arms, she just wouldn't let go. Keyomi, her mother, took her crying while I tried to get my things together to leave. There has always been a special place in my heart for that beautiful little girl and her family, who gave such a terrible war one beautiful, unforgettable moment.

Edward Herold

———— • ————

Dear Mr. Brokaw:

I've been meaning to write to you for a long time to tell you about my father, a member of "The Greatest Generation." My father was part of that generation who never made it home from World War II. Yeoman 1C Joseph Raymond MacDonald was killed on February 21, 1945, in the Pacific. His ship USS *Keokuk* was hit by a Japanese plane. Seventeen servicemen were killed. There was no body to be sent home. I was born April 12, 1945 (the day FDR died). My father also left a wife and my older brother, who was 2 years old. Growing up without a father seemed normal to me because it was not something that was taken away. My mother remarried when I was 16. She is 86 years old now, and my stepfather is a wonderful man.

My father was 32 when he died. He was in the Navy Reserves and called back to duty near the end of the war. We never talked much about him growing up, and there is a lot I don't know about him. The enclosed letter was given to me by my mother about 15 years ago. It was the last letter my father wrote, three days before he died. I read it every year on Memorial Day, cry a lot and think of what a hero he was. My three teenage daughters also know their grandfather was a hero. I have the flag given to my mother, my father's medals, Purple Heart and campaign medals, and a picture of him in his Navy uniform. I served in the U.S. Air Force from

1964 to 1967. I was fortunate to be sent to the Hickam Air Force Base in Hawaii. I was also fortunate to visit the memorial cemetery in Hawaii, and I found my father's name engraved in stone. It was quite an emotional experience.

I am very proud to be a veteran and prouder yet when I think of the ultimate sacrifice my father made.

Thank you very much.

Sincerely,
Mr. Lorne J. MacDonald

USS Keokuk (AKN)
At sea in Pacific
18 February 1945

Gerry dear:

Tomorrow is D-Day at Iwo Jima—right on Japan's front doorstep—we will go in and lay nets sometime during the assault. That is why I am writing this letter.

I have faith in God to help us through to victory but am prepared to die for America and face our Lord if He so wills it.

We had Divine Services today and prayed for strength to make the invasion a success—thanked God for the blessings He has bestowed upon us right along. One of the hymns we sang was "Mother Dear, Oh Pray for Me and Never Cease Thy Care"—we hope she heard our plea.

Task Force 58 of our immense fleet is smashing Japan's mainland today with 1,500 planes launched from its carriers—also our paratroopers have landed on Corregidor—all this gives us confidence that we will take Iwo Jima.

Our prayers tonight will be for the 4th and 5th Marines under "Hawking-Mad" Smith—as they are the boys that will hit the beach first from our landing craft—while we Navy men try and knock out the guns they are facing—with our firepower. May God be with the Marines one and all.

My sweet life to date for me has been full—the best years were with you, my love—and our little Ray. I hope he never has to go to war—that the world will see how futile it is and never let it happen again. I hope Ray grows up to be a fine upright young man—and our baby to come Suzanne or another boy will be as nice as Ray and the pair of them will always be good to the best mother in the world. Most men haven't had a sweet wife and baby like mine. I am so proud to fight for you.

My other blessings have been fine parents like your own and a brother and sister both dear to me.

I didn't intend to write this letter—thought it would be like trying to imitate Commander Shea of B.C. or be too dramatic—but my married shipmates and I agree that it is manly and human to think of your loved ones when danger is near.

Through the actions of the invasion, many thoughts will wander to you and the good folks who pray for us out here, and it will give me strength because of your faith.

God who rules the mighty wave will decide our fate—so bravely we will face it.

God bless you, my darling wife, and watch over you always. Kiss Ray for me and tell him how much I love you both.

Daddy Ray

———— • ————

Dear Tom:

I was an army nurse in WWII, served mainly in Saipan (in Mariana Islands) and Okinawa (in Ryukyu Islands), in the Pacific Theater of War. While in Saipan, we received many Guam casualties. I worked in an abdominal infantry ward—many of the shells and shrapnel penetrated the fronts of their abdomens and came out their backs, resulting in their having to have colostomies. Often peritonitis followed because of severity of wounds. I remember those patients as being so young—just 18 years old—and so terribly ill.

From Saipan, our hospital (75th Field Hospital) went to Okinawa, where the front lines were about five miles from our hospital area.

We received casualties who were given first aid by corpsmen on the battlefront, put on stretchers and brought to ambulance and then to a field hospital. To get them to the ambulances, the litter bearers many times had to crawl on their abdomens and drag the litters on the ground as bullets and shrapnel were so low.

When we received casualties they were still in combat fatigues (uniforms). I remember one casualty's face was burned to a black crisp. It blinded him—was caused by a flamethrower. Another had three limbs missing—there was about 6 inches of black bone showing on each stump. His remaining leg (from inner aspect of thigh to below knee) only a piece of thin skin was holding on his combat boot, which had flopped to one side.

This describes but two of the forty casualties brought that day to the ward I was on.

Our unit was scheduled to go to Japan, but then a bomb was dropped and invasion wasn't necessary. (Everyone felt that Pres. Truman made the right decision as we didn't start the war.) We all felt that they would have used it if they had the technology first.

Sometimes my grandchildren con me into showing some of the snapshots I have to their history class. When I show pictures of the cemeteries, I always mention that each little white cross symbolizes someone's son, husband, father, or loved one, and should never be thought of as a mere statistic.

Okinawa is only about 40 miles long and 7 miles wide, what a tremendous price we paid for it—casualty wise.

Sincerely,
Marie Mobley

———— • ————

Dear Mr. Brokaw:

I am a 75-year-old WWII vet with progressive leukemia. My purpose in writing is that I realize the horrific campaign on Okinawa has its anniversary 1 April (invasion occurred 1 April 1945).

I will never forget climbing down the rope ladder from the transport into the landing craft below—how many times we

Robert Kleinsmith, Okinawa, 1945.
(Courtesy of Robert Kleinsmith)

banged into the hull! To recount the seven months after would require a novel. A couple of events stick in my memory like yesterday. During one advance of the 24th Corps, 96th Infantry, we were on the reverse slope of a small hill when an errant Navy F4U (Corsair) flew over and dropped a 500-lb. bomb, coming right at the hill of our position. I owe my life to Army Cpl. Al Kinsella, who knocked me flat into a ditch when he also saw the bomb. In all these years I have never been able to locate Cpl. Kinsella, to whom I will be forever grateful. It was Kinsella who waved his poncho at the next two Navy Corsairs (rockets and strafing) to say "hey, we're the good guys!" And they backed off.

Sincerely,

Dr. Robert A. Kleinsmith

Robert Kleinsmith (right) and Fred Otto, Okinawa, 1945. (Courtesy of Robert Kleinsmith)

———— • ————

Dear Mr. Brokaw:

Having read your book *The Greatest Generation*, I am pleased to enclose my World War II memories.

Once I started writing, I was amazed how easily my memories flowed.

Ironically, there was a moment a few days ago when I thought that jungle rot itching had reappeared, after having been gone over forty years. Fortunately my memories had taken me a little too far.

My four children, having received only bits of information while growing up, are most thankful for finally getting the fuller story.

Having written these memories, I will use them as a springboard (backward and forward) to write my autobiography.

Sincerely,

Victor Goehring

On a September evening in 1940 I was driving to high school to participate in a band practice for the Grape Festival Queen Coronation Pageant. I had the radio on, and in a campaign speech for his third election, President Franklin D. Roosevelt said, in his nasal voice, "I have said this before and I will say it again and again and again: your boys are not going to be sent into any foreign wars."

I was only 14 at the time, and it had no impact on me then, but the voice and words were later repeated in my mind many times.

December 7, 1941, on a Sunday, while we were driving home from church, it was announced over the car radio that Pearl Harbor had been bombed. The next morning, December 8, the superintendent of Lodi High School, LeRoy Nichols, called an assembly of all the students. The program started by everyone singing World War I patriotic songs such as "Smile, Smile, Smile," etc. Then we listened to the radio—live—President Roosevelt's declaration of war, whose words will live in infamy.

Following this a talk was given by a naval recruiting officer, urging students to volunteer for the service. The part of his talk I remember most was when he said "You sophomores and juniors are going to win this war." I was a sophomore age 15 at the time and said to myself, "You must be crazy."

On April 7, 1944, I reached age 18 and registered for the draft immediately. Europe had not been invaded yet. Three weeks after my Selective Service registration, I appeared on orders from the President of the United States for my physical examination at Sacramento.

My basic training at Camp Roberts, California, started August 14 and ended December 21, 1944, a period of seventeen weeks. The temperature at first reached as high as 114 degrees Fahrenheit and toward the end of it was freezing on some days.

Victor Goehring in uniform after basic training at Camp Roberts, California, 1944. (Courtesy of Victor Goehring)

In early January 1945, I was stationed at Fort Ord, California, for approximately two weeks. We were issued heavy winter clothes there and sent on the train to Fort Lawton, Washington. Because of the heavy clothing, we believed we would be sent to Germany. I had especially hoped to be sent there since I could speak the language.

We were in Fort Lawton approximately three weeks when one day we turned in all our winter clothes and were issued khakis and suntans. We knew then which direction we were headed. Shortly thereafter we boarded a ship at Seattle called the USS *Pickaway,* No. 222.

Our first stop was Honolulu. What impressed me most as we entered the harbor was the Nisei working on the docks, probably loading or unloading ammunition or strategic supplies. I immediately was reminded of the Nisei in the states relocated from a much less sensitive area than Honolulu. Some of my best friends were Nisei who were relocated.

I remember a visit to downtown Honolulu—I could not buy a drink with my buddies because I was only 18.

In Oahu we were stationed at Schofield Barracks. After being there two weeks we boarded the USS *Pickaway* again. We had a long voyage, and the ship never sailed a straight line—it zigzagged regularly to avoid detection by the enemy.

The voyage from Hawaii to Saipan took about three weeks and was the longest nonstop voyage prior to arriving at Okinawa. We had no official information where we were going until several hours before disembarkment from the ship in Okinawa.

Approximately two days before we arrived in Okinawa, an announcement was made over the ship's loudspeaker that President Roosevelt had died. Everyone on the ship was immobile for a while. We were stunned hearing that our commander in chief was dead. I have never witnessed such a somber group of people as after that announcement was made.

Victor Goehring, 1998.
(Arthur Greenburg Photography, Inc.)

I arrived on Okinawa approximately D plus 22. The front line was located approximately 30 miles south from where we got off the boat.

The second day I was sent to the battlefield along with other replacements, in a canopied 6 × 6 army truck. The ride was about 30 miles, and the road was muddy the entire length. Tire tracks from the wheels in the mud made movement slow, and in some places the trucks had to back up to continue.

Added to the scenery were the returning trucks we passed, most of them with either wounded soldiers or corpses. I was reminded of one of the soldiers on the ship coming over remarking, after he read a book about the 17th Infantry, 7th Division, at Kwajalein, what a great outfit it was and he hoped to be assigned to it. Since all of us in the convoy were assigned to the 7th Division, I wondered if he still had that opinion after seeing the wounded soldiers and corpses of the 7th Division returning from the battlefield.

I finally arrived at my permanently assigned unit as a combat rifleman at approximately 5:00 p.m. It was 2nd Platoon (13 people), Company C, 32nd Regiment, 7th Infantry Division. Upon my arrival, the unit had just finished dinner (rations) and was in serious briefing for an attack the next morning. At this time I had been on the island about 42 hours and had never previously met any of the soldiers in the unit. After the briefing for the attack, we positioned ourselves in foxholes for the night. This was the end of my 2nd day in Okinawa.

The following morning we commenced an attack for the capture of a certain hill. Fighting was fierce. Casualties were heavy. We were isolated. Supplies, including our food rations, didn't come as scheduled that evening. We had semisweet chocolate bars in our pockets as emergency rations for our dinner. Fortunately the resistance subsided the second morning. We were then able to retrieve our wounded and retreat.

Every soldier not a casualty was involved in carrying out our wounded, and I personally helped carry one soldier on a stretcher. I was physically weak from not having any sleep or adequate food the night before, then helping to carry a wounded soldier on a stretcher called for more strength than I normally would have been able to muster. I could scarcely walk myself. The trek to the rear was one of the most trying physical ordeals of my life. Compounded with that we were instructed if we encountered any enemy fire—such as a sniper—to hit the dirt. Fortunately, none occurred. If I had hit the dirt, I doubt I would have had the strength to get up. We arrived at our destination with our wounded without further incident.

After about a week at the front our regiment pulled to the rear for rest and recuperation.

My unit was at rest about two weeks. During this period we received replacements. One of the replacements was Ben Daschiell. We had much in common, and he became my favorite buddy. He was about a month younger than I, had just graduated from high school, and was admitted to U.C. Berkeley. At that time I had no idea I would ever go to Stanford, so I didn't hold this against him.

We returned to the front line together with the new replacements who joined the unit during rest period. The first attack after the rest period was very short (maybe 15 minutes), but it was the fiercest exchange of fire I experienced in the whole campaign.

In the attack Ben Daschiell was killed in approximately the first five minutes of fire. Ben was the closest buddy I had in the whole war. We knew each other only about ten days, but our bond was strong. The rifle Ben was firing when he was killed was the rifle I used up until the time I was assigned to radio operator.

Upon my discharge from the army, I took the first week to visit Ben's parents in Weott, California. They were grateful to talk to someone who was present when their only child got killed. It was so tragic to face the parents who lost their only child, who had such a promising future.

———— • ————

Dear Mr. Brokaw:

I am hopeful you may consider this letter as my tribute to World War II veterans and in particular to my late husband. He served faithfully and honorably from September 24, 1942, until his discharge October 14, 1945. Before he was sent to sea duty on March 8, 1944, his service was at Great Lakes Naval Training Station (boot camp), thence to Bureau of Naval Personnel, Arlington, Virginia, where he remained for 16 months. I might add during his service he advanced from Yeoman 3/c to Yeoman 1/c, studying while on duty every chance he could manage.

We were married October 28, 1942, on his ten-day leave from boot camp, and then I followed him to Arlington the first week of December 1942 and was able to get a job at the Pentagon. We were so blissfully happy even though his BuPers assignment was tenuous at best, and we treasured the time we were so fortunate to have in Arlington.

The male servicemen in his V6 section were being replaced by WAVES, so he was assigned to the crew of the USS *Rall* (DE-304) and left for California in March 1944. The ship was to be commissioned April 8, 1944, and he with the other yeomen had to get the

"My Sweetheart": Members of the crew of the USS Rall, *1944.*
Bill Robinson, Virginia Robinson's husband, is at the extreme left.
(Courtesy of Virginia Robinson)

office in order and process the orders of the crew gradually being
assigned duty on the *Rall.* After commissioning and shakedown
cruises, it left Mare Island for Pearl Harbor and the South Pacific.

The *Rall* was assigned to the Third Fleet and so was engaged in
all its actions throughout the islands of the South Pacific.

During his duty on the *Rall,* my husband was the recipient of
the Asiatic-Pacific, the World War II, and the American Campaign
medals with three Bronze Stars and the Good Conduct Medal.
Their luck in action held out until April 12, 1945 (the day we also
lost our president), when they were hit by the famous "suicide
plane" the Japanese were using, but not before they scored by
downing three of them. A destroyer got a fourth one, and the fifth
one in the attack hit the *Rall.* That hit resulted in 21 deaths and 38
injuries out of the *Rall's* small complement. His best buddy's body
was never recovered, for the shrapnel from the 500-pound-bomb
explosion fragmented anything in its way. He helped treat and give
morphine shots to many of his close comrades, and that took a big
toll on his strength and stamina. He personally was only bruised
and shocked by the carnage. It changed his outlook on life, he assured me in one letter of a few days later. One can only imagine the
horror of such experiences and the effect they would have.

After some temporary repairs at a harbor facility near Okinawa, the *Rall* was sent back to Pearl Harbor, but their shipyards
were so full they were then sent on to Todd Shipyards at Seattle,

Washington. My husband got a 20-day leave and came to Phoenix, Arizona, where my parents and I had moved. It was our first time together in over 14 months of being apart. The ship had just gotten back to Pearl Harbor and was being readied for more action when Hiroshima and Nagasaki were bombed. He felt he had been saved from future injury or even death, for he had become fatalistic about his chances of survival.

My husband died of a sudden heart attack March 13, 1978, at the age of 59 years. Our son and daughter were only 25 and 19 years old respectively then. Our four grandchildren were born after his death and so never will know what a dear, sweet husband and father he was. To that end I have, since last year, been word processing and printing over 350 letters he wrote me. He was a diligent correspondent, which helped keep us close and him able to cope with his fears, uncertainties, and constant stress. Up until his death, he still had nightmares from what he had gone through, though they were decreasing in intensity and frequency.

The letters will be his legacy to his children and grandchildren, and I hope they will treasure them in years to come. They are also a tribute to a much-missed husband, an honorable citizen and a true American veteran.

I thank you for the "greatest generation," of which I consider myself and my late husband, William Robinson, honored members. My war work was important too, and I hope everyone who follows us will remember how, after the war, we went to work rebuilding this nation and reestablishing our future, without self-pity and recriminations. We knew our duties and did them as best we could, and for that we can feel proud, for a job well done.

Thank you sincerely,
Virginia Robinson

P.S.   I have enclosed a copy of one of his letters, which will give you some idea of the depth of his love for me and his thoughts, in general, of his life "out there."

USS Rall under repair at Okinawa after a Japanese attack, April 1945. (Courtesy of Virginia Robinson)

Saturday night
March 31, 1945

Dearest little sweetheart,

Happy Birthday, darling! And—many happy returns of the day! I wish I were there to celebrate with you, angel! We would really paint the old town red!

This makes two birthdays you've had since I've seen you, darling, and I don't think I could bear to be away another one. It has been the loneliest and most disheartening period of my life, that is for sure. Even though we grow older in years, darling, we have the consolation of knowing that our love for each other burns a little brighter each time it is fanned by time, whether it be minutes or years. Knowing this, I have the patience to continue plodding out here until I can be with you again—forever. If we do survive this war, darling, surely no obstacle can ever pull us apart after it is over. Although we are suffering right now, we can think back with pride to the hardships and heartaches that we endured for each other because we so loved each other. It is true that our absence from each other is time wasted, in one sense of the word. On the other hand, we can and will more than live the wonderful future doubly as intense as we would have otherwise. To say that absence makes the heart grow fonder is a gross understatement as far as I am concerned. I loved you terribly before I had to leave you, but my love for you now has dwarfed my former affection for you. It hardly seems possible, darling, but it is true just the same.

When the war is over and I am with you again to *stay*, I don't care if I never see another person but you as long as I live. I shall be content to just stay near you and love you completely for the rest of my life. That, my darling wife, is a promise!

I must close now, angel, as it is almost time for me to be relieved of my watch. We have been under way for a week now, and sleep is beginning to be a priority once more. I'll slip into a big, beautiful dream of you tonight, sweetheart, to make up for not being able to be with you tonight. Good night, darling, and always remember how much

I love you,
Bill

Dear Mr. Brokaw:

I want to share a bit of the WWII period with you as I am sure others have been wont to do since your book was published.

Our parents came to America from Albania, our father in 1912 and our mother in 1920. They met, married and established a good and loving home in Tennessee as American citizens. Our father died in 1934—Depression!! Our young 28-year-old widowed mother raised me and 3 brothers alone by sheer tenacity—a characteristic of her people.

Lieutenant John Furge, brother of Margaret Sheffield. He was killed on May 17, 1945. (Courtesy of Margaret Sheffield)

In WWII two brothers [joined the] U.S. Navy and 1 brother, U.S. Army Air Force. My brother John Furge was a fighter pilot in the Pacific. He was extremely intelligent. Wanted in the Air Force. He was 1″ too short but had made 98 out of a possible 100 on the entrance exam. The recruiter told him—go home, get a burr haircut and eat lots of bananas and come back in 30 days. He did. They measured him by the top of his *hair* and he made it. In the Pacific he had 34 missions from Saipan over Tinian, Rota, Guam, in his P-47 Thunderbolt. Most of the pilots had girlie paintings and names on their planes. John painted his own plane—*All American*—in red, white and blue. From Saipan he went to Iwo Jima and got his favorite plane, the P-51.

Here he flew in escort of B-29s to the Japanese mainland, Tokyo and other places. The flight was extremely dangerous as the P-51 was lessened in weight by armor removal, so it could carry extra gas for the more than 150 miles over water. He had made several flights. But on May 17, 1945, he was shot down over Tokyo. It was a terrible loss of a fine young man. Our pilots today profit from lessons learned and sacrifices made in each flight endeavor.

At the same time my husband was in the infantry with the 1st and 3rd Divisions in North Africa, Sicily and Italy. He was missing in action for more than 8 months. Came home, thank goodness, having been severely wounded and still paying the price.

We members of the "greatest generation" have been there and endured. We are stronger, have a true sense of responsibility and wonder how the generations of our children and grandchildren will live up to their legacy.

Sincerely,
Mrs. Margaret F. Sheffield

—— • ——

Dear Mr. Brokaw:

I think that it's important for the future to better understand how the Depression and WWII enriched the values of the "greatest generation."

For the past year, I've been writing my WWII memoirs, "So Young—At First." My war experiences culminated dramatically when our crew witnessed the dropping of the atomic bomb on Nagasaki.

Coming of age during the great depression and the Second World War united us with a common purpose and common values—duty, honor, economy, courage, service, love of family and country, and responsibility for one's self.

Reading the letters I sent to my wife while I was in combat (she saved them all) showed how true this was, now 54 years ago.

Sincerely,
Jack Schwartz

From March to May 1945, our crew made 10 bombing missions from Guam to Japanese-held islands, Marcus, Woleai and Truk. In early June 1945, our Heavy Bomb Group was transferred to Okinawa to begin raids on the China and Japan mainlands. By August we had made over 10 of these raids.

After flying more than twenty missions together, the crew had developed a special rapport. Our ball gunner was everyone's favorite. His real name was Jack Meyer. We called him Moxie because he had so much. Lithe, muscular, compact, and at five feet four inches he was almost small enough to fit comfortably in his reserved seat—the ball turret. This turret, retracted for takeoffs and landings, wasn't easy to get into. I can remember the strain Moxie showed while curling, turning, and cringing to get into position. But once in place, he grabbed the handles of two 50-caliber machine guns, twisting them up, down, right and left, and the turret would rotate accordingly. As our appointed observer on missions, he slowly and constantly spun the turret, searching for enemy fighters and concentrations of flak.

"Wow!" This was the universal reaction of my squadron as soon as we learned that the atomic bomb had been dropped on Hiroshima on August 6, 1945. Maybe the peace process would begin and the end of this terrible war was in sight.

No. Three days later, the war was still on, and at 6 a.m. we were mustered to the squadron briefing hut to learn about our next mission.

"There are still too many active fighters flying out of Iwakuni. Your orders are to bomb its airstrip and destroy any fighters they have in revetments," said our briefing officer.

At 7:40 a.m. August 9, 1945, our formation of twelve B-24 bombers of the 7th Air Force, 11th Group, 431st Bombardment Squadron, took off from our base in Okinawa. As navigator of the lead airplane, I charted the course to Iwakuni, a Honshu naval base on the Inland Sea across from the Japanese islands of Kyushu and Shikoku. This was a strategic target, in contrast to some of our recent missions aimed at heavily populated cities and causing many civilian casualties.

The raids on cities involved as many as two hundred bombers, each carrying 4,000 pounds of napalm bombs. Napalm exploded on impact into fiery jelly clinging and burning everything it touched, causing an incredible amount of smoke, fire, and suffering. Even from 8,000 to 9,000 feet, we could visualize the soaring, spreading fires killing or maiming all in their path, including women, children, and the elderly. None of us felt good about these missions, but we desperately hoped that they would help to hasten the end of hostilities.

Our earphones were always in place, encouraging chatter. This day our pilot, Captain Art George, cooled it with a stern "pipe down." We were flying at 9,000 feet along the east coast of Kyushu, opposite Nobekoa, on our way to the Inland Sea target when Moxie cried, "My God! The earth's just exploded!—Look out at nine o'clock!" (The clock system identified where an object was in relation to the fuselage, the nose representing twelve o'clock.) We all rushed to the nearest port on the left side. We saw the top of a sun-bright fireball spouting shards of vivid red, blue, and orange flashes. As it faded, it broke off into a towering mushroom cloud that continued to climb way above us.

"Where the hell is that from, Jack?"

"Come on, Schwartz, work those dividers."

"Wish it was Palace Tokyo—the damned war would be over."

"That's the worst napalm raid I ever saw."

As navigator I was expected to know the answers. I recorded the time of the flash in my log as 11:03 a.m., but a dense ground fog blanketed the terrain, making it impossible to follow the base of the spiraling cloud down to its origin.

Estimating the bomb cloud's height to almost 25,000 feet, I said to the crew, "Right, it looks like another napalm raid. Probably Kumamoto—60 miles away."

The crew became quiet as we progressed up to Iwakuni. The urgency of getting to our target, bombing it, and coming home in one piece had taken over our thoughts.

At 12:15 p.m., we turned from our initial point twenty miles west of Iwakuni and steered into our final run. Heavy flak bursts began to crowd us, soon filling the airspace we had to fly into. To bomb accurately, the bombardier needed at least 45 seconds of straight and level flight. It's amazing how long 45 seconds can seem, but at last, at the cry of "Bombs away" from Puddle, our bombardier, we veered sharply to the right, diving to lose altitude, evasive action to defeat the accuracy of the Japanese gunners.

As soon as we were safely south of the target and had one more mission nearly completed, the crew relaxed a little and began more discussion.

"That must have been an atomic bomb."

"That must be what Hiroshima looked like."

"Yeah, even the worst of napalm bombs never burned like that."

"Jack, couldn't it have been one of the cities on our list?"

A week ago the pilot and I had been given a top-secret list of five cities to which we were not to fly within 50 miles under any circumstances. Hiroshima and Nagasaki were two of them.

"Nagasaki was due west of us then—but by almost 85 miles, for God's sake," I said. "That means the cloud had risen nearly 50,000 feet. I really doubt that."

Moxie said, "Trust me, that was the real thing."

We landed at Yontan Field, our Okinawa base, at 3:30 p.m. When we climbed out of the plane, Pop Weiss, our crew chief, greeted us with "They dropped the second atomic bomb on Nagasaki at 12:00."

"Oh no, Pop, it was 11:03," I replied, with the conditioned reflex of the designated timekeeper. And that was when it really sunk in, what an incredible event we had witnessed.

———— • ————

Dear Mr. Brokaw:

I am a World War II veteran whose enlistment papers for the United States Navy Reserve, dated 28 September 1944, list my age as 17 years and my physical characteristics as follows: height, 6 feet; weight, 156 pounds; eyes, negro; hair, negro; complexion, negro; and color, US NEGRO. Even though I never fired a shot at an enemy of my country and was never fired upon by one, I voluntarily placed myself in harm's way to be employed as necessary to aid the successful conclusion of the greatest war known to mankind, and I number myself among the members of that great generation.

William Holton with his mother while on leave, 1945. (Courtesy of William Holton)

I was 14 years old when the Japanese attacked Pearl Harbor. Until this attack, I was largely unaware of the war clouds that had gathered on the European scene and other parts of the world, and I was surprised and incensed at the Japanese attack. From this time until I became old enough to join the service, the war consumed all my attention as images of warfare and individual valor heightened not only my sense of patriotism and duty to my country but also my anxiety that it might end before I could get into it.

Even before my 17th birthday on April 29, 1944, I began a relentless effort to get my mother's consent for me to join the US Navy. My father died in 1936, and my mom had promised him that she would see to it that all his five kids would graduate from high school, and she said she wanted to keep her promise to him. At times, she forbade me to mention the subject to her. At other times, out of complete frustration, she adamantly refused to discuss the subject and maintained that she would never sign her name to any paper that allowed the government to send her son anywhere to get his head blown off. After four months of almost daily pleadings, however, Mom finally re- alized that my volunteering was some- thing I simply had to do.

I met her at the recruiting station in the post office on a sunny afternoon, and with trembling hands and tearful eyes she penned her signature. We walked home without saying anything to each other. I'm sure that each of us was won- dering if we had done the right thing. I was always a good and obedient son and felt guilty and sad for causing my mother such heartache and pain. I know it took a lot of courage on her part to let me go into a world of which she knew very little and over which she would have no con- trol. My uncertainties about leaving home for the first time centered around family considerations, but never did I ever harbor any reservations concerning my patriotic duty or my intention and ability to carry out those duties with honor and integrity.

William Holton in 1946.
(Courtesy of William Holton)

Subsequently, I completed recruit training at Great Lakes Naval Training Center, Illinois; basic engineering training at Hampton Naval Training School, Hampton, Virginia; assignment to Logistic Support Company 505, Shoemaker Receiving and Dis- tribution Center, California; embarkation to ComServPac, Pearl Harbor, Hawaii; and finally invasion of the Japanese homeland. I was excited to be in a combat theater and it appeared that, at last, I might accomplish my greatest desire: to fight heroically for my country. This dream was shattered, however, when two well-placed nuclear bombs brought an abrupt end to our war with Japan and the devastating inferno that was World War II. The end of the greatest of all wars was also the end of the greatest adventure of my life, and I had mixed emotions when it ended before I had proven myself *to myself* in combat. But I have long reconciled my- self to the fact that it was my young age and not my lack of courage or resolve that negated a more valorous role for me this great War.

I continued my service in the peacetime Navy until May 1948, during which time I was assigned to duty first on the repair ship USS *Amphion* (AR-13) and later aboard the auxiliary gasoline tanker USS *Noxubee* (AOG-56). Both of these ships were home-based in the Norfolk Navy Yard and permitted discriminatory practices inherent in the surrounding community to variously determine the treatment of colored general-service personnel assigned to newly integrated ship's companies.  During the War all units were completely segregated, and intermingling of Negro and White personnel on an operational basis was rare. On a ship of more than 800 ship's company, where one is the lone colored fireman in the general service, a whole new set of problems are guaranteed, as are strategies for fighting demeaning practices without compromising one's moral and intellectual integrity, while at the same time maintaining adherence to established regulations.

William Holton in 1998. (Courtesy of William Holton)

For my overall service to my country, I was awarded the American Campaign Ribbon, the Pacific Campaign Ribbon, the Philippine Liberation Ribbon, the Navy Good Conduct Medal, and the WWII Victory Medal. I am tremendously proud of the opportunity afforded me to serve my country in war and in peace, and I wear these awards proudly at every appropriate event.

Sincerely,
William F. Holton
MOMM3/c, USNR
(1944–1948)

——— • ———

Dear Mr. Brokaw:

A book you have written concerning letters of WWII citizens prompted the enclosed.

Like so many others of my generation who participated in WWII, I am in awe to have survived such a turbulent century and humbly grateful to be a survivor greeting the new millennium.

Sincerely,
Charles G. Westwater

THE LAST AIR STRIKE BY THE UNITED STATES NAVY
IN WWII: AUGUST 15, 1945

My U.S. Navy flight log for August 15, 1945, reads, "Character of flight: Strike Tokyo, type of machine: SB2C-4" (a dive-bomber). It proved to be the last U.S. naval air offensive of World War II against Japan.

We had been at sea off the coast of Japan almost two months, attacking airfields and naval installations. For pilots and aircrewmen, the continuation of naval air strikes in our single-engine aircraft over heavily defended land installations bred a wary fatalism. A recent series of air strikes on the Kure naval base, from whence the Japanese ships had sailed to bomb Pearl Harbor four years earlier, caused losses of 133 aircraft and almost as many aircrews. The suicidal battle for Iwo Jima and the carnage of Okinawa inured us against hope for a quick end to the war.

On that August morning, our plane left the carrier deck in a murky overcast. After circling to get into formation, we headed due west for Tokyo. The orders were to strike selected targets in Tokyo not yet obliterated by the B-29 heavy bomber raids. Some talk had been circulating, really rumors, of a possibility the war might soon end—something about a bomb of unimaginable destructive force. Skeptics that we were, we retorted: "Golden Gate in '48."

Charles Westwater and Jay Cooke, October 1945:
"First day back from overseas."
(Courtesy of Charles Westwater)

Only a month had passed since I turned nineteen years of age, but the images I acquired as the radioman-gunner of a navy dive-bomber would become the unending mental video for which there is no erase button. At the time, I couldn't foresee all that. Like most of my shipmates, I experienced a cynicism the lot of men in their forties. My resignation expressed itself in a simple yet forthright prayer. It was a lone, plaintive cry: "Let the war end one day sooner."

To this day, in my mind's eye, I can see the gradual unfolding of the horseshoe bay leading to the city of Tokyo, and ten miles from the target hear the radio order: "Jettison all bombs, unarmed." Someone questioned the message with: "What's up?" only to be told: "Good news." My wingman, Doug Page from NYC, rolled back his Plexiglas cockpit cover and in celebration fired his Smith & Wesson .38 revolver into the air. Less in jubilation than in stunned awareness of the answer to my prayer, I stared at the unarmed bombs falling to the bay below.

That evening, the fleet had one of its strongest air attacks from disgruntled Japanese officers contesting the conclusion of hostilities. As I stood on the catwalk bordering the flight deck of the carrier and gazed at the phosphorescent wake alongside the ship, a sailor from the engine room came alongside. We discussed the events of the day. Aware that my conversation lacked the usual conviviality of flight crews with ship's company, I asked him would he like a drink.

From time immemorial alcohol has been a postcombat soporific, and the U.S. Navy continued this tradition by offering a small medicinal cup of brandy to pilots and aircrewmen returning from air strikes. I had saved some of mine for just such an event as this night. After producing the half-pint or so of brandy, I gave it all to this unknown sailor from belowdecks, who registered surprise at my largesse. An overwhelming gratitude had motivated me in what would become a lifetime of trying to say "Thanks."

Charles G. Westwater

*Air Medal presented to Charles Westwater in 1945.
(Courtesy of Charles Westwater)*

———— • ————

Dear Mr. Brokaw:

World War II was a special time. My husband and I were both teenagers when it started, and as soon as he turned 18, he enlisted in the Army Air Corps. He had a most interesting experience as a young pilot in the CBI theater. Right after the bombs were dropped on Hiroshima and Nagasaki, several crews in his squadron were moved from their base in Ledo, Assam, and transferred to Rangoon.

Shortly after their arrival they were informed that one plane in their group was going to be selected to make the first trip into the Japanese-held territory of Saigon to take in some United States agents and medical doctors and supplies so that preparations could begin for the evacuation of our American prisoners of war and also to provide medical assistance as quickly as possible to the critically ill prisoners being held by the Japanese. The plane selected was piloted by my husband and pilot Harold Kiser, who lives in Shingle Springs, Ca. They were both quite young, unmarried and had no dependents, so perhaps that is why they were chosen. Their commanding officer warned them that since the war was not officially over and the peace treaty with Japan had not yet been signed, there were concerns for the safety of their flight and the reception they would receive from the Japanese. Their C-47 was unarmed and unescorted, and their only weapons were their side arms, .45 automatic pistols.

When they were about 50 miles from Saigon, two Japanese Zeros approached their plane. They hoped the Japanese pilots knew the nature of their mission (which had been arranged by the Red Cross). The two Japanese Zeros flew past them, turned and, flying wingtip, guided them to the Japanese base at Saigon.

After landing, the Japanese soldiers removed their side arms and the C-47 crew watched as Japanese soldiers unloaded the plane and the passengers met with a Japanese interpreter. The Japanese military took the pilots and crew members to a hotel and placed them under guard over night. During the night there was rioting and gunfire outside the hotel—so perhaps they were under guard for their own protection.

The next morning they were escorted back to their plane, their side arms were returned and the plane was loaded with the most seriously ill American prisoners, ready to be transported to Rangoon. One prisoner had a huge tumor on the side of his head, and another prisoner said he had been hit very hard with the butt of a Japanese rifle, causing a severe injury which developed into a tumor because he was never given any medical aid! The American doctors asked the pilots to fly the plane as low as possible in hopes the tumor would not rupture. Many of those wounded had been under forced Japanese labor, building the railroad line and the connecting bridge on the river Kwai. After safe return to Rangoon, the former prisoners were transferred to a large C-54 hospital plane, part of the Air Transport Command.

William Nielsen with a C-47 just after completing training at Malden Air Force Base, Missouri, in 1944.

The crew of William Nielsen's C-47 watch as Japanese soldiers unload medical supplies, Saigon, August 1945.

William Nielsen (far right) and a group of friends in Bangkok, Thailand, August 1945. (All courtesy of Helen Nielsen)

With the mission to Saigon safely completed, the next day the same crew was given the same test mission into Bangkok and brought out the first group of American prisoners held there. Their third day's flight was to an obscure Japanese prison camp in the jungles of Siam. They were used to makeshift jungle landing strips and were able to bring out the Americans most in need of urgent care. These first three flights with just one plane were evidently made to be certain the flights could be carried out safely and without risking more than one plane until the safety factor was established. After these test flights were completed, all the American C-47 crews who had been transferred to Rangoon were involved in large-scale flights into these areas until all of the American war prisoners were evacuated. The large number of flights were beginning as the peace treaty documents with Japan were being signed.

Most sincerely,
Helen Nielsen

———— • ————

Dear Mr. Brokaw:

I have just finished reading *The Greatest Generation*.

I am not at all certain that the generation of which you write fits the title of your text. Let me explain. The circumstances of the time demanded a positive response from my generation. If the dates were changed a couple of decades, that would have been the generation.

Herrick Roth in Kyoto, Japan, October 1945. (Courtesy of Herrick Roth)

No one I knew of my generation wanted war. No one wanted to be drafted into the Army of the United States. I certainly did not, yet my draft number was the only number FDR's hands touched (Henry Stimson, Secretary of War, drew the next 9999). I used to joke, "I won a lottery—but guess which one!" So I was in the first draft call of Colorado's Draft District 10. The draft board knew I was in the last named of ten or twelve "nonessential" industries (public school teaching). However, they were sympathetic to my request to let me finish the school year so deferred me from the district's first (March) draft call to July 1941.

Herrick Roth and his baby daughter spend Christmas week 1944 with her great-grandfather (left) and his friend Colonel Jensen in Hot Springs, South Dakota. (Courtesy of Herrick Roth)

At my entrance post, Ft. Bliss, Texas, we all took tests, including typing. I had not elected to take typing in high school, but my business teacher in our class of 39 persons insisted that another young man and I, both overloaded with extracurriculars, learn to type. She taught us in ten hours—ten days when she had to extend her after-school hours from 5 to 6 pm to teach us. We both thanked her many times over. My typing performance at Ft. Bliss classified me to be in the Signal Corps at Ft. Monmouth, NJ. Five months later, Pearl Harbor! Two days later, every college draftee at Ft. Monmouth was enrolled in OCS.

Because OCS needed teachers, beginning in March 1942 for 23 months I became the assistant director for the map reading and field wire divisions. In a way, that was laughable—we had 600 students every three months. Most of them were Regular Army and had been in combat, particularly in the South Pacific. I learned more from them than they possibly could from me.

While at Ft. Monmouth, three times I received overseas orders. The first two orders were rescinded when something else came to light in the Army's computer system.

Finally, I received overseas orders to the Pacific in April 1945. After spending a month in Hawaii and another two months from there via Eniwetok as three different troopships broke down in that period, I arrived at the Manila, Philippines, Staging Area, where I immediately boarded an APA troopship bound for Wakayama, Japan. As one would say, a funny thing happened on the way to the forum. Two days before our scheduled arrival in Wakayama, a bomb was dropped on Hiroshima. Our landing (wading for a mile in the bay) went exactly as scheduled. But no one was firing on us. Via Osaka and Kyoto, we finally reached our destination—Kure-Hiroshima. From Columbus Day to Christmas Day in 1945, I was in charge of one of the two crews of 50 GI's to go into the hills around Hiroshima and try to get the names of the persons who had "vanished" (vaporized is the term now scientifically used) in Hiroshima. Each week, I carried the packet of names our crew had put together from the survivors in those surrounding hills (most of whom spoke perfect English because it was the second language in Japan's public schools for two decades prior to the bombing of Pearl Harbor) to MacArthur's headquarters in Tokyo. When I received my orders on December 25 to go to Nagoya to come home, we had delivered over 48,500 names.

I was discharged on January 26, 1946, at Ft. Logan, CO, which still exists today, immediately adjacent to Denver's SW boundary. I began teaching the same day, since it was the first day of the second semester. My principal was delighted that I was in uniform. Two others had returned to teaching there before I returned, and he asked them to wear their uniforms (we had variety—one Navy and one Seabee).

I was plain lucky. 55 months in the Army and not a scratch. I lost one of my closest friends who was drafted when I was—he was in the North African campaign. His entire platoon had been wiped out.

I always stand in awe of the unknown power which has created our lives.

Respectfully,
Herrick S. Roth

— • —

Dear Mr. Brokaw:

I joined the USM Corps in Jan. 1940. One of my first duties was on the USS *Yorktown*. It was not long before we found ourselves in the South Pacific. I was on her when she was hit in the Coral Sea battle. I saw combat in several places, Roi-Namur and Iwo Jima.

It was on my Saipan tour of duty where the baby came into the picture. In a combat zone is not where you think of finding a 2-day-old baby. Her mother had been killed, and the baby was in a basket under a tree. We (three of us) took her for 2 days until we found a priest (chaplain) to give her to. We used a surgical glove and just 3 small holes in one finger and gave her Carnation milk, water and a tiny bit of sugar. We did keep her alive. The chaplain took her and did assure us she would be well cared for. We called her Baby Girl.

Fred Irwin

—— • ——

Dear Mr. Brokaw:

I am an old soldier who has withstood the hardships of the Depression and World War II, during which I spent 3½ years as a POW. I endured sickness and health problems caused by slave labor camps, wounds, and beatings.

I am one of the very few that survived the Bataan Death March, still living. Also, my story is different from most because my job took me to the front lines daily and I saw more than most men.

Very truly yours,
Glenn D. Frazier

World War II ended with Japan on September 2, 1945. I was a Japanese prisoner of war in a slave labor camp on the western coast of Japan, about 500 miles by rail from Tokyo.

Now to get out and try to adjust to a life that for four years I never thought would happen. My thoughts would drift back to the Bataan Death March: the times that my body was so badly beaten and sick, until I feared that I would not live another night.

Now I could go back to the good old U.S.A. to see my family and friends. To enjoy freedom and not wake up every couple of hours to check to see that things were all right. Maybe to realize that I was still of the living, without the threat of the Jap guard's rifle butt slammed against my head. Maybe I would not have to look forward to a small bowl of wormy rice or hear the sound of Jap guards yakking at a fellow POW trying to go to the slit trench to relieve himself. Maybe to have a bath at least once a week and not go six months or so with salt water and no soap.

How would I be able to sleep without the body lice crawling up and down my body. Without them, after three and one-half years, I would feel all alone. The thought of sleeping in a bed by myself was out of the question.

In the winter, having enough covers to keep you warm, where the circulation gets into your toes and fingers, without sleeping piled up like pigs in a pigpen. Being able to walk into a barbershop and get your hair cut, without dull scissors pulling the hair out of your face. Being able to sit down with my family to eat a meal; at one time I would have given my life for that one privilege.

Wondering if the girl I left behind was still there waiting for my return. Being able to purchase a clean undershirt, or a pair of shoes without cutting holes in them for my toes to stick out. Oh, how would I be able to handle the fact that I did not have to ask for permission to go to the slit trench or to the bathroom.

No more would I have to guard my spoon, so I would have a way to eat the watery rice. No more would I have to shake the one next to me in the morning, to see if he had made it through the night. Even just to conceive the reality that I might not be beaten or killed today.

All these things were so real for us every moment, for so long. Then we knew that Allied forces would have to invade Japan before the end could come. The Jap guards had standing orders, the minute an invasion took place on the mainland, to

Glenn Frazier, following his discharge and return to the United States in 1945. (Courtesy of Glenn D. Frazier)

shoot all POWs. We had accepted this fate long before now. The only thing we had to look forward to was feeling that the Japs would get what they deserved, that their defeat would serve as a lesson to all evil governments that waging war against others, then treating their prisoners as though they were animals, like the Japanese did, [is wrong].

Now I was told we were going home, and we knew the war had changed the world. A little fear for the future ahead crossed my mind.

After, the thought sinking into my mind, "You are going home, it's over!" Can I live with freedom, after all of this? Can I adjust from the horrors of war and the brutal treatment I received while being a POW? Can I lay down my guard and walk with pride and hide the feelings that come over me remembering how I felt sailing under the Golden Gate Bridge and seeing the land I never expected to see again?

Then the thoughts of how many fallen buddies that were not able to come back brought tears to my eyes. The mothers, dads, sisters, and brothers that would wait patiently at the pier, hoping to see their loved ones coming down the gangplank, running into their arms. The ones that would wait for months, going back to each arriving ship to wait for their family member to return and never seeing him get off any ship and wondering if he was dead and where his body lay on foreign soil. Never to understand the cruelty of how he may have been treated as a POW. How long will it take me to realize that I am free again. Free to choose where I go and free to do what I want to.

The return to my hometown was such a wonderful experience. Everyone in the whole town turned out to greet me that day. My brother also returned home the same day. His duty was in Europe, and this was the time after almost four years for our own reunion. After I saw him, the reality of the end of the war finally sank into my head.

My parents told me my brother had called from Atlanta to tell everyone he was returning home and told me about the joy in his voice when he knew I was alive. So for the next few weeks, day after day, we had personal visits from family, friends, and people that we had never met that came by to welcome us home.

Many people would ask what I was going to do now, and all I could think of was enjoying being free, and how good it was. There was nothing but good from all of my family and friends. Things were wonderful, but then came the time to go to my room alone and close the door and get into a clean bed with clean sheets and turn out the lights. The room was dark, and I dropped off to sleep.

Soon my mind would go back into the past. The slightest noise would find me sitting straight up in bed, looking for the Jap guard that may have shot or hit a POW. But now instead of my subconscious mind working to adjust to being free and safe, it went back to what had been a way of life in the past. It was hard to wake up and know where I was, and to realize that my life was not on the line. Then I would have to tell myself that I was home and safe. Some time after that the nightmares started, and they became a part of my life. It was easy to justify drinking until I passed out. Trying to drink my thoughts away.

While I was in the hospital in San Francisco, I was told by the doctor to go out and act normal and all would be fine. It was hard to keep that in mind when my dreams were as real as when I was actually living these horrible times.

I would awake feeling lice running all over my body. I would jump up and turn the lights on to examine my clothes because it felt so real.

It was not something I could talk to anyone about, since they would surely have thought I was crazy. It would have been a complete waste of time. Night after night I would struggle with the problem of readjusting. Each morning when I would awake, I was as tired as I would have been back in the prison camp. While these dreams were going on, it was a real-life experience again. Then waking up, trying to go back to sleep without getting back into the same battle for my life. This kept me from getting the sleep my body badly needed.

How could I answer someone's question Are you enjoying being home? Could I tell them it was hell? No, so my mind would send mixed signals.

After being trained to fight the war, then having to kill to save my life and others around me, I got to the point that I believed I had become a killer. I would lie in wait for a chance to kill a Japanese. And when I did, it filled my heart with excitement. I was proud to be able to kill another, and that became a way of life. When a day passed and I missed a chance to kill, I felt like I had failed to do a good job. Then coming back to a small, quiet town where shooting a rabbit was maybe the biggest thing to happen in a day, it was impossible for me to live a normal life. The nightmares nearly every night would bring back another real-life experience. I could not separate my feelings from the past. It was a time I could see a fine line between killing and not killing. My thoughts would bring me to a point of thinking that maybe to kill someone would make things easier. I would think that I needed to kill to satisfy a hidden urge in me, and to get that monkey off my back.

Maybe if I had been able to kill a few Japs after my prison camp experience and then return home, it may have helped. It was impossible to discuss this with anyone. It was an everyday fight to keep these thoughts out of my head, and there was nowhere to turn to get help. Then going to bed each night knowing that I was going to face the Japs again, hiding under bridges, running, jumping off embankments into the water, hiding under cars, being shot at, where there was no way to defend myself, the same as during the three and one-half years I was a POW.

The horrors of the war were with me every day and night for the next twenty-nine to thirty years. At times I wished I had never come home. How peaceful it would be to lie in a quiet place and find the peace that comes only with death.

Glenn D. Frazier
Ex-POW, Survivor of Bataan Death March

———— • ————

Dear Tom:

Enclosed please find a copy of a very rare letter. It belonged to my father, Kenneth Earl Mitchell, and was written on the 30th of March in the year of 1946.

Kenneth Earl Mitchell was one of the 317 survivors of the USS *Indianapolis*. The ship, as you know, carried the parts for the first atom bomb.

The letter (written right after the war and soon after my dad returned to Mishawaka, Indiana) was being sent to a Ray Hornbuckle in Southern California. Dad passed in 1980, and I think Mr. Hornbuckle died a few years ago.

Fondly,
Earl Dean Mitchell

Mishawaka, Ind.
March 30, 1946

Dear Ray:

I sure was surprised and glad to receive your letter. I have wondered how I could get in touch with you, as I realized there were things you would like to know about our old gang. Ray, there were so few of us left I cannot believe yet that it is true. That men we learned to know and like so well had to die such a hard way. It was hell to see men give up all hopes of being rescued. And many men did just that; others went crazy, and that was a very terrible sight to see and remember. Ray, I along with the men that were saved was so very lucky. God spared us. Can we ever repay him I wonder. I along with 175 men spent five days and nights in a kapok life jacket. Of the 175 men I was with, we only had 63 saved. Men of our old gang who were with me were Strain, Schollter, Righter, John Wallace, Kozik, Rothman, Dean, Shorty Cane, all these men died out there. Lederman, Aulschuler, Kenley, and myself were saved. We were picked up and taken to Peleliu by the *Cecil B. Doyle*. Other fellows were taken to Samar. We were all moved to Guam later, where we learned about what happened in other groups. Their hell was just as bad as ours. Groce died in Tommy Reid's arms, he knew he was going. Condon was killed outright, as were a couple of new men. Heggie was trapped in the aft mark 28. By the way, his mother died the last of October from a broken heart. Ray, I wish there was good news I could give you about E. J. Wallace but there is not. He died in the same group that Groce did. I know it must have been a terrible shock to his wife and family. One thing I cannot forget is that Strain, Schollter, Righter, Wallace and Kozik died the last day before we were rescued. That sure was a bad thing. Sure hurt me, because we sure stuck together out there, prayed together, and hoped together. The first few days we kidded one another and talked a lot about home. Well, Ray, I will close for this time, realizing there is much more to tell you, but will leave it to later. Excuse my writing, Ray, I am a little nervous yet, but I will be OK. And I do get pretty blue when I write about these fellows. About the men you would like information on, Ray, write and I will do my best to tell you. Hope Mrs. Hornbuckle is fine. Tell her hello for me. My wife and son are well, and they sure were glad to have their old pappy home once again. Sure am glad that you made chief. But you are a good boy, Ray. Stay like that always. Oh yes, if there is anyone you would like me to write to thinking it might help them a little in their sorrow, I will be glad to do it. Will close now, hoping to hear from you again real soon.

Kenneth Mitchell in 1944.
(Courtesy of Earl Dean Mitchell)

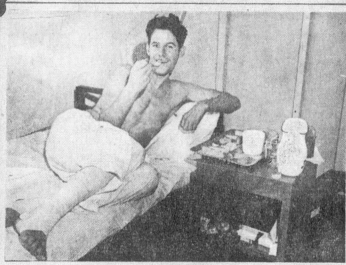

ENJOYS MEAL IN HOSPITAL.

Seaman 1/c Kenneth E. Mitchell, of 706 West Grove street, Mishawaka, enjoys a meal in a Pacific naval base hospital, where he is convalescing. Mitchell is a survivor of the cruiser U. S. S. Indianapolis, sunk off the Philippines just a few days before the Jap surrender. He saw action on Iwo Jima, Okinawa and participated in strikes against the Jap mainland. His wife, Mabel, and son, Earl Dean, reside at the Grove street address. Before entering the service, he was employed as a foreman for the Ball Band plant.

Kenneth Mitchell in a Pacific naval base hospital
in 1944 convalescing after his ship, the
USS Indianapolis, was sunk; he'd spent five days
and five nights adrift in a life jacket.
(Courtesy of the South Bend Tribune,
South Bend, Indiana)

Kenneth Mitchell with his son, Earl Dean Mitchell,
on leave in Mishawaka, Indiana, 1944.
(Courtesy of Earl Dean Mitchell)

I will try to answer any questions you might like to ask. So long for this time.

    Your old shipmate and friend,

                        Kenny Mitchell

I am sure this list will bring a tear to your eyes like it does mine.

                              Ken

Men that died:

Condon	E. Golf
Meagler	Farber
John Wallace	Batson

E. J. Wallace—I did not see him at any time.

McCoskey—He refused to leave the ship.

Groce	Baker
Tosh	Rothman
Dean	Gries
Taggert	Durey
Kozik	Jerimeyer
Schollter	Menchaff
Strain	Doss
DeFoor	Denny
Franklin	Poyner
Sedina	Lt. Jenny
Hamman	Lt. Crews
Heggie	Lt. Swartz
Kroegler	Shorty Cane
Righter	Al—and all other Radar T.
Campana	

Saved:

Jerkawitz—not spelled right, Jerk

Underwood	Anderson
Lederman	Kenley
Ault	Gettleman
Aulschuler	Rogers
Reid	Mitchell

ABOVE: *Dressed in overalls and a bandanna, "Rosie the Riveter" was introduced as a symbol of patriotic womanhood in the 1940s.* (AP/Wide World Photos)

RIGHT: *A road sign typical of the home front spirit.* (Reproduced from the collection of the Library of Congress)

Part Four

•

THE HOME FRONT

WHEN AMERICA WENT TO WAR IN EUROPE AND THE PAcific, it went to war at home as well. It launched an attack on all fronts to produce the arms, planes, ships, uniforms, medical supplies, food, and all that was required to support the millions of men and women in the armed forces. That effort was by every measure as critical to the success of the Allies as the daring of the commanders and the warriors.

The magnitude of the challenge and the response of the American industrial machinery were reflected in the opening months of the war. The historian John Morton Blum has written, "By the time of Pearl Harbor, military spending had already reached a monthly rate of $2 billion. In the first six months of 1942, federal procurement officers placed orders for $100 billion of equipment, more than the American economy had ever produced in a single year." By the peak of the war, military needs constituted 37 percent of all production and services. The gross national product almost doubled during the war years. Unemployment went from 14.3 percent in 1937 to 1.3 percent in 1943.

The war defeated Fascism and helped liberate America from the Great Depression. And it changed the American economy beyond the bottom line. Labor unions increased their membership by more than four million during the war years, securing their place in the mass-production industries such as steel, rubber, and automobiles. In the heartland, farmers were planting and harvesting fence to fence, tripling their income.

But this was not a free-market triumph. At every stage the U.S. government was involved in ordering, financing, and coordinating the home front economy. The Selective Service and War Manpower Commission determined how labor resources were allocated. Some skilled workers of draft age were allowed to stay out of uniform so they could build new planes or produce more combat boots. In 1941 the Office of Price Administration was instituted to control prices. The War Labor Board and the War Production Board were created and then placed under the Office of Economic Stabilization, which in turn was folded into the Office of War Mobilization. It was all designed to assure that the demands of the war effort were satisfied, while limiting profiteering and inflation.

Consumer items were in short supply. Detroit stopped making automobiles. Gasoline was rationed. So was meat. Americans found themselves eating horse meat; one Milwaukee market sold eight thousand pounds in a day and a half. Butter was replaced by margarine. Women applied makeup to their legs to compensate for the absence of stockings. Families were encouraged to save string, tin, rubber bands. Christmas toys were often homemade. The motto was "Use it up, wear it out, make it do, or do without." Mary O'Hearn Armitage remembers the way her hometown of Lawrence, Massachusetts, was transformed during the war years by "sugar and gas rationing . . . blackout curtains, automobile headlights painted in half-moons with the residue of melted down 78 rpm records, [and] neighborhood air-raid wardens."

Radio became the medium for entertainment and, especially, information about the war. More than nine hundred radio stations blanketed America, and more than half of them were affiliated with a network. When the famous newscasters of the day—Edward R. Murrow from London, H. V. Kaltenborn from New York, Lowell Thomas—came on the air, it was a signal to listen. The radio networks also became a quasi-government voice. The Selective Service used radio to spread the rules about the draft. Government manpower needs were broadcast. Even the most isolated American was keenly aware of the urgency of the war effort.

It was also a rich time for other forms of entertainment. Book sales rose 20 percent each year after Pearl Harbor. There was a huge appetite for books about history, military matters, and the new technology the war effort encouraged. Once the fighting heated up, battlefield accounts were in great demand. The popular war correspondent Ernie Pyle had an instant bestseller with his book *Here Is Your War* in 1943.

Hollywood jumped into the war shortly after Pearl Harbor, turning out films with patriotic themes designed to keep up morale at home. *Since You Went Away, Bataan, So Proudly We Hail,* and *This Is the Army* were among the big attractions, and the collective film output drew in an estimated ninety million moviegoers a week, about a third more than before the war. Some of these movies endured well beyond the forties. *Casablanca* was in many ways the perfect World War II film, even though it contained not one combat scene.

Hollywood stars were enlisted as promoters of war bonds, the government promissory notes that paid 2.9 percent a year and attracted millions of small investors, who had the dual reward of saving their money while financing the war effort. Some stars—such as Henry Fonda, Clark Gable, and Jimmy Stewart—volunteered

JULY 2, 1940

Congress passes the Export Control Act, directed against Japan, allowing the president to restrict exports of material, including raw materials, considered vital for U.S. defense.

JAN. 7, 1941

FDR establishes the Office of Production Management, headed by William Knudsen, to coordinate and expedite defense production.

MAY 15, 1941

Nylon stockings are introduced at about $1.15 a pair. By Aug. 1941 silk stockings are rationed.

MAY 20, 1941

FDR establishes the Office of Civilian Defense, under the direction of New York Mayor Fiorello La Guardia.

MAY 27, 1941

FDR proclaims an unlimited national emergency, saying; "I call upon all the loyal citizens engaged in production for defense to give precedence to the needs of the nation to the end that a system of government that makes private enterprise possible may survive. I call upon all our loyal workmen as well as employers to merge their lesser differences in the larger effort to insure the survival of the only kind of government which recognizes the rights of labor or of capital. I call upon loyal state and local leaders and officials to cooperate with the civilian defense agencies of the United States to assure our internal security against foreign-directed subversion and to put every community in order for maximum productive effort and minimum waste and unnecessary frictions. I call

JUNE 14, 1941

FDR freezes all Italian and German assets in the United States.

JUNE 16, 1941

FDR orders all German consulates in the United States closed by July 10.

JUNE 24, 1941

FDR promises U.S. aid to the Soviet Union.

JUNE 25, 1941

FDR establishes the Fair Employment Practices Commission to prevent racial discrimination in defense work.

JUNE 28, 1941

FDR establishes the Office of Scientific Research and Development.

JULY 1, 1941

The Federal Communications Commission allows commercial TV to begin. NBC becomes the first commercial TV operation in the nation.

AUG. 14, 1941

FDR and Winston Churchill issue the Atlantic Charter.

AUG. 28, 1941

FDR establishes the Office of Price Administration to control prices.

OCT. 1941

FDR establishes the Office of Facts and Figures with Archibald MacLeish as director.

DEC. 7, 1941

Japan attacks the American fleet at Pearl Harbor, Hawaii.

for military duty. Stewart flew twenty combat missions as a command pilot.

While Franklin Roosevelt relished the role of commander in chief, the war years were a difficult political balancing act for him. In 1942, congressional Republicans made significant gains in midterm elections, capitalizing on voter worries over defeats in the Pacific, higher taxes, and wartime shortages. The New Deal of the Great Depression began to wind down as a result of improved economic conditions and steady Republican opposition.

In 1944 the Republicans nominated New York governor Thomas Dewey as their presidential candidate. Roosevelt, seeking a fourth term, left the selection of his vice-presidential candidate to his party's convention. Responding to the increasingly conservative tone in the country, Democrats selected Missouri senator Harry Truman as FDR's running mate. Roosevelt campaigned on his record of wartime leadership and the strong economy. Dewey could do little except attack governmental inefficiency and claim that Roosevelt was too old for the job. In the end, voters rejected Dewey's youth (he was forty-two) and arrogance. One critic said that Dewey could strut sitting down. FDR's vote totals were not as large as those of 1940, but they were greater than expected, proving the president still had wide support.

American culture during the war years presents a contradictory picture. On the one hand, much of the nation's cultural product celebrated democracy. Americans insisted that the war was a contest between democracy and totalitarianism, tyranny and freedom. Radio listening groups, which first emerged in Great Britain, blossomed in the United States. By listening to radio programs together and then discussing their content, people engaged in national politics. One historian has pointed out that children learned about the value of group activities in books such as *Susie Cucumber: She Writes Letters,* in which neighborhood children learned to work together to achieve a common goal. Music did the same thing. In 1942 the Music Educators National Conference changed "The Star-Spangled Banner" to a pitch everyone could sing.

Common ground was an American ideal. According to the popular stereotype, the war was the apotheosis of the great melting pot. But the true portrait of America on the home front was far more unsettling. Following the attack on Pearl Harbor, Japanese Americans, many of them pillars of their communities, were suddenly suspect. In February 1942, less than ninety days after Pearl Harbor, the president signed Executive Order 9066, authorizing the detention of approximately 110,000 Japanese in ten internment camps in Western states. On the West Coast, which had substantial Japanese American populations, whole neighborhoods were emptied overnight as families were herded, under armed guard, aboard trains that would take them to bleak resettlement camps in the high desert of Arizona, the plains of Wyoming, and other isolated areas.

Young Japanese American men were given the opportunity to enlist, and many served with distinction. In 2000, twenty-two Asian American members of the famed 442nd Regimental Combat Team, made up almost entirely of Japanese Americans, were awarded the Medal of Honor for their courage during combat in southern Europe.

For America's African American population, World War II was at once a difficult and a liberating time. Difficult because they had to fight their way into uniform and into the jobs the war created. Liberating because the war started to change the racial landscape in America in a way that made it possible to begin the journey that led to civil rights legislation twenty years later.

But it wasn't easy. A. Philip Randolph of the Brotherhood of Sleeping Car Porters had to threaten a mass march on Washington to pressure President Roosevelt to address discrimination in the defense industries. FDR created the Fair Employment Practices Committee to enforce Executive Order 8802 forbidding such discrimination. This was the beginning of a mass migration out of the subsistence jobs of the South to the better wages in Detroit, Pittsburgh, Gary, Chicago, New York, and the other manufacturing centers of the North.

In the military, most African Americans were assigned to unskilled jobs as stewards on board ships or as hospital orderlies. They were segregated during basic training, and even black officers were denied admittance to the officers' clubs on most bases—though, incredibly, some German and Italian prisoners of war shipped to the United States were admitted.

When blacks were given the opportunity, they performed well in combat. The Tuskegee Airmen, an all-black fighter pilot outfit, had an enviable record. The 332nd Fighter Group fought alongside Patton's best troops in the drive on Berlin. Despite those performances and countless others, the American military remained di-

DEC. 8, 1941

FDR calls December 7 "a day which will live in infamy." The United States declares war on Japan.

DEC. 9, 1941

FDR tells the American public: "We are now in this war. We are all in it all the way. Every single man, woman, and child is a partner in the most tremendous undertaking of our American history. We must share together the bad news and the good news, the defeats and the victories, the changing fortunes of war."

DEC. 11, 1941

The United States declares war on Germany and Italy.

1942

In the so-called Little Steel formula, the National War Labor Board allows wages to rise 15 percent over the levels of Jan. 1941.

The world's largest office building, located near Arlington, Virginia, and called the Pentagon, is opened; it houses more than 25,000 workers.

JAN. 1942

The War Production Board, headed by Donald Nelson, is established to coordinate production of war matériel.

The Office of Production Management bans the manufacture of cars and light trucks after Jan. 31.

FEB. 19, 1942

FDR signs Executive Order 9066, which will remove Japanese Americans from their homes in Pacific Coast states to internment camps in inland areas. More than 100,000 people will be relocated. The evacuation will be ruled constitutional by the U.S. Supreme Court in 1944.

APR. 18, 1942

FDR creates the War Manpower Commission, headed by Paul V. McNutt, to manage labor resources.

APR. 28, 1942

The General Maximum Price Regulation places controls on civilian food items, ensuring that prices cannot exceed the highest prices charged in March of this year.

MAY 1942

Sugar rationing begins because imports from the Philippines have ceased and the shortage of shipping makes transportation from other sources difficult.
War ration books are issued, one for each person.
Gasoline rationing begins on the East Coast.

MAY 15, 1942

FDR signs a congressional act establishing the Women's Auxiliary Army Corps (WAAC).

JUNE 12, 1942

FDR appeals for old tires, rubber shoes—anything made of rubber.

JUNE 13, 1942

FDR establishes the Office of War Information, with Elmer Davis as director.
The Office of Strategic Services (OSS), forerunner to the CIA, is established with William Donovan as director.

JULY 1942

The Congress of Racial Equality is founded by pacifists.

JULY 30, 1942

Congress authorizes the women's naval reserve, known as the WAVES.

vided along black and white lines until Harry S Truman as president signed the desegregation order in 1948.

Although it was not clear at the time, the war years were the beginning of the end for widespread gender discrimination as well. American women had been expected to stay home, raise the children, and defer to their husbands. Those who did work outside the home were largely confined to so-called women's jobs, such as schoolteaching or secretarial or clerical assignments. There were exceptions, of course, but the women who defied convention and set out to build careers in male-dominated professions such as the law, medicine, business, or politics were generally subjected to demeaning observations along the lines of "Shouldn't you be home having babies?"

When the men marched off to war, however, the acute worker shortage forced the culture and the government to suspend their gender discrimination and actively recruit women to the workplace. By 1944, 37 percent of all adult women—19,370,000 altogether—were in the workforce in some capacity. For the first time in American history, married women outnumbered single women on the employment rolls. They were also moving into new assignments. By 1943, women made up 90.8 percent of the new hires at Detroit's 185 war plants. In shipyards, Rosie the Riveter became an icon of the "all hands on board" spirit of the war years. Emblematic of that spirit were women like Esther Barger, a riveter for an airplane plant in St. Louis, and Jane Branston, who worked as a research chemist at the National Cash Register Company in Dayton, Ohio, who wrote to me about their contributions to the war production effort.

However, discrimination didn't vanish. There were very few organized efforts to provide day care for working mothers. Salaries remained two-tiered. In the auto industry in 1943, men made, on average, 50 percent more than women while working only a few more hours per week.

In 1945, when the war was over and the returning veterans were eager to find jobs, women were the first to lose their places on the auto assembly lines and in the aircraft plants. They were moved aside in research laboratories and sent back to cover society events in newspapers. But the role of women in American life had been unalterably changed. The foundation was in place for what became the modern women's movement.

Historians, economists, and sociologists are still measuring the effect of the war years on the development of the modern U.S. political, cultural, and economic landscape. California was no longer the Far West to returning farm boys from the Great Plains or city kids from the Midwest and the East; it was the land of year-round sunshine and good jobs in new industries. Black workers who had gone north seeking employment settled in. Texas oil, the fuel of the booming postwar economy, was an elixir to entrepreneurs and workers alike. Cities began to grow in the Rocky Mountain West, where space and natural resources were magnets. Florida ceased to be a sleepy backwater.

The American industrial colossus that had produced tanks, planes, trucks, ships, and weapons of every caliber night and day for four years emerged from the war mightier than ever. It was big business in every sense of the phrase: the Big Three automakers; big steel; the big networks—CBS and NBC; the big airlines—TWA, Pan Am, and United. In key sectors, a handful of companies prevailed. The domestic extension of the military structure had won the war: massive organizations with strong hierarchies, strict lines of accountability, codes of conduct, and little tolerance for improvisation.

The war had been won, at a terrible cost, and America had been transformed. The nation was ready to produce a new generation, the baby boomers, and to leave the difficult days behind. And Americans were ready to put all they had learned during the war into building good and useful lives for themselves and their families, and a strong America for the seemingly limitless future.

OCT. 2, 1942

Congress passes the Stabilization Act, expanding the power of the Office of Price Administration to regulate agricultural prices.

OCT. 21, 1942

The Revenue Act of 1942 calls for a huge tax increase, including a 5 percent tax on all incomes over $624.

NOV. 1942

Nobuo Fujita became the only flying officer of the Imperial Japanese Navy to bomb mainland American soil, dropping bombs on Oregon forests intending to create a firestorm that would spread down the coast.

DEC. 1, 1942

Gasoline rationing begins nationwide. An "A" sticker receives the lowest allocation, four gallons a week. A "B" sticker receives a supplementary allowance. A "C" sticker signified essential driving and receives an additional allowance. Automobile traffic does decline, but train travel becomes more crowded and uncomfortable. Gasoline rationing also gives rise to a black market.

DEC. 31, 1942

Frank Sinatra appears at New York City's Paramount Theatre to huge audiences of shrieking teenage girls. "Not since the days of Rudolph Valentino," Time magazine noted, "has American womanhood made such unabashed love to an entertainer."

1943

Henry Kaiser makes ships by mass-production methods. Between 1941 and 1943 construction time for cargo ships is drastically reduced.

Dear Mr. Brokaw:

On Sunday, December 7th, 1941, my family left early in the morning for a picnic at our then isolated secret spot in Van Cortlandt Park in the Bronx. We had a wonderful day. I was a happy ten-year-old, enjoying a wonderful cold but sunny day, with parents, brothers, and uncles, aunts and cousins. It was complete with steaks over an open fire, roasted mickies and football. As day waned and darkened, we drove back home along strangely empty streets. I remember my father commenting on the lack of Sunday traffic. We stopped at Grandma and Grandpa's house, and from the moment we crossed the threshold, life as we knew it would never be the same.

"Quiet!" yelled Grandpa. He and Grandma were glued to the Philco. "The Japs bombed Pearl Harbor!" Somehow, even at ten, I knew the severity of that horrifying statement. Two uncles were already in the service, one whose number was picked in the 1940 draft lottery by President Roosevelt. He had finished jump school and was now an instructor at Fort Bragg. The second enlisted immediately after the first was drafted and was at Fort Leonard Wood in Missouri in some sort of special infantry training. Both were in the very first groups deployed overseas to the Pacific. Awesome decisions were made that night at Grandma and Grandpa's. Within a week eight of my family were off to war.

Thus began my truly life-shaping years. I followed every battle in every theater of the war. My room was lined with maps, on which I would record the very latest available movements by division or fleet. Every command was noted in my still childish hand, indicating specific leadership, command strength as I knew it from papers or radio. I even had the audacity to write to various generals and admirals when I thought that I had a worthy suggestion or two. Amazingly, a number of them wrote thoughtful letters back.

Each afternoon after school, everyone rushed for home, not for mitts, bats

Donal Brody at age ten, collecting scrap metal to donate to the war effort, New York City, fall 1943. (Courtesy of Donal Brody)

and balls as in the past but for wagons and sacks so we could scrounge the garbage cans and alleys for cans, bottles, tires, paper and anything else required for the war effort. In the spring it was kapok for life preservers.

Donal Brody (right) with his parents and his brother. (Courtesy of Donal Brody)

Every evening after schoolwork, it was time for V-mail, at least one or two every night, to our fighting relations now spread out all over the Pacific and Europe: Peleliu, Guadalcanal, Tinian, Sicily, Anzio, Normandy and other now familiar places. Everything was always "okay," which we much later found to be untrue as the wounds mounted. But, thank God, they all returned, much, much worse for wear, but the terribly sad Gold Star, [I say this] thankfully and with the utmost humility, never flew over any of our homes. Book upon book of saving stamps were accumulated until $18.75 was amassed in each and converted to a $25 war bond.

And finally it was over. The boys came home, and we kids greeted and watched them with awe and sometimes bewilderment. We had no real understanding of what they had gone through, so we really could not comprehend the actions of the local still-in-uniform hero, with a Distinguished Service Cross, two Silver Stars and three Purple Hearts on his breast, which now also displayed the Ruptured Duck, suddenly throwing himself prone on the street in front of an advancing trolley car and shooting at it with his cane. Fortunately, we knew enough not to make fun of this valiant man but to help him up as he lay crying in front of the now-stopped trolley. We wiped his uniform off and walked, very silently, home with him. We saw them stumble out of taverns drunk and we also saw them go back to work or to school, and we cherished and honored them all.

World War II taught us kids passion, zeal and total dedication to the cause. It taught us, in some small way, to be "men of the

AUG. 6, 1945

An atomic bomb is dropped on Hiroshima.

AUG. 9, 1945

An atomic bomb is dropped on Nagasaki.

AUG. 14, 1945

The War Manpower Commission lifts its controls.

Japan agrees to an unconditional surrender.

SEPT. 2, 1945

MacArthur receives the formal surrender of the Imperial Japanese government on the USS Missouri. *The war with Japan officially ends.*

house," to be more mature, to be more appreciative of our free country.

It was a terrible period of history, but what incredible lessons we learned, we the children of the war years.

Cordially,
Donal Brody

——— • ———

Dear Mr. Brokaw:

I was born in 1938. My father was not in the war but worked such long hours in the oil industry that we never saw him much. However, we were blessed with the knowledge that his life was not in jeopardy.

I still get chills up my spine when I hear a fire whistle go off in the middle of the night as I recall the air-raid warnings we experienced when our defenses were tested. My father was an air-raid warden on our street in a suburban Philadelphia community, and his responsibility was to check that all the lights were out on the street. While he was out doing this, my sister and I would huddle close to my mother in the basement while she tried to explain what was happening. She told us that this was just a test and that no harm would come to us. Then, we would pray for all the members of the armed services, President Roosevelt, and all the little children in Europe who were really experiencing bombs falling on them. Oddly enough, many years later, when I was a flight attendant on international flights, I spoke with my German- and British-born colleagues for whom I had prayed. Their stories were chilling. How lucky I was.

Sincerely yours,
Dana Boyle Hawa
(Mrs. Joseph S. Hawa)

War Bond stamp album purchased by Dana Boyle. (Courtesy Dana Boyle Hawa)

—— • ——

Dear Mr. Brokaw:

I was 10 years old when Pearl Harbor was bombed, and I remember very well my dad saying to me, "Honey, there's going to be a terrible war." How right he was. A couple of years later I was in the high school band, and I remember well marching downtown to play for "the boys" as they boarded a bus to go to Cleveland for physicals for the army.

My grandfather was the superintendent of schools in our town, and as these young men would come home on leave, they would often stop in to visit with him. One young soldier, not much more than 18 at the time, said he had come to say good-bye and added that he knew he would never come home alive. This prediction was sadly true.

Sincerely,
Nancy Cope

—— • ——

Dear Mr. Brokaw:

As the oldest of three children, conceived at the Alameda Navy Base and born on another Navy base in Memphis, I have felt a part of my parents' story right from the start. I was named after Maureen O'Hara, one of the most popular stars of the 1940s. Dinah Shore was my father's favorite singer, and he had a lifelong crush on her. My parents' favorite song was "Deep Purple," and they married on a whirlwind furlough in June 1943 on a hot summer day in Detroit, their hometown. They were high school sweethearts and lived two miles apart from each other. From a young age, I have pored over my parents' photo albums from that period, proud of my handsome father in his leather bomber jacket and his radioman earphones and of my beautiful mother in her platform heels and deep-red forties lipstick.

My father gave up his summers fighting fires in the national park system and interrupted his college education at Michigan State to enlist after the bombing of Pearl Harbor. He tried to join the Marines as an expression of his desire to fight, but a heart murmur kept him out, to his great disappointment. My grandfather wanted him to sign up for officers' school when he joined the Navy, but Dad wanted to be one of the "grunts." He was 20 years old. He asked my mother to marry him after he enlisted and wrote many letters of longing to her during the war, all of which she kept and shared with me recently.

My parents are still in Williamston and at the center of their children's world, even though we are busy professionals scattered over the country with lives of our own. When they celebrated their fiftieth wedding anniversary, in June 1993, we put their engagement picture, my dad in uniform, on mugs for us all. We played forties tunes and reminisced about a wedding so rushed no pictures were taken. They still have friends they had then. They don't speak about the war unless prompted, and my father remains tight-lipped about most of it. He feels nothing like a hero. He's just glad he made it out alive so that he could be with my mother and have the family he'd always wanted. He doesn't like war and the hoopla that goes with patriotism. He's a peace-loving man now, modest, gentle, and wise.

Sincerely yours,
Maureen Honey

Keith and Betty Honey, parents of Maureen Honey, in 1942. (Courtesy of Maureen Honey)

———————— • ————————

Dear Tom:

I was only 10–11 years old in 1941, and when a list of names appeared in our local paper requesting mail from the States to cheer up our boys overseas, I immediately took to the idea of corresponding with our boys and felt that I was doing my part for the war effort. What a rewarding experience it was. I took part in our school's program to fill boxes for our servicemen with the small necessities that they welcomed. My letters were filled with cheerful and humorous happenings about my family and our home plus cartoons cut from the newspaper. Anything to cheer them up. My responses were filled with "thank-yous" and prayers for me and my family. They were so grateful. A few were from the Boston area, and upon their return to the States on furloughs, two sailors visited me one day. They made the 30-mile trip to meet me to personally thank me for bringing a little brightness into their lives. I was so happy to meet these two boys. We hugged and cried together, and they were so handsome in their bell-bottomed pants. I instantly became a "swabbie" admirer. They thanked me over and over for making their mail call something to look forward to. When we finally said our good-byes, we were unaware that one of them would never return. You see, he was killed when his ship was torpedoed during his next tour of duty in Japan. I continued writing letters to the boys until the war ended in 1945.

When I was 16, I met my own GI. He was not engaged in active duty but was sent to Germany for the cleanup. We corresponded for the next 2 years, and upon his return (he came from my hometown) we got married. We raised 5 children, 11 grandchildren and 1 great-grandchild.

Sincerely,
Claire Ignacio

— • —

Dear Mr. Brokaw:

My dad, W. A. Loveless, was 41 when W.W. II started and was too old for the draft. He was named high school principal in Albany, Georgia, when the current principal, B. D. Lee, after training at Fort Benning, GA, was shipped to the island of New Guinea to fight the Japanese.

FAR LEFT: *Al Loveless, five years old, in his backyard in Albany, Georgia, wearing his miniature Air Corps officer's uniform.*

LEFT: *Al Loveless with one of his many model airplanes.*
(Both courtesy of Al Loveless)

During W.W. II the girls and boys of Dad's high school took me on scrap and paper drives and even to a dance, whose proceeds, after paying the band, went to war bonds. Many years later I was told the band at the dance was Tommy Dorsey's. I do remember a skinny singer with the band—could it have been Frankie Sinatra?

One day in 1944 I looked out the window of our house in Albany, Georgia, and saw a dust cloud, some distance away, coming down our street. Out of the dust materialized scores of men marching in formation and talking to each other in guttural voices. Years later I found that these were German prisoners who were picking peaches and doing other agricultural work in our community. These former members of Hitler's Afrika Korps and Wehrmacht were scattered all over the Southland in various camps.

Mother and Dad were very patriotic during the war years. Hardly a weekend went by without Mother's inviting young American and RAF pilots in training at Turner Field to our home for a home-cooked meal. To a man they took a fancy to a hero-worshiping little boy such as myself and gave me all kinds of military memorabilia.

Dad had to teach one biology class as well as perform his duties as principal, and during class time it seemed incredible to me as I sat in an honored seat in the front row, spellbound as he paraded hero after hero who had fought in the war and were home on furlough. There was Jack Stausell, who showed us the knife he used to kill a Japanese soldier who jumped into his foxhole. Then there was Zeke Bass, who flew the Hump in the Himalayas accompanied by a dachshund dog and armed only with a 45-cal. pistol.

Sincerely,
Al Loveless

———— • ————

Dear Mr. Tom Brokaw:

I was about 10 or 11 years old when World War 2 started. I'm a Mexican American born in Fort Morgan, Colorado, where there was a lot of discrimination, and yet my brother enlisted in the Air Force and went to war for a country that we love but where a lot of white people did not want us in the theaters or restaurants.

My brother was a sergeant, came back and got married and lived in Glendale, Ca. until 1970, when he died of cancer.

I guess I'm trying to tell you that not only white or black people went to that war or any other.

You don't know how hard it was to put all this down on paper. I wrote it and rewrote it because once down on paper it seemed so insignificant.

Sincerely,
Mary Ellen De La Torre

————— • —————

Dear Mr. Brokaw:

In the summer of 1942, I was thirteen years old and had just completed the 8th grade. All of the men were serving in the War, and the crops on the farms in New Jersey were rotting. Our school in Bloomfield, N.J., asked students to serve in the U.S. Crop Corps and help save the farms.

Four of us enrolled and were transported by bus to the Pine Barrens near Toms River, N.J. On my first day on the blueberry farm, I bent over and picked blueberries in the hot sun for eight hours. When I straightened up at the end of the day, I had huge blisters all over the back of my neck. The teacher supervising us said, "Oh, dear, I forgot to tell you to wear a big hat."

We lived in a hospital on one of the empty floors and ate our meals in the basement. Each morning an old truck would pick the students up, and we would pile into the back of the truck and sing raucous songs en route to the blueberry farm.

At the end of three weeks our tour of duty was over. I was paid $13.00 and received a Crop Corps certificate.

This was my first foray into the realities of the workaday world, and I will never forget it.

Sincerely,
Carol E. Isselian

————— • —————

Dear Mr. Brokaw:

My parents came to this country in the late 1920s from Mexico to escape the persecution of the Catholics. My sisters and I were born in Los Angeles, California. My mother and father loved this country because it gave them sanctuary and lived the rest of their lives as patriots and citizens.

War Ration Book No. 3.
(Courtesy of Zelpha Simmons)

When war was declared in 1941 my father went to enlist in the Merchant Marines, but, because he was 41 years of age at that time, he was told instead to go home and take care of his family. However, he was invited to work for the draft board and was later recognized for his effort.

Memories come flooding back of the public's participation in the war effort: rationing, collecting scrap metal, buying savings bonds, our neighbors working in the factories, my father planting a Victory Garden. Every morning in the Catholic school that I attended, we would begin the day by saluting the flag and praying for the safety of the young men and women who were so far away from home.

I remember the day President Roosevelt died; I came home from school and found my mother sobbing at the terrible news. He had been our strength and protector!

Brave and noble men and women live among us, and we should continue to honor them with respect.

Most sincerely,
Ms. Trinidad S. Jiménez

———— • ————

Dear Mr. Brokaw:

On December 7, 1941, I was three weeks away from turning thirteen, and my sister was almost nine years old. Of course, my family, community and state had been involved in prewar activities for some time—saving chewing gum wrappers made of tinfoil, collecting tin cans, baling wire, scrap metal, etc. Immediately after December 1941, our lives changed drastically; uncles (my dad's three brothers and two brothers-in-law and my mother's brother and two brothers-in-law), neighbors, teachers, and eventually high school classmates volunteered or were drafted into military service. Some served in places we had either never heard of or could only imagine where they were. We were given ration books to buy gasoline, groceries, and clothing items, when we could afford them.

My dad and mother ran a laundry, and we lived in the back of it. Before long, Dad couldn't find parts to repair the washing machines and had to close the laundry. We moved into a rented house, and he and Mother found work at other places. Mother clerked at a grocery store and moved into a job at the high school administration office. Dad worked as night watchman at Avenger Field.

My high school days were colored by war efforts and letters and packages to relatives and friends away from home, some for the first time and some who left behind wives and small children. My dad was 36 years old at the time, and, although he was required to register for the draft (I have his registration cards, sent to him periodically updating his status), he was at the edge of the draft age and was never called up. Once when he went for a physical, he was given a "flat-footed" qualification, something that would keep him from being a foot soldier. But he took his role very seriously being one of only a few males left at home and considered himself a custodian and peacekeeper among two large extended families. Mother's family all lived within ten miles of each other in Nolan County, but Dad's family were in Mitchell County, west of us. When gasoline and tires permitted, he usually managed to help out most of the households, tend to crops, work outside jobs, etc.

I am a product of the edge of your "Greatest Generation" and, again, thank you for recognizing the spirit and courage of so many great men and women.

Sincerely,
Myrna Saunders Qualls

———— • ————

Sugar ration coupon.
(Courtesy of Zelpha Simmons)

Dear Mr. Brokaw:

I grew up in North Oakland, near the Berkeley line.

San Francisco and Oakland were major embarkation points for the West Coast for men heading for the war in the Pacific. Thousands of servicemen roamed the streets of Oakland at night, particularly on weekends.

My folks had a big empty house, with us kids gone. (I joined the Navy in 1942 and was in until August 1946, mostly in the South Pacific.) They loved hosting the servicemen on weekends, and there were many "repeaters." Genuine friendships developed. Last year, in preparing to move to Pasadena, I found my mother's old guest book in which the men signed their names and hometowns. Many wrote words of appreciation for their hospitality. There were men from Army, Army Air Corps, Navy, Coast Guard, and Marine Corps. Some of the men were from big cities: Chicago, Boston, Baltimore. Others were from smaller towns and hamlets: Denison, Iowa; Walla Walla, WA; Brainerd, MN; Cambridge, NY; Caldwell, NJ; and Medford, MA. In all, men from 33 states signed that guest book. After the war, several of the men stopped by Oakland on their way home, to thank my folks for their kindness.

Cordially,
John A. Hammond

———— • ————

Dear Mr. Brokaw:

May I offer a wartime activity that I feel deserves your consideration. This is from my letter to our grandchildren:

Madeline Fenton in her USMC (WR) uniform, summer 1944, Washington, D.C. (Courtesy of Madeline Thomas)

An example of the way people worked to encourage the servicemen and women was at North Platte, Nebraska, which was on the main rail line between the East and West Coast, and a fueling station for the trains. In 1942 the housewives at North Platte, Nebraska, had heard that the troops comprising the Nebraska National Guard were coming through, so they got busy and baked cakes and pies and cookies and fixed coffee and tea for the troops aboard the train. As it turned out, it was the Kansas National Guard, but the ladies fed them, regardless. Thus began a tradition that lasted until the war ended in 1945 and the trains no longer carried the troops. Every troop train was met by ladies with all kinds of goodies. Word spread, and ladies from towns all over Nebraska, Kansas, Colorado and Wyoming took their turns bringing cookies, tubs of fried chicken, birthday cakes, etc. During pheasant season, they brought fried pheasants. Another fueling station for the trains was at Dennison, Ohio, and the same hospitality prevailed.

I am a native of Nebraska and served in the Women's Marine Corps during World War II.

Sincerely,
Madeline Fenton Thomas

THE WHITE HOUSE
WASHINGTON

TO MEMBERS OF THE UNITED STATES ARMY EXPEDITIONARY
FORCES:

You are a soldier of the United States Army.

You have embarked for distant places where
the war is being fought.

Upon the outcome depends the freedom of your
lives: the freedom of the lives of those you love—
your fellow-citizens—your people.

Never were the enemies of freedom more
tyrannical, more arrogant, more brutal.

Yours is a God-fearing, proud, courageous
people, which, throughout its history, has put its
freedom under God before all other purposes.

We who stay at home have our duties to
perform—duties owed in many parts to you. You will
be supported by the whole force and power of this
Nation. The victory you win will be a victory of all
the people—common to them all.

You bear with you the hope, the confidence,
the gratitude and the prayers of your family, your
fellow-citizens, and your President—

Franklin D Roosevelt

"You will be supported by the whole force and power of this Nation": Letter from FDR issued to all soldiers on their way to Europe, November 1944.
(Courtesy of Dolores Leathers)

Pvt. Delmer Leathers Wounded In Action

Mrs. Delmer E. Leathers received a telegram from the War Department informing her that her husband, Pvt. Delmer E. Leathers, had been slightly wounded in action on December 3 in Germany. She also received a letter from her husband dated December 5 in which he stated he was somewhere in Belgium in a hospital with a slight shoulder wound from shrapnel. He said he is getting along fine.

Pvt. Leathers entered the army on March 1, 1944 and took his basic training at Camp Blanding, Fla. After a 10-day furlough with his family in September he went to his port of embarkation. He was sent to England, then to France, Belgium and in November into Germany.

Pvt. Leathers reports that his outfit is called the "Double Dueces" one of the fightingest in his area. They have received one presidential citation and another is on the way, Leathers writes.

Newspaper article about Delmar Leathers being wounded in action.
(Courtesy of the Daily News, Boonville, Missouri)

WESTERN UNION

CLASS OF SERVICE

This is a full-rate Telegram or Cablegram unless its deferred character is indicated by a suitable symbol above or preceding the address.

1201

A. N. WILLIAMS
PRESIDENT

(40)

SYMBOLS

DL=Day Letter
NL=Night Letter
LC=Deferred Cable
NLT=Cable Night Letter
Ship Radiogram

The filing time shown in the date line on telegrams and day letters is STANDARD TIME at point of origin. Time of receipt is STANDARD TIME at point of destination

KBB2 FT=CAMPEDWARDS MASS FEB 24   1945 FEB 26 AM 8 43

MRS DELMER E LEATHERS=
        600 SIXTH ST

ITS A LONG STRETCH FROM NO MANS LAND BACK TO YOU BUT I MADE
IT. WELL AND SAFE. SEE YOU SOON. LOVE=
        PVT DELMER E LEATHERS.

"I made it": Telegram from Delmar Leathers to his wife, Dolores, upon his return to the United States in February 1945.
(Courtesy of Dolores Leathers)

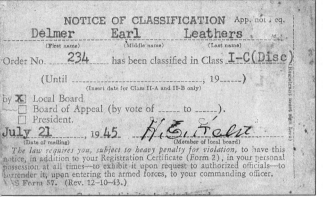

Classification card issued to Delmar Leathers on July 21, 1945.

Delmar Leathers (front row, right) in basic training, Camp Blanding, Florida, 1944. (Both courtesy of Dolores Leathers)

Dear Sir:

My husband was drafted in 1944. We had been married in 1937, and by the time he had to go, we had 4 children and a baby on the way. He took his training in Florida to be sent to the South Pacific. Last-minute orders [came,] and he was sent to Europe. They arrived in England in late October with summer uniforms. They were outfitted with winter outfits and sent across to France, and on to where the 1st Army 4th Division was fighting, into the Hurtegen Forest area—mud, snow and shelling all the time.

I had been writing every day, and while he was in the States he did too. Then his letters became farther and farther apart, until finally three weeks went by and I did not hear from him. I was very worried but had to keep up a front for the children. They sensed something was wrong. And then, just before Christmas of that year, a telegram [arrived] telling me he had been wounded and was in a hospital in England with frozen feet and a shoulder wound. It was Feb. of 1945 before he was shipped back to the States. The whole time he was in hospitals they kept talking of taking his feet off due to the frozen condition. But he kept refusing. He came home with his feet intact but suffered the rest of his life in cold weather.

When he came home in July of 1945, we took up our lives and routines. While he was gone I grew up in more ways than one. He had left a 23-year-old girl really and came home to a 25-year-old woman who had to make decisions on her own for the first time in her life, keep things going while he was away and raise five children, take care of an invalid mother and, on the small allotment from the army and my mother's S.S.I. check, feed and clothe seven people and deal with rationing, shortages and the worry of not knowing what was happening to him. But my being raised a child in the Depression years came into good play as I had learned very early in life that money did not grow on trees, so to speak. By the time he came home I had paid off the bills we owed and saved $1,000.00.

When my husband came home he was amazed I had done so well. Needless to say, I was too.

Oh we had adjustments to make, as all did at that time. We had 56 years of marriage before he passed away in 1993.

All during the time he was gone I remember listening to the radio news programs and reading any account I could lay my hands on that mentioned the 1st Army 4th Division, which was his outfit. I used maps published in *Life* magazine to follow the reports.

I was only one of many women who, though not in uniform, also served.

Sincerely,
Dolores Leathers

———•———

Delmar and Dolores Leathers in October 1944, before he was shipped to Europe.

Delmar Leathers upon his return to the United States on medical leave, 1945. (Both courtesy of Dolores Leathers)

Dear Tom Brokaw:

I was born in 1921, married in 1939, my husband left in 1943, landed in the Philippines finally, as a Seabee. Our daughter was 3 when he left, 6 when he came back. He went into the plumbing and heating business, we had 3 more children, lost the youngest at age 32 to cancer. One thing we truly learned was how to work and taught our children the same.

I was a billing clerk in a shoe factory when my husband left for the service. So many boys had to leave that the office was sent back to the mother plant, and we were asked to take men's jobs. I learned

Howard Rump, on leave from boot camp, and his wife, Dorothy, at home in Lebanon, Pennsylvania, with their daughter Darlene, 1943. (Courtesy of Dorothy Rump)

Dorothy and Earl Rump's daughter Darlene, in front of
the family's 1942 Packard.
(Courtesy of Dorothy Rump)

to trim uppers before the welt sewers got them; it was a dangerous job with 2 round cutting wheels, but I was lucky and had no mishaps.

We are in our 60th year of marriage, my husband 81 and I, 78. We lived in an era like no other and proud of it!

Sincerely,
Mrs. Dorothy A. Rump

———— • ————

Dear Tom:

Both in the service and on the home front there was a light side that at times momentarily relieved the worries and stress of that era. With a fiancé and a brother in the Air Force in Europe, and another brother in the Pacific (who received the Bronze Star) to worry about, I wanted to support the war effort.

At 5'1" and 90 pounds, the military didn't want me. I was attending college in Beaumont, Texas, and went to work for the Maritime Commission at Pennsylvania Shipyards. In addition to a number of civilian departments, the Navy and Coast Guard maintained offices there. I worked in public relations and was assistant editor of a bimonthly publication, *PennShip Log.* The entire shipyard was my news beat.

The superb paint department personnel turned out expert camouflage work on the ships. I knew where they were clustered in a river basin, yet when I went home by train on weekends to Louisiana, I would look out the window and saw no ships.

One day the superintendent of the paint department, visiting with my boss in the adjacent office, overheard my lament to a friend that my sister had made (on my landlady's sewing machine) my lovely formal gown to wear to the annual ball at Hotel Dieu Hospital, where she was in nurse's training, and my old white sandals looked scuffed. I didn't want to spend a precious ration coupon for a frivolous pair of shoes. As he came by my desk, the superintendent told me to "bring those sandals to work tomorrow and someone will pick them up." Two days later they were returned to me— beautiful silver sandals with sparkles on the high heels! I felt like Cinderella at the ball.

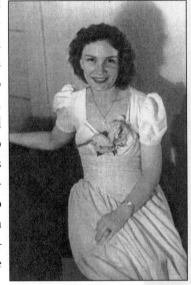

Hazel Parks in Beaumont, Texas, 1944. (Courtesy of Hazel Parks)

The Louisiana Maneuvers—the largest ever peacetime military exercises—was staged the summer of 1941. The South Dakota 109th Engineers, C Bn., from Camp Claiborne was the first wave of military forces to occupy my hometown. I met my future husband, Jack Parks, who was from Rapid City.

In early 1942 Jack shipped out to the ETO, where the 109th went from Northern Ireland to North Africa and on to Italy. Following his separation from the service after V-E Day, we were married August 31, 1945. Our son, Donald, born July 3, 1947, carried on the family tradition of responding to the military call to duty. He served three tours of duty in Vietnam and made the Army a career.

Best wishes,
Hazel R. Parks

———— • ————

Dear Mr. Brokaw:

I thought you might be interested in this excerpt from my memoirs of World War II:

I was 19 years old when the United States went to war. Within a short time I was working as a Red Cross nurse's aide, and I served as a hostess at the Servicemen's Center in Lawrence, Massachusetts, my hometown. On February 28, 1942, while still a civilian, I went to work in Washington, D.C., where I joined my older sister, who already was working in the House of Representatives. I worked in the Disbursement Department of the Army Signal Corps. About six months after I went to Washington, my younger brother joined the Navy, where he took part in three invasions and had three battle stars. On the home front my mother joined the Massachusetts Women's Defense Corps and with neighbors tended a Victory Garden. Both my parents helped sell war bonds with local dignitaries and patriotic movie stars, among them Dorothy Lamour and James Stewart, who visited Lawrence while traveling across the country on bond tours. My parents also helped to entertain troops that were stationed nearby.

Mary O'Hearn while working as a Red Cross nurse's aide, 1942.

When my sister and I went back home for visits, we saw changes: sugar and gas rationing, oleomargarine replacing butter, blackout curtains, automobile head-lights painted in half-moons with the residue of melted-down 78 rpm records, neighborhood air-raid wardens, a scarcity of beef and recycling, and we heard of plane spotters on Lawrence's highest buildings. I re-member a new mother in the neighborhood whose anx-iety was relieved when my mother produced a bottle of Karo syrup for her infant's formula. The young mother had exhausted all avenues trying to find the scarce and precious commodity. Now we knew why a family in the neighborhood had, since before 1939, quietly been giving shelter to refugees from Germany.

The most noticeable change was undefinable. The neighbor-hood was very quiet, a palpable, uneasy stillness caused by the ab-sence of young men and the anxiety of their parents. All the young men we had grown up with and whom we loved and cherished as childhood companions had gone to war. And when the dreaded and terrible news was brought to a family that a dear son would never return home, as happened in our neighborhood, neighbors were the strength and constant source of comfort for the sorrowing and dis-believing family.

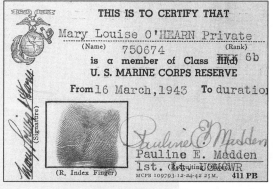

Marine Corps Reserve I.D. card issued to Mary O'Hearn on March 16, 1943. (Both courtesy of Mary O'Hearn Armitage)

Although wartime Washington was exciting, my sister and I had the feeling that there was more that we could do. By August of 1942 we were talking of join-ing a women's reserve branch of one of the services, and on March 17, 1943, we enlisted in the newly formed Marine Corps (WR), "to release a man for ac-

A victory garden in Lawrence, Massachusetts, being tended by Louise and John O'Hearn (extreme left and second from the right) and their neighbors Myrtle and Bill Malloy, July 1942.

John O'Hearn and his two daughters, Sergeant Mary O'Hearn, USMC (WR) (left), and First Lieutenant Margaret O'Hearn, USMC (WR) (right), on their first leave, May 1944.

Mary (center) and Margaret (left) O'Hearn being sworn into the USMC Women's Reserve by First Lieutenant Pauline Madden, March 16, 1943.

Mary O'Hearn in USMC (WR) rain gear, 1944. (All courtesy of Mary O'Hearn Armitage)

tive duty." Our parents approved of our decision without reservation and actually encouraged us to join. My father had been in the Navy in WWI, had worked with yeomanettes and had a positive attitude toward women in the service. They had to sign for me; I was not yet 21 years old. A bit of a fuss was made over us because we were the first sisters from our area to enlist together.

Mary O'Hearn in uniform while attending storekeeper's school at Indiana University, immediately after boot camp, summer 1943. (Courtesy of Mary O'Hearn Armitage)

We left home in May of 1943; my sister to Officers Candidate School at Mount Holyoke College in South Hadley, Massachusetts; she had her degree. I went to enlisted men's boot camp at Hunter College in New York; I had left college. In later years being a Hunter College Boot became a mark of distinction.

In September of 1943 I arrived at the Cherry Point, North Carolina, Marine Air Station. It was there that I had my first real taste of military life. This place was dry and ugly, not hostile, but certainly not welcoming. It had a look of raw-boned efficiency that intimidated me. We were billeted in wooden barracks, double bunks and about 88 women to a section. By now I could do calisthenics just like everyone else. We exercised at dawn in sleepy formation. I had never been up this early in my life, and I was impressed by what I had missed. Though the days were parched, there was beauty in the moist and scent-filled beginning of each new day. For this prebreakfast torture we had to get out of bed, dress in fatigues and fall into formation. Hair rollers were hidden under hats, pajamas under outer clothing. I lost my slippers during a sloppy execution of "To the rear march!" and never found them again. At this stage of my military career I became a chow hound: I always had breakfast. The scene was right out of Bill Mauldin: a new day before sunup, a mess hall that merged with the bleak background and outlined against it the sloped figures of fatigue-clad men wreathed in cigarette smoke. No conversation, just a time for slow thoughts, cogitation and anticipation of good, black coffee.

Mary O'Hearn Armitage, MC(WR) 750674

Dear Tom:

Carl and I were married on November 3, 1940. It was 3 years before he went to the service. Prior to this he was a farmer, and he went to school to be an airplane mechanic in St. Louis, at Lambert Field. I went to work in the airplane plant, the plant on Goodfello St. in St. Louis.

I drilled holes for the rivets to be put in and was also a riveter until Carl went into the Army Air Corps. [Then] he moved me back home to Carrier Mills, Illinois, 35 miles east of Carbondale, Illinois.

He served in England and did his 25 missions.

It was a long lonely time for me. I was very lonely but tried to make the best of it.

It was a sight and a pitiful one as most of the young men went to the service. A lot of them went to the Pacific (theater). In fact the only ones left farmed or worked in the coal mines. There were hardly any men left in this little town.

The women, wives of the men, would gather early to wait for the mail to be put up at the little post office. Oh how we wished for a letter but were disappointed most of the time.

I wrote my husband every day while he was away. He didn't get most of my letters, and when I heard from him he always asked me why I hadn't written.

I would go to the show or movie once a week to see and hear the Hearst Metrotone News that they showed. Then I would walk to our apt. I didn't stay to see the movie, for I was afraid to be out alone at night.

Carl made his missions over Germany, had a lot of holes in their plane every mission but one.

I said many a prayer for him and all the people who were in the war. Thank God my prayers were answered for him and his 3 brothers.

Carl and Esther Barger, November 1943, near St. Louis, Missouri.
(Courtesy of Esther Barger)

Carl and Esther Barger, October 2000, in a photo taken for their sixtieth wedding anniversary.
(Courtesy of Olan Mills)

*Carl Barger (front row, extreme right) with his flight crew in front of
a training plane in Ardmore, Oklahoma, 1944.
(Courtesy of Esther Barger)*

They all came back, none of them injured. It was a miracle, I
believe. Those were troubling weeks and months for all of us.

Thank you so much,
Carl & Esther Barger

———— • ————

Dear Tom:

As a teenager I would listen to my little radio after going to bed
and hear the commentators tell us about Hitler's march through
Poland and other countries and lie there and wonder if the world
was coming to an end soon. I was working at my first job in Dallas
at age 21 on that "day that will live in infamy." I rolled bandages, attended nurses' aide classes, knitted for Bundles for Britain and
later for our own boys, was a USO Victory Belle, attended war
bond rallies on the streets at lunch hour and dated flyboys stationed at nearby airfields. We listened to their stories of learning to
fly and cried with them sometimes—never about going overseas
but because they had "washed out" of flying school. Sometimes
they would become glider pilots. It was an exciting but sad and bittersweet time.

I met my future husband, Jake, who was a sailor on leave visiting his family and introduced by a mutual friend. He had been in

Nurse's aide Frances Fulmer Hamrick in uniform for making surgical dressings for the Red Cross, 1943.

Jake and Frances Hamrick sight-seeing, January 1945.

Jake Hamrick (second from the left) and three buddies outside their Quonset hut in Londonderry, Ireland, 1943.

U.S. NAVAL PERSONNEL SEPARATION CENTER
NORMAN, OKLAHOMA

He's coming home!

This is the news you have been eagerly awaiting to hear. Your husband is being separated from the United States Navy this week after months of honorable service to his country.

This week has been crammed full of interviews and lectures in which we have explained his rights and benefits as a veteran, and have suggested a few things to prepare him to resume his place in the community.

My earnest prayer and hope is that his return to civilian life will be happy and that he will be successful in all his undertakings.

Very Truly yours,

Elbert Cole
Chaplain, USNR.

"My earnest hope is that his return to civilian life will be happy": A form letter from the U.S. Naval Personnel Separation Center in Norman, Oklahoma, informing Frances that Jake was going to be discharged. (All courtesy of Frances Hamrick)

Ireland a couple of years working on telephone systems for LSTs, which he would not learn until later were being readied for the invasion of Europe. He was back in the States for further training before reassignment. I took a week's vacation from my job to go by Greyhound bus to Washington, D.C., to be married as he was stationed there. Therein lies a tale often told—when my week was up, I started my trip back to Dallas on the bus. It was January and snowing, and somewhere in the hills of West Virginia, we could go no further and spent the night at a service station–restaurant. During the long night, I got to thinking I might not see Jake again and I didn't want to leave him now. As we boarded the bus the next morning, I asked the driver if he would flag down the first bus we passed going back to Washington, that I wanted to go back. He did, and as he put me on it he told the driver, "Here is a lovesick war bride wanting to go back to her husband." I arrived in D.C. with $10.00 in my purse, having spent all we both had during the week. I rode the streetcar back to our friend's apartment and got in touch with a very surprised husband. That time I stayed until he went to Philadelphia for the commissioning of his new ship, the USS *Little Rock* (a light cruiser), which would head for the Pacific after the shakedown cruise.

We've raised 2 beautiful girls, but I learned about boys because we have 4 grandsons. The younger generation should read your book—not because we are a great generation but because of the quiet courage and sacrifices so many thousands of young people made, which have brought them whatever security is in the world today.

Most sincerely,
Frances Hamrick

——— • ———

Dear Mr. Brokaw:

To honor the men and women who daily risked their lives, often in deplorable conditions, is most appropriate. Also in line for praise are the members of my generation who fought World War II stateside. They, too, own the glories, the griefs and the heartaches of that era.

Many men tried to enlist in the armed forces but were kept in this country because their work made them vital to the national effort. I worked as a research chemist in the laboratories at the National Cash Register Co. in Dayton, Ohio. Several of my colleagues were in this position. It was hard to handle because of certain resentments of men not in uniform.

Others who were in uniform were kept here on various bases because their skills were especially suited to certain assignments in the States. I am now married to my second husband, whose orders for overseas duty were three times canceled by the Seventh Service Command Headquarters, Omaha, Neb. because he was a master sergeant in charge of a classification interviewing section, Signal Corps/Medical Corps Replacement Center, Camp Crowder, MO.

For hundreds of thousands of people, young and old, life was on hold. We dealt with long working hours, shift changes, fuel, food and clothing shortages, now vaguely remembered. We learned delayed satisfaction to a degree not imagined by the next generations.

I do not mean to diminish the men and women who daily risked their lives in combat but feel that it should be noted that it took a large national effort and a change in lifestyle to sustain our fighting forces abroad.

Sincerely,
Jane M. Branston

———— • ————

Dear Mr. Brokaw:

We were in Times Square on V-J Day, and I always claim that as the most exciting day of my life. When I would see aerial pictures of the crowd, I knew I could find my sister, cousin, three sailors from Floyd Bennett Field and me if only I could get a still blown up. We were right in front of the Coca-Cola sign, Felix the Cat was over my left shoulder, Bond Clothes and the smoke-ring-blowing Camel ad on our right.

I've always said 1925 was the best year to be born. I was too young to marry but old enough to date.

Kindest regards,
Joyce Merrifield Steele

Joyce Merrifield and Bill May, 1944.
(Courtesy of Joyce Merrifield Steele)

Esther and Stanley Lewin in Paris, 1993.
(Courtesy of Stanley Lewin)

Dear Tom:

In January 1943 the Navy accepted me into the V-12 program, under which I was called to active duty in July 1943. After a year we were sent on to midshipman training and commission as ensigns in the USNR. There I was at age nineteen, going on twenty, and on the way to the Pacific Theater for duty aboard the submarine USS *Euryale* (AS-22). Having gotten into the Pacific as Europe wound down and the A-bomb development was reaching its culmination, and delivery not long thereafter, we were spared the need to participate in the invasion of Japan, for which we were loading at Subbase Pearl. We were sent to Japan in September 1945. Sasebo first, then Kure.

I returned home to Detroit and after a period of adjusting to the changes required was told by Wayne [State] University that the credits I earned at Central Mich and Supply Corps School as a midshipman qualified me for my bachelor's degree. On to graduate school at Wayne while working part-time at the university as a veterans' counselor dealing with the G.I. Bill influx.

Indirectly, the veterans' organization AVC was the path to meeting my wife to be. During the third week of May each year, it is traditional for Detroit area veterans' organizations to sell poppies as a remembrance motif and a fund-raiser to further veterans' programs. One evening while doing that in May 1947, I found myself in competition with two women selling poppies for a JWV (Jewish War Veterans) auxiliary. As we talked, I learned that both women had lost their husbands during the battles of WWII. Later, over coffee at Lou's River Deli, I obtained the phone number of one of the women and managed to wrangle a Friday night movie date. We've been dating since that poppy time 52 years ago—and married for going on 51 years (June 20).

My wife, Esther B. Lewin, was married in 1940 to Leonard L. Lewis, a Detroiter who was a journalist and reporter. He was working for the *Pontiac Press* when he volunteered in 1942 for the U.S. Navy. He was commissioned as a landing officer and assigned to

LEFT: *Stanley Lewin on leave in Detroit before departing for naval duty in the Pacific.* RIGHT: *Esther Lewin at the grave of her first husband, Ensign Leonard Lewis, Normandy, 1993.*
(Both courtesy of Stanley Lewin)

duty in Chicago, and then in October 1943 he was assigned to an LST and sent to England in preparation for the invasion of Europe. Esther and Leonard had been blessed with the birth of their first child in August 1943; Linda, their daughter, was 3 months old when her father was sent to England. Lt. (jg) Leonard L. Lewis was killed at Omaha Beach sometime between June 6, 1944, and June 8, 1944, as he was serving in the capacity of landing officer for his LST.

Esther was among some 23,000 U.S. widows or family members who were asked in 1948–49 whether their loved ones would be reburied at Colleville-sur-Mer or returned to the U.S. for burial. The decision was a difficult one, but her choice was the American military cemetery overlooking Omaha Beach. Although it took many years, eventually we had the opportunity to visit Europe, France and Normandy. After seeing the grave and the marble Star of David marking, it was definitely her feeling that the choice was the right one.

Sincerely,
Stanley Lewin

ABOVE: *People crowded Times Square in New York City on May 8, 1945,
as the V-E Day celebration continued into the night.*
(AP/Wide World Photos)
RIGHT: *World War II veterans from various branches of the armed services
salute a passing American flag during a V-E Day Parade on Saturday,
May 6, 1995, in Kansas City, Missouri.*
(AP/Wide World Photos)

Part Five

·

REFLECTIONS

WHEN JAPAN SURRENDERED IN AUGUST 1945, FOLLOWING THE surrender of Germany three months earlier, America was reborn. It had survived a decade of economic calamity followed immediately by almost four full years of world war. The cost was staggering and tragic: 292,131 Americans, most of them young, were killed. Thousands more returned home damaged either physically or emotionally.

But there was no time for grief or mourning. America was engulfed by a surge of relief that the hard times were over, followed immediately by a wave of determination to get on with the good times. After all, the United States had emerged from the war intact; it had lost far too many citizens on distant battlefields, but its government, economy, culture, and physical infrastructure were whole. Indeed, the war years had made the United States a full-blown colossus in the world economic and political arena. Moreover, it had a population of eager young citizens tempered by depression and war, impatient to reap the rewards of good jobs, families, and communities.

Before the war had ended Congress passed the Servicemen's Readjustment Act of 1944, better known as the G.I. Bill of Rights, one of the most important legislative acts in American history. It promised returning veterans a year of unemployment insurance when the war was over, economic assistance for education, and low-interest home loans. In a way not even the most visionary member of Congress could have imagined, the education aid transformed America as millions of veterans who had never dreamed of college returned from the war and rushed off to campuses across the country. They jammed into temporary housing and stood in the aisles of crowded classrooms in undergraduate and graduate institutions alike. Former President George Bush, a son of wealth and privilege, recalls that when he returned from the Navy to attend Yale, he and his wife, Barbara, shared a kitchen in a small apartment with two other couples.

By 1950, when I was ten, America had a new generation of teachers, businessmen, lawyers, and doctors on the job and moving into the new pattern of life developing in the suburbs, where schools and shopping malls joined the homes that were sprouting, like freshly planted gardens, from cleared tracts of land.

This is the time in America that I and other members of my

generation experienced most directly and remember best, the time when the war was over and people wanted to get on with their lives, and did not talk about the war much, or at all.

In addition to providing assistance with education and housing, the G.I. Bill also aided those who wanted to develop a craft or trade, and the building boom generated a voracious appetite for workers trained in refrigeration and air-conditioning, for electricians, mechanics, and plumbers.

It was a golden time for the American worker that reached well beyond the prewar centers of manufacturing and industry, such as Pittsburgh, Detroit, Cleveland, Toledo, and Buffalo. The Sun Belt states—California, Arizona, Texas, Florida—with their felicitous combination of space, agreeable climate, and economic opportunity, were especially popular destinations. My uncle Richard, who was in the Coast Guard during the war, did not go back to the high plains of South Dakota when peace came. He settled in Long Beach, California, which always seemed a little exotic to those of us who remained in the Midwest. Now, more than a half century later, my mother has retired to California, my youngest brother lives there, and, since two of our children were born there during my early days with NBC in Los Angeles, the Golden State will always be part of the Brokaw geography.

When the war was over, my father, a skilled operator of heavy construction equipment, was tempted by the stories of good jobs and high wages in Texas, but my mother wisely reminded him that with three boys, all under the age of seven, it was better to play it safe. She was thinking long-term, and the postwar boom in public works projects was an ideal solution for our family's economy. The mighty Missouri River meandered through South Dakota, regularly flooding farmland and generally going unharnessed. Congress authorized a massive flood control and hydroelectric project that meant four enormous new dams on the Missouri. One was to be constructed on a wild stretch of the river in the middle of the Yankton Sioux reservation, near an old cavalry post called Fort Randall.

My father went to work for the U.S. Army Corps of Engineers, the federal government's muscular construction firm, which in those preregulation days was largely unchecked by environmental restrictions or organized opposition. The Corps had deep pockets and big ambitions, so when it was assigned a project the dirt flew, concrete poured, and the landscape was transformed in short order. We moved to a town that had been efficiently assembled on a river bluff overlooking the Missouri. Living there was a working-class dream, especially for children of the Depression. The temporary homes were small but comfortable; all the streets were paved and they led to a new, modern school, a complete shopping mall, an interdenominational chapel, a hospital, and a large movie theater. One end of the community was reserved for a larger trailer park that housed the families who came from across America to get in on the good wages and steady work the winning contractors were providing.

Construction on the dam went on seven days a week, twenty-four hours a day, for six years, and it was a cornucopia of prosperity for the workers. They were able to buy their first new automobiles, expand their wardrobes, save for college educations for their children, and look beyond their last paychecks to a more stable future. It was a time and a place bursting with the promise of just rewards for hard work.

While I treasure memories of growing up in such a Huck Finn setting, I realize that life there was insulated from many of the changes sweeping across postwar America. Apart from a few Sioux Indian friends, I lived in an all-white culture where everyone had a job and seldom was heard a discouraging word about the virtues of the United States, past and present. The American Legion was a major presence in our lives, a sponsor of Boy Scout troops, baseball programs, and an annual good citizenship award, which I won as an eighth grader. There was an emphasis on patriotism in daily life and in the public schools. We said the Pledge of Allegiance every morning in class and absorbed lessons in American history that were emphatically triumphant. Everyone was expected to be a productive, churchgoing citizen, and those who strayed from the norm were remarked upon in unkindly terms.

Even though we were settled in the middle of a Sioux reservation, we were embarrassingly ill informed about the Sioux culture or the federal government's abuses of the local tribe's rights. Moreover, since we were in a location too remote to receive a television signal and a good daily newspaper, we were disconnected from the passions generated by McCarthyism and the rising tide of resistance to racial segregation. The landmark U.S. Supreme Court decision *Brown* v. *Board of Education of Topeka*, declaring that racially segregated schools were unconstitutional, had no direct bearing on our white-bread lives. Nonetheless, it was shocking to hear the derisive comments about Negroes from families moving in from the South.

Many of the heroes my father admired and held up to me— Jackie Robinson, Jesse Owens, Joe Louis, and Bill "Bojangles" Robinson—happened to be black. Moreover, my father's own humble, earn-your-way life had made him intuitively sensitive to the plight of the disenfranchised. So the word *nigger* was an obscenity that I regularly protested. Once I got into such a heated argument with the mother of a friend that she threatened to stop the car and make me walk home. I was just twelve.

Still, the big events of the postwar world seemed light-years away. Korea was a war we saw in brief flashes on the newsreels before the main feature at the local movie theater. When Harry Truman fired General Douglas MacArthur for insubordination, I remember that even in our quasi-military community there was a general feeling the president was right. Truman was a family favorite, so this act was for me a memorable first lesson in political courage.

When work on the Fort Randall Dam was completed, we moved downstream to Yankton, South Dakota, and another Corps of Engineers project, Gavins Point Dam. It was my first full-blown civilian community, since we had lived mostly on an Army base or in that temporary town with Army-base overtones. With that move, the war receded evermore from our thoughts. We were able to get television signals for the first time, and there were two local radio stations, where I would find work as a teenager and college student. My parents bought their first home, for $11,500, and for our compact living room they purchased a Zenith black-and-white television set, which provided a picture of life beyond our rural surroundings.

The prime-time entertainment programs for the most part showed an America that was an all-white patriarchy. *Father Knows Best, The Adventures of Ozzie & Harriet,* even *Gunsmoke* were simple morality tales in settings devoid of poverty, real anger, people of color, or much in the way of references to the war we had recently lived through. Our community was organized around a *Saturday Evening Post* version of Main Street, where local retailers, doctors, bankers, and car dealers, all men, met in morning coffee groups to argue politics, discuss business, gossip, and informally determine the division of power within the town. During my high school era most of these men were World War II veterans, although that part of their lives was seldom part of their public résumés, and we never heard them talk about it. They were better known for their political or religious affiliations—Catholic or Protestant was a major dividing line in small-town America in the 1950s.

Dwight Eisenhower was in the White House, and a young, ambitious Californian, Richard Nixon, was his vice president. Ike, the Kansas farm boy, was a comforting presence, extending his World War II role as commander and father figure. But news programs also brought stories of a young Negro minister named Martin Luther King, Jr., who was organizing boycotts in Montgomery, Alabama, and of a blustery new boss of the Soviet Union, Nikita Khrushchev, who proclaimed, "Whether you like it or not, history is on our side. We will bury you." In school we were regularly reminded that in the event of a nuclear attack we should shield our eyes and take cover beneath our desks. Although there were no bomb shelters that I was aware of in Yankton, there were designated civil defense shelters in public buildings.

In 1956 a new book caused a considerable stir. *The Organization Man,* by an editor at *Fortune,* William Hollingsworth Whyte, Jr., was an insightful and provocative critique of the conventions of General Motors, General Electric, IBM, Procter & Gamble, Rotary Clubs, and the Chamber of Commerce, where individualism was suppressed in the interests of belonging and mass marketing. In my crew cut, button-down shirts, and chinos, I was a working-class wanna-be for that culture because it seemed to be the promised land of social and financial security, the two great goals of Depression-era parents for their children. I remember an advertisement for a three-button suit, what we called, even on the prairie, an Ivy League model. The copy said, "For the young man who wants to make $10,000 a year by the time he's 30." My father at the time was making $5,200 a year, supporting a family of five and saving money. My mother worked to provide extras for my brothers and me, so the idea of $10,000 annually by thirty!—it was a dizzying sum and, I thought, probably unrealistic.

Then fault lines began to develop across the orderly American landscape. A young man born in a small town in Mississippi gave voice to a new form of music, rock and roll. When Elvis Presley came into our living room via that Zenith television set, he won my heart and appalled my parents. About the same time James Dean appeared on the movie screens of America in *Rebel Without a Cause,* forcing those of us in crew cuts and letter jackets to reconsider the usual trappings of big men on campus.

The postwar era of regimentation was giving way to a time of youthful rebellion and other challenges to the traditional rules of business, politics, and culture. When John F. Kennedy, dashing scion of a fabulously wealthy Irish American family and a World War II hero, did an end run around party bosses for the Democrats' presidential nomination in 1960, he transformed modern politics. His narrow win over Vice President Nixon was due in part to his superior command of the most powerful new tool in the public arena, television. Chet Huntley and David Brinkley on NBC and Walter Cronkite on CBS, trusted guides in their nightly appearances in our living rooms, showed us a world most Americans had never seen close up before: political primaries, conventions, and general campaigns, including the first television debate between presidential candidates.

When John Kennedy said in his inaugural address that "the torch has been passed to a new generation," he was speaking of the young men and women who had survived World War II. But he also seemed to be speaking to my generation, signaling that we no longer had to play just by the rules of our elders; we could find our own way through life and career.

It was a heady time, and it was coming directly to me on that black-and-white television screen. I had my nose pressed against that screen, fascinated and inspired by what I was seeing, thinking that maybe I, too, could become one of those dashing network correspondents and ride the winds of change that seemed to be sweeping the world. The Soviet Union and the United States were in a race into space, and I took it as a personal responsibility to our team to be in front of a television set when one of our astronauts lifted off. I became a passionate advocate of the rights of Negroes, who were taking to the streets first in the South and later in urban areas across America.

Then, on November 22, 1963, came the shattering news bulletin out of Dallas. I read it on the air in Omaha, Nebraska, where I had gotten my first news job after college and marriage to Meredith, a hometown girl of exceptional brains and beauty. I interrupted a noontime talk show for women. Shots had been fired at the presidential motorcade. President Kennedy was being rushed to a hospital. He was dead! I distinctly remember thinking, This doesn't happen in America. But it did, of course, and it was the beginning of a tumultuous passage in our collective lives that now seems surreal: Vietnam; hippies and the drug culture; passage of the Civil Rights Act; the assassinations of Dr. Martin Luther King, Jr., and Robert Kennedy; the Black Panthers; the election of Richard Nixon as president twice and Ronald Reagan as governor of California twice before he, too, became president; the musical *Hair;* the Beatles, the Rolling Stones, Bob Dylan, Jimi Hendrix.

As a child of the 1940s and '50s, I had always thought I would serve in the military; indeed, at one point I thought it might be a career. In 1962, though, when I was turned down for the draft and officer training in the Navy, I was happy to move on because there was no urgent call to service. Within two years that had changed, as President Lyndon Johnson began to expand the U.S. presence in Vietnam. At first I defended the war because, well, stopping Communism was important and, besides, when America goes to war, it's right and just, isn't it?

By then Meredith and I had moved to Atlanta, where I came to better understand the complex culture of the American South and its strong loyalties to the military. When the young black activists John Lewis, a sharecropper's son (now a congressman), and Julian Bond (now the head of the NAACP) issued a statement through the Student Nonviolent Coordinating Committee expressing their opposition to America's involvement in Vietnam, there was hell to pay. Bond was temporarily denied his recently won seat in the Georgia legislature and endured a lynch-mob climate as he walked through the halls of the ornate capitol. At the other end of the spectrum, Secretary of State Dean Rusk, a Georgia native, was the principal speaker at a rally called "Affirmation: Vietnam" that drew thousands of flag-waving, cheering defenders of the war.

By 1966 I had my own serious reservations about Vietnam, but I admired my friends and relatives who were in uniform. As the divisions in America grew deeper during the war years, I was personally buffeted by the turbulence generated by the veterans of World War II and the protesters, including their own children. The flag burnings, bitter condemnations of the American system, and defiant rejection of their parents' personal codes of conduct by so many baby boomers were for me at once deeply troubling and fascinating. I was a straight-arrow husband married to a woman with whom I fully expected to spend the rest of my life. As the father of three daughters I was a cheerleader for women's rights, but I also wanted my daughters to know the rewards of a loving marriage like the one Meredith and I enjoyed.

In my professional life I was spending late nights documenting the Free Speech movement in Berkeley, the antiwar protests in Chicago during the 1968 Democratic convention and in 1972 at both parties' Miami conventions, the drug culture in the Haight-Ashbury section of San Francisco, and the communal life of Southern California. I had easy access to Jerry Brown, later California's free-spirited governor, as well as Ron Ziegler, Richard Nixon's White House press secretary. I cheered and wept when America put Neil Armstrong on the moon. I was in a rage when one of my best friends from college was killed during his second tour in Vietnam. On weekends I'd put on peasant shirts and bell-bottom trousers and take the kids to the local hippie fairs, but on weekdays I was back in uniform: coat, tie, and serious expression, albeit framed by a mop of long hair.

World War II, which had been the incubator of many of our lives, faded almost entirely from the national consciousness, even as veterans of that war continued to dominate almost every aspect of American life. Richard Nixon, and Senators Bob Dole, Gaylord Nelson, Daniel Inouye, Frank Church, Mark Hatfield, George McGovern, and Strom Thurmond were among the politically influential veterans. The U.S. House of Representatives, governors' offices across America, and big and small city halls also had a high proportion of veterans. Jefferson Airplane, Janis Joplin, Otis Redding, Joan Baez, and Ray Charles were the new stars of the pop culture, but they could not diminish the place of such World War II favorites as Frank Sinatra, Bing Crosby, Bob Hope, and John Wayne. Gloria Steinem was getting a great deal of attention for her role in the women's movement, but the mother of that transforming idea in modern American life was Betty Friedan, a member of the World War II generation. In the 1960s and '70s the top executive suites of American business began to fill up with World War II veterans, men for the most part, now in their forties and fifties. University faculties and administrative offices were laced with veterans.

Yet World War II seldom emerged as a topic of conversation outside the VFW and American Legion Posts that, too, were beginning to lose their prominence on the American landscape. There were too many distractions. The war in Vietnam inflicted deep wounds until it finally wound down in a torrent of relief, guilt, and rage. I went to Washington to cover the Nixon White House, which was engulfed in Watergate, a two-year political and constitutional crisis that ended only with the first resignation by a president in American history. America's first three presidents from the World War II generation were John F. Kennedy, Lyndon Johnson, and Richard Nixon, whose personal and political lives were all destroyed by gunfire, war, and perfidy on a grand scale.

As my own life and career advanced, I continued to focus on the present and the future without giving much thought to the past. Occasionally I'd marvel at the material advances of my generation, especially those of us who'd grown up in the harsh economies of rural America. Most of my childhood friends owned homes, sometimes two, and a couple of cars, and they had traveled widely. Increasingly, America was a culture defined by the young, especially that great mass of baby boomers, the offspring of the World War II generation. They weren't much interested in the adventures of their parents. Ben Bradlee, the legendary journalist and a World War II Navy veteran on the USS *Philip,* a destroyer in the Pacific, said that when he brought up the topic of experiences in World War II, his kids would roll their eyes and say, "Uh-oh, here comes the Big Two." So he didn't talk about it much. Neither did the millions of other men and women who had gone through that trying time.

By 1984 these veterans were in their sixties or seventies, winding down their professional lives or retired; they had become grandparents and senior citizens. Many seemed a curious presence in that go-go decade of the '80s, even as their own—Ronald Reagan, George Bush, Caspar Weinberger, George Shultz, and Donald Regan in the two terms of President Reagan—still ran the country. That year I went to Normandy to participate in an NBC documentary on D-Day, the Allied invasion of Europe. I was accompanied by veterans of that invasion and their wives—schoolteachers and priests, lawyers and members of Congress, Republicans and Democrats. They were uniformly modest about their achievements four decades earlier, grateful to have survived when so many of their friends had not, and understandably emotional as they walked again on those windswept beaches that had been so murderous when they had first encountered them.

When President Reagan made his memorable speech from a bluff overlooking the beaches during the commemoration ceremonies, and television cameras focused on the weathered and grandfatherly faces in the audience before sweeping across the neat rows of white crosses and Stars of David in the nearby cemetery, it was a rich and deeply affecting portrait of courage and honor. I returned to America with a renewed sense of all that I owed my parents and their generation. I began to write and lecture about those men and women and all they had been through. By the time of the fiftieth anniversary of D-Day, in 1994, I had decided what I thought they represented, no less than the greatest generation any society has ever produced.

Those thoughts were expanded into two books that have changed my life and, I gather, the lives of that generation, their children and grandchildren. I cannot go anywhere in America without people wanting to share their wartime experiences, without hearing children and grandchildren describing, often in husky, emotional tones, their new appreciation of all we owe the Greatest Generation. The stories and the lessons in this book have emerged from long-forgotten letters home, from reunions of old buddies and outfits, from unpublished diaries and home-published memoirs—and though one might have thought that the passage of time and the vagaries of memory might have rendered these accounts less than 100 percent accurate, I have found, to my great pleasure, that, allowing for human fallibility, the accuracy as well as the spirit of these witnesses is supported by the record. Schoolchildren have been assigned to interview their grandparents or others in their communities who went through those difficult times. Service clubs and charitable organizations have honored local members of the Greatest Generation.

During the long presidential campaign of 2000, at one time or another all the candidates referred to the obligation we have to the Greatest Generation. The historian Stephen Ambrose, who is in many ways the literary godfather to this generation, Steven Spielberg and Tom Hanks with *Saving Private Ryan,* Senator Bob Dole and the World War II memorial, the many new and republished books about that time, have kept the war and the people who won it where they belong: front and center in our memories.

As the stories in this album of memories remind us, it truly was an American experience, from the centers of power to the most humble corners of the land.

That lesson in the enduring strength of joining together to create strength and find a common ground comes to me in unexpected times. Recently I visited a New Mexico pueblo, the home of the Acoma people on a sandstone mesa an hour west of Albuquerque. The Acoma have been living on this site for more than four hundred years, and during the Spanish occupation a large, spare, but hauntingly beautiful mission was constructed for Roman Catholic services. Out back there is a small, simple cemetery with perhaps a hundred grave sites. Nine of those sites are the final resting places of World War II veterans from this small tribe.

This album of memories and the two books that preceded it reflect and honor the lives of those nine people, and all the others who died, and all who lived during the Depression and World War II, two of the greatest trials any society has ever known.

Dear Mr. Brokaw:

My dad, Morris Adelman, was a Navy lieutenant during the war. He fought in the Pacific on the U.S.S. *Electra* and landed on the beaches of Japan. I knew very little of his time in combat as he preferred to speak of his training beforehand in San Diego and Hawaii, and, right after the war, driving to Los Angeles through the orange groves of Orange County. Occasionally he would mention a fellow officer, but even that was rare. My mother discouraged me from asking him anything about it.

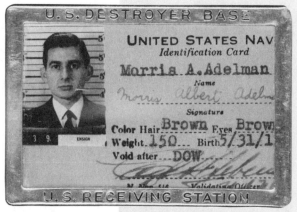

Navy I.D. card issued to Morris Adelman.

Dad just turned 83. Recently I moved him from his home of over 36 years outside of Boston to an assisted living facility. During my clean out I discovered his files from the military. I took them back to Los Angeles with me and reviewed them a few days ago.

My father is a writer and an economics professor emeritus at M.I.T. who traveled the world extensively. I always felt he could express himself in an eloquent manner, none as dignified as the incident I read described in a report he wrote regarding the death of one of his landing crew. They were going through a channel and there was an explosion. My father and the soldier (named Hershel Burrell) *sitting right next to him* jumped up together. Burrell said, "I think they hit me, sir," then fell as my father grabbed him. A shell had exploded right over the boat—and Burrell had sustained a fatal wound in the back by a projectile. My father and the other men tried to save him, but by the time they made it back to their ship, it was too late.

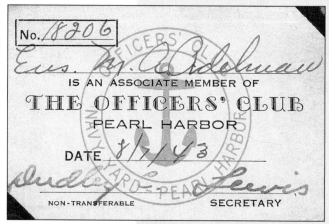

Included in the file was the copy of a letter from my dad to Burrell's parents. My father wrote: "It would be foolish to think that anything we could say could diminish the grief that you must feel now. But you do have the right to know that your son died facing forward like a man and a sailor and that he was at least spared

Officers' Club card issued to Morris Adelman in July 1943.
(Both courtesy of Barbara Adelman)

any pain. He is at rest at the foot of a mountain that looks a good deal like some of the hills in his own New Mexico."

While studying the report and letter I had to keep reminding myself that this wasn't some novel or movie—it was my father's life. I realize how close I came to not being here—if Dad had been sitting a little more to the right or left it would have been an officer writing to *his* mother. I have greater admiration than ever for what he must have had to deal with and the sacrifices he made to do what was necessary, without asking for anything in return.

My mother, Millicent Linsen, grew up in New York City and became a WAC in February 1943. I think she signed up out of a combination of duty to her country, a quest for adventure and, being 29 and still single (having watched most of her friends get married), she was feeling a need to change her life. In any case, she always referred fondly to being in the service and of some of the friendships she made and kept for years afterwards.

Millicent Linsen at Sheppard Field.
(Courtesy of Barbara Adelman)

Since Mom had administrative and secretarial skills, she was given a job in one of the offices at Sheppard Field, Texas, where she was ultimately stationed. She wrote to her aunt Clara that, while she enjoyed her position, it was starting to bore her and she was eager to learn more, to advance, but knew that was virtually impossible since "promotions were for the men." She wrote to Clara describing thoughts of having a career after the war as a commercial photographer. Photography was her hobby and passion at the time. I think she feared she would never marry, since few women seriously entertained thoughts of being married with children AND having a career in those days. After the war she returned to New York City, worked in other offices, and continued photography as a serious hobby until one day she quit her job and decided to visit a friend in California. Mom took another courageous step for a single female of the time—in 1949 she flew cross-country, alone, on a trip that would result in her meeting the love of her life, my father, with whom she was fixed up on a blind date. Dad was about to return to Boston and his position as an economics professor at M.I.T. They were engaged a few months after meeting and she returned to New York to plan their wedding and her move to Boston.

That was the end of her career aspirations. She did what most 1950s women did—raised a family and worked in the home, while my father taught at the University. I know she never regretted her decision although she never got rid of her camera and equipment. It was only when I was cleaning out Dad's house earlier this year that I came across them and donated them to someone who was genuinely interested. Mom and Dad were married for almost 46 years until her death, in 1995.

I must admit that reading your first book gave me tremendous insight into what men (and women) of Dad's generation thought and why they behaved in many of the ways they did. They won the war—they were, in a way, invincible. Then they returned to the States and did what was expected of them—work hard and raise a family. When my mother was dying five years ago, Dad refused to get any help in the house until the very end because in his mind he was doing what "a man was supposed to do" . . . take care of his wife and family. That was his commitment, as it had been to his country years earlier.

Millicent Linsen at Sheppard Field in 1943. (Courtesy of Barbara Adelman)

And, just recently, when I had to become the parent and help my father into what likely will be his last residence, I had far more patience and strength than I ever thought possible. He deserved the respect.

Sincerely,
Barbara Adelman

———— • ————

Dear Mr. Brokaw:

I am a child of the '60s, one of those who grew up with very conservative parents and of course who served in "the war." . . . Mom was at home and Dad was a Marine in Europe and Korea.

When I say Dad, I am really talking about my stepfather. My biological father left us when I was quite young, and a few years later my mom met and soon after married this huge, impressive, yet wonderfully warm man named John Howard. Shortly after they were married, I was adopted and took his name. I was always interested in just what it was he did during the two wars he served in, but he was always somewhat vague and even humble in discussing it. He would simply say, . . . "Well, son, I just went over there and did what was right."

As I grew through my teens and into college, it became apparent that Vietnam and the draft would be something I would have to deal with. Sure enough, the letter came one day, my college deferment wouldn't hold out any longer and I was "invited" to visit with my draft board. I shortly thereafter opted to join the Navy, with the intention of doing a few years of service and returning home. For reasons too numerous and unimportant to the real purpose of this letter, I decided to make the Navy a career.

Over those Navy years I had the opportunity to travel to dozens of countries, learn to speak several languages and begin to really understand the depth and extent of what my dad and his fellow soldiers, airmen and sailors accomplished around the world. It really is astounding, the sacrifices, the efforts and the successes of these young men and women. *They truly did do nothing less than save the world.*

Something happened that helped me to understand what my father was really about and what service to man and country really meant and how important my service was to my father.

I served aboard the USS *La Salle* during the hostage crisis in Iran, and we were at many times the only American ship in the Persian Gulf. There we were, a big, white, floating listening platform that monitored Iranian communications and actions during that tense time. I was literally in the radio room listening to the conversations of both the leaders in Washington and the men on the ground at Desert One when it all went wrong and President Carter had to order our men out. I can't even begin to describe what the next weeks and months were like, as we literally feared that the Iranians would blow us out of the water. It was letters from my mom and dad that got me through this time, but especially my dad, who knew the pressures of conflict and fear. And I assure you, I was afraid. He let me know that it was OK to be scared. Thousands of miles away, this old, retired Marine still served his country and helped a stepson through another war in another faraway place.

Shortly after the Iranian conflict I returned home, a highly decorated Navy man with a chest full of ribbons and the stride and confidence that only a returning military man can muster. I learned immediately after my arrival stateside that my dad had been diagnosed with cancer of the spine. He didn't want to tell me this while I was abroad because he didn't want to add to my worry and concern. I made arrangements with my mom to come home right away, and she made only one request of me. She asked me to wear my uniform. My brother met me at the airport in Richmond, VA, and took me to the Veterans Hospital there in Richmond, where Dad was undergoing treatment for what we all knew by now was a fatal affliction.

When I walked into his room, he was asleep, and I stood at the foot of his bed simply watching him, old, sick, thin and much smaller than I ever remembered. I stood there for quite some time, just watching him and reflecting back on the life of this man who took me, my mom and brothers and sisters into his life and gave us his name. A man who never once wavered in his love for us or his country, and seemed to always be able to understand what I was going through and how to help get me through it.

At some point he finally opened his eyes, and I shall never forget what he said. I will tell you now that all the medals, ribbons, warfare qualifications, awards, diplomas, degrees I have ever received have paled in comparison to that frail, proud man opening his eyes and looking at me and saying, . . . "Oh my, just look at you. I am so proud of you. Thank you, son." We buried him not long after that, and I remember thinking what a pity it was that more people hadn't gotten to know this man. Of course what I learned from your book was that there were, and are, thousands of John Howards all over our country, and children and grandchildren are, in many cases, just now learning about the magnificent things they accomplished.

I have a son now, and although I have since retired from the Navy and work at the Centers for Disease Control and Prevention, I hope that I will serve my son as the same beacon of integrity, compassion, understanding, vigilance and strength that John Howard did. I think of him every day of my life and am thankful that he went into harm's way to ensure that the grandson he never got to meet would walk among the free.

Warm regards,
Robert Howard

———— • ————

Dear Mr. Brokaw:

I wanted to share with you a different kind of war story, one involving another member of this special generation, my father, Wilbur (Jack) Leslie Brimm, Jr., who died on May 5, 2000. While sorting through my father's private papers, my brother and I came across the enclosed letter, written in 1945. As you will note from his heartfelt plea, here was a man who wanted deeply to do his duty and serve his country. However, at age six, whooping cough had left him blind in one eye, a condition that ultimately prevented his enlistment in the armed services.

Just as many of the men in your stories never spoke freely about their involvement in the war, my dad never mentioned this letter. As I've learned, during the war years he worked tirelessly on the home front, did his civic duty, and met the responsibilities of a devoted father and husband. In fact, my parents were married 59 years, and my father worked for the same insurance company in Memphis, Tennessee, for over 40 years. Interestingly, after working all day, he attended night law school, hoping that a law degree would help him get into the army.

I do not want to take anything away from those brave men and women who fought and died in WW II, as well as those who returned to become productive citizens, but not once in our years together did I ever question my dad's courage, his sense of duty or his honor. I know, if given the chance, he would have served his country bravely and with dignity. The legacy of *duty and honor* that he left for my brother and me and for our sons and daughters and for their sons and daughters is another shining example of why many consider this particular generation of individuals to be the Greatest Generation. Thank you for allowing me to share with you my father's letter and a few thoughts regarding his life.

Sincerely,
Jack L. Brimm

May 7, 1945

Gen. Joseph Stilwell
Army Chief of Staff
War Department
Washington, D.C.

Dear Sir:

My name is Wilbur L. Brimm, Jr. The purpose of this letter is to see if there is something that you can do towards my getting in the Army. I have written many letters to officers of the Army to see if there was something that could be done, but I have received no reply from any of them.

I have been turned down 3 times in the draft, once under the Volunteer Officer Candidate Program, and about 7 times on voluntary enlistment. The only physical disqualification that I have is defective vision in my left eye. But to offset that I say this, in 1940 I was in the CMTC training at Fort Oglethorpe, GA. At that time I qualified as expert on the rifle, pistol, and light machine gun. This vision defect does not mar my shooting.

I have one brother in the service, and I feel there is something that I must do towards winning the war. I realize that at this time the war in Europe is over, and that Japan remains. But that would be the sole purpose of enlistment, to fight Japan. I have had many sad moments about not being in the service, and I really want to get in.

Now what I want to know is this, can you or anyone else possibly do anything to help me. I would sign a waiver relieving the government of liability on my eye, or I would do anything to get in the service. My right eye is perfectly normal, and the loss of vision in the left eye does not affect it.

I hold an Ll.B. degree, and with my training in ROTC, and CMTC, I feel that I may be of some value to the service and my country.

Thanking you in advance I remain,

Yours truly,
W. L. Brimm, Jr.

11 May 1945

Dear Mr. Brimm:

The feelings which give rise to your letter of May 7th are sympathetically understood, and your desire to serve your country during this war is deeply appreciated.

However, the present need of the Army is for loss replacements, necessitating procurement of men who are physically qualified for full combat duty. While your letter does not state the extent of your eye defect, the fact that you have been turned down so frequently on enlistment would seem to indicate a serious physical defect, and that you are probably not physically qualified for combat.

In view of your earnest desire for active military service, I regret that I cannot give you a more favorable reply, but I am certain that you can be of much real service on the home front—in services which are essential and which contribute greatly to the overall effort of the country.

Sincerely yours,
J. W. STILWELL
General, U.S.A.

— • —

Dear Mr. Brokaw:

I was born two months after the attack on Pearl Harbor, the sixth son of Italian immigrants. My oldest brother, Carmen, the namesake of my father's brother who was killed in World War I, was just shy of his sixteenth birthday and a rough-and-tumble guy who was eager to join the fray. So eager, in fact, that he begged my parents to sign for him to enlist in the Marines. They, of course, refused, so Carmen reluctantly bade his time, finally enlisting on his eighteenth birthday in March of 1944. After basic training Carmen came home for the last time, and a picture was taken of me holding his hand, looking up at this handsome guy resplendent in his beloved uniform. This is my bond with him, the image that remained with me and haunted me my whole life.

We were quite poor; my father had no formal education and rarely worked. When he did, the little he earned didn't go very far, but in our neighborhood enclave of "paisans," there was plenty of homemade pasta and red wine; lots of music and laughter and a camaraderie that unfortunately no longer exists. So, when the telegram came, the music and laughter ceased, and the long period of mourning and sorrow began. I often wonder what would have been if Carmen had not died on the sands of Iwo Jima.

They brought his body home in 1949 to a house paid for by his insurance, $6,000.00, I think. This I remember clearly; the Marine bodyguard, the folded flag, the coffin in the corner of the living room. The sorrow, the tears, and the overwhelming grief. Then off to the attic to open "Carmen's box," with the Purple Heart, the letter from his captain, and the letter from the chaplain who assured

Carmen Perna with his parents,
Anna and Giustini,
Middletown, New York, 1944.
(Courtesy of Don Perna)

*Carmen Perna with his aunt Pauline,
his brothers Don (left) and Tony (center),
and Pauline's daughter Jeannie.*

*The burial site of
Private Carmen Perna
in Iwo Jima.*

NAVMC-HQ-PD

CARMEN JOSEPH PERNA

who lost his life while in the service of his country
has been reported buried

GRAVE 343, PLOT 1, ROW 7, FOURTH MARINE
DIVISION CEMETERY, IWO JIMA, VOLCANO ISLANDS

D. Routh
Major, U.S. Marine Corps

Marine Corps report of Carmen Perna's interment.

*Memorial card issued by the Marine Corps
at the wake of Carmen Perna, March 1948,
Middletown, New York.
(All courtesy of Don Perna)*

MEMORIAL CARD FOR THE SOULS OF
OUR FAITHFUL DEPARTED

O God, Whose property it is ever to have
mercy and to spare, we humbly beseech Thee
in behalf of the souls of Thy servants, the
men of the 23rd Marine Regiment, whom
Thou hast called out of this world, that Thou
wouldst not deliver them into the hand of
the enemy, nor forget them forever, but command the holy angels to take them and lead
them to the home of Paradise, that forasmuch
as in Thee they have put their hope and trust,
they may not endure the pains of hell, but
may come to the possession of eternal joys.
Through Christ Our Lord. Amen.

23rd Marine Regiment   4th Division.

my mother that Carmen had received Holy Communion before his death. He sent a card with a note to my mother every Easter and Christmas for many years, and she kept them all.

The family never wanted to talk about the circumstances of Carmen's death; how was he killed? did he suffer long? who was with him when he died? Although I read everything there was about Iwo Jima, the older I got, the more guilt I felt. So, I started accumulating names of men from the Fourth Division and writing and calling them in the hope they could answer my questions. They were all wonderful to me, but Carmen was a replacement and his first battle was Iwo, so no one knew him. This became an obsession to me, constantly in my mind, and I had to find some sort of closure. Then God intervened.

My wife, Marie, and I and our three daughters were living in Montvale, New Jersey, in the mid-1980s. Marie had a Bible study group that she met with weekly, and on one occasion an elderly woman asked that the group pray for her brother who was celebrating his 50th year in the priesthood. She mentioned that he was a chaplain in World War II, and that he had recently retired. After the meeting, Marie asked the woman where her brother had served as a chaplain, and she said he was with the Marines in the Pacific campaigns. He was the priest that had written so many times to my mother! He was the chaplain in the very famous photo of the Marine kneeling on Mount Suribachi, waiting to receive Holy Communion.

The chaplain's sister arranged for a private Mass to be said in her home by her brother for my mother, brothers, and my family. In his homily, he said that all who died on Iwo Jima certainly went straight to heaven, for they had spent their time in hell on that tiny island. For me, the words lifted the heaviness that had filled my life and left me with a sense of closure. For my mother, it was the chance to thank in person the kind man who kept her in his thoughts and reassured her that her son had died in a state of grace.

The war changed many lives. Those that came home lived forever with the memories of those they left behind. Those that did not come home left behind loved ones whose lives were never again the same.

Very truly yours,
Don Perna

— • —

Dear Mr. Brokaw:

I am a 26-year-old doctoral candidate in human development and family studies at Auburn University. In years, I am far removed from the Greatest Generation, but I have been fortunate enough to have many opportunities throughout my life to share the company of the generation. I wholeheartedly agree with your assessment of their collective character.

As I read about the work ethic, the standards, the determination, and the spirit of these individuals, I immediately thought of my grandfathers—one who deeply wanted to serve but was denied because of a childhood injury and the other who was a stateside Naval doctor. But, I wasn't thinking about them in WWII. I was thinking about how hard they both worked and how I learned from them to do one thing and do it well and to completion. I was thinking about the long hours worked and how after a 12-hour day they still had time to play with me when I visited. I was thinking how I've learned from them the need to take care of ourselves and our families and always do what needs to be done without complaining. I think that now I understand a little better where that all comes from.

I began talking with my parents, and we generated a long list of those who served our country during the war and who have shown me, many times, why they are a part of the greatest generation. One of the things you point out in many of the people's stories you tell is how they are modest, almost reluctant, about acknowledging their contributions. This is the humility that has been shown me by those of this generation.

Sincerely,
Malinda Colwell

— • —

Dear Mr. Brokaw:

My father was a pilot with the Army Air Corps who fought in North Africa during World War II. He was killed several months before I was born. After his death, my mother continued to receive letters that had been written by him. Soon after, my mother had a nervous breakdown and quit eating. At the time she was pregnant

Bob and Dorothy Nichols, September 1941, in Salem, Alabama.

with me. My grandmother had to coax her into eating. The minister of our neighborhood church praised Mother for being stoic and not showing her feelings. Needless to say, this was the worst advice to give someone who was grieving the loss of her beloved husband.

Then I came along in the middle of my family's grief. Besides my mother, I lived with my grandparents, three aunts and an uncle.

My relatives walked on eggshells around me. I was discouraged from talking about my father's life and death. It was just too painful for them to talk about my father, and in those days people didn't seek out grief counseling. Their way of handling the grief was to deny that he had ever lived.

I look like my father. Whenever my mother looked at me, there was no eye contact. Her mind always seemed to be far away. I never had her complete attention. She seemed to hear only half of what I was saying. The words and feelings faded in and out. She looked past me, over me, or through me. I felt as if only a part of me existed. Our relationship was like this until the day she died. My other relatives, although they meant well, also tried to keep my mother from thinking about my father's death. He was never mentioned. I found the flag from

Bob Nichols, St. Louis, 1941, while working as a flight instructor. (Both courtesy of Barbara Howell)

his coffin folded on a shelf in the closet and the telegram my mother received informing her of his death. I felt confused and wondered where I fit in. People were uncomfortable around me, and I was anxious around each of them. We were a family who never shared feelings.

Bob Nichols, pilot, serving in the North African desert in 1942.

Born to a grieving family, I developed into a grieving and sad child. I knew that my father had missed most of his life and I was the only one to live for him and for myself. He was an angel. How could I live up to that? How was I to fulfill the gift of life for him? I did not want him to be forgotten. I felt that his memory was being erased.

My mother remarried when I was eight years old.

I had to repeat the 2nd grade. By this time, I was a very angry, confused and sick child. Whenever I asked my mother about my father, she would cry or get mad. I avoided the subject and my feelings about my father's death. I continued to have mixed feelings about myself. My face was a constant reminder of the father who according to my family never existed.

Dorothy Nichols and her daughter Barbara in St. Louis, Missouri, 1944. (Both courtesy of Barbara Howell)

I am not saying there weren't happy moments when I was growing up. But even during my happiest times, I felt anger, confusion and anxiety. I had no control over these feelings. Now that I am 57 years old, I can say that these feelings over a period of years translated into clinical depression. Today, I am doing well as a result of therapy and medicine.

I wanted to share with you some of the effects of WWII on the family of a loved one who never returned. I have the utmost respect for all those who served. It is my hope that someday the stories of those left behind, the families of those men and women who died for their country, will be told.

With love and appreciation,
Barbara Howell

———— • ————

Dear Mr. Brokaw:

My husband, Harold, died just one year ago February 9th. As a WWII Army veteran, he had spent four years in the service of our country. There is so much that I do not know about those years—as you noted, most of the men who were in the thick of battle never discussed their war experience very much. I have heard him tell about being in North Africa before going ashore in Sicily. Also he told about how, in crossing the Alps, donkeys carried the mortars, and with one slip, over the side fell the donkey and its load. As a 1st

First Lieutenant Harold Newkirk.
(Courtesy of Rosa Lee Newkirk)

lieutenant he served as a chemical warfare unit commander in five major battles in Italy, France and Germany.

He did not receive any physical injuries, but he was hospitalized in Paris as a result of all the battles. He did receive a disability pension because of these "injuries." He probably never did get over the effects of fighting the war—many a night I was wakened in bed by him hitting me—no doubt he was still fighting the enemy in his sleep.

I still feel that one thing that contributed to his death was the condition of his lungs. The doctor really didn't agree with me, but once when I commented about the situation to Harold, he said, "That's what they are paying me for," and that was all that was said.

So many of your remarks about the men and women of our generation rang so true about Harold. He was very frugal. He sent money home (we weren't married then) when he was overseas, and upon his return he was able to buy a new bright red Dodge with that money. Was he ever proud of it!

When Harold entered the service, he had just finished embalming school and had passed the state board to receive his funeral director's and embalming licenses. Later his greatest ambition for our children was that they attend college and receive a degree. He always regretted that no one in his family had urged him to do so.

Since your book related to how the depression affected our generation, I want to tell you about a couple of recent circumstances which emphasize this point. My cousin, who is the same age as our children, couldn't get over the fact that I wiped off a perfectly good piece of aluminum foil so that I could use it again. Upon his chiding me, I remember that I said, "You didn't grow up in the depression."

Harold Newkirk.
(Courtesy of Rosa Lee Newkirk)

This past Christmas I visited my daughter and her family in Illinois, and, of course, we roasted a turkey. The next day I proceeded to boil the turkey carcass in order to make turkey soup like my mother always made. My daughter had never paid any attention to how we made the soup, which she always thought was so good. She couldn't believe how it was made. Using the broth and the turkey that was picked off the bones, I simply added rice, celery and onions. With a chuckle, I called it depression soup, as during my childhood nothing was wasted. Her husband still talks about that good depression soup.

My husband always made sure that there was a flag on my father's grave as he was a WW I Marine. Now I am the one to see that there is a flag on each of their graves.

Sincerely,
Rosa Lee Newkirk

———— • ————

Dear Mr. Brokaw:

As a Vietnam veteran, I have long been struck by the contrasts between the sacrifices made in this conflict and those offered in World War II. I was an artillery officer with the First Infantry Division from November 1966 to November 1967, and served both as a forward observer with the infantry and a fire direction officer in battalion artillery. The First Division's area of operation was the Third Corps, from south of Saigon north to the Cambodian border. I was fortunate enough to return unscathed after my tour.

Some people today may be unaware that everyone who went to Vietnam had a 365-day commitment . . . a beginning . . . a middle . . . and an end. Some chose to remain for a second tour, with attendant bonuses and increases in rank and experience for the career soldiers, and similar rewards for those who simply wished to serve. Every one of my acquaintances (even Major Carl Vuono, my battalion executive officer, who rose to the rank of Army chief of staff in the late '80s) knew exactly how much time he had left.

The contrast between this and the World War II commitment is obvious, overwhelming, and humbling. Their commitment was open-ended, unknown, and courageous beyond belief.

A dinner conversation with my family was prompted specifically by your book and by a recent experience I had with one of my customers. My company sells process instrumentation. Fred works for a plumbing supply house in Groton, Connecticut, and I visit him periodically in maintaining our business. He is an older and somewhat wizened man, totally unassuming. In the course of our conversation, Fred mentioned that once a year he returns to Oklahoma for the reunion of the 45th Infantry Division. There are only about 80 men left who return, but they all have a good time when they get together. I pressed him about his experience, and he said that he was also in the artillery, and that he served 600 days in combat, up the boot of Italy and into central Europe. Roosevelt finally had to halt his division's progress. They were running out of gas, and the political situation dictated that they pull back.

Six hundred days . . . open-ended . . . no defined tour . . . no 365-day calendar . . . just one objective and then the next objective and then the next . . . until it was over.

I'm sure you stand with me in awe and salute all the Freds of this and other generations. Their courage and the humility with which they display it will remain a testament to all those who ever served in uniform. I will forever be grateful and in awe, and mindful of Milton's sonnet "On His Blindness": "They also serve who only stand and wait."

Sincerely yours,
P. Thomas Oberholtzer

— • —

Dear Tom:

I've just read your book *The Greatest Generation*. Your generalization of that particular era of people who pulled together was right on the money.

And I would like to add one more rubber band which helped pull us all together: *music*. We had the world's greatest bandleaders of all time: Glenn Miller, Artie Shaw, Benny Goodman, you name them. And the music they put together was magnificent. "Moonlight Serenade," "Don't Sit Under the Apple Tree," "A Nightingale Sang in Berkeley Square," etc. They kept us marching through the Depression and WW II.

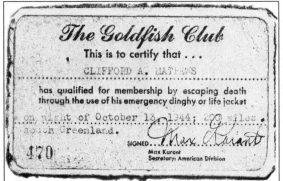

Goldfish Club card issued to Clifford Mathews for having been rescued at sea.

When I was small, I contracted polio, which left my right leg shorter than my left. Around three years old I came down with an abscessed ankle, which fused the right ankle solid. I walked with a slight limp and a hip-hop on account of my ankle not bending.

When I took my physical to go into the service, I was ushered into a huge gym with about one or two hundred draftees and enlistees. One doctor asked me if I had anything wrong with me. I said no. Then the drill instructor started putting all of us through calisthenics while four or five doctors observed us. I *passed* and was classified 1A. So you see what a difference time makes!

I went into the Navy at 17 and wanted to fly. They said that I was too young! I must be 18. So they assigned me to an Aviation Ordinance School, figuring a little background would not hurt. When I turned 18, they told me I was too late with too little. The pilot training program was overloaded, and it would take years to get in.

I told them to forget it, finished up ordinance school and signed up for aerial gunnery. After I finished Aerial Gunnery School, they assigned me to Ft. Lauderdale, Florida, to be trained as a gunner in a TBF Avenger torpedo bomber. After finishing flight training, I was assigned to operational Squadron VC-69. The

"He's Got Wings": Newspaper article about Clifford Mathews, 1943.
(Both courtesy of Clifford Mathews)

He's Got Wings

Representative of the large group of aircrewmen who received their wings Wednesday, except for his photogenic freckles, is Cliff A. Mathews, AOM3c, whose home is in Pasadena, Calif. Like the majority of those graduating from operational training, he's 18 years old, and enlisted in the Navy last summer, soon after receiving his high school diploma. Besides their wings, all of the men are receiving certificates symbolic of successful completion of their training.

squadron served on four aircraft carriers, the *Wake Island, Bogue, Guadalcanal*, and *Mission Bay*.

My first radioman that I was assigned with got injured so badly on one flight that he could not fly again. The second one was killed when we dove into the water nose first in the middle of the night. I thought I was a goner, but I survived and was picked up by the USS *Neunzer* DE-150. A large iceberg was nearby, which tells you how cold it was. Looking back on that tragedy, it had to be our fault; after all, who in their right mind would take off on Friday the 13th in Plane #13? We did.

Sincerely,
Cliff Mathews

———— • ————

Dear Tom:

Your book really brought tears to my eyes—remembering growing up during the tough years of the Depression and then into World War II. I was one of the younger members of that generation. A matter of a year or even a few months meant the difference between being in combat and possibly getting killed or surviving the war. Many of my friends in the high school class ahead of me never came home.

Over fifty-four years ago I was a senior at Atlantic City High School, Atlantic City, New Jersey. World War II was continuing after five years. All my friends and I could not wait to enlist in the armed forces. We were the last of the innocents—we had no understanding of the horrors of war until much later. To us it was the great adventure, the time of big band music, girlfriends and patriotic fervor—a very romantic era. At age 17 I went to New York City and enlisted in the U.S. Navy on April 27, 1945. My parents had to sign for me since I was underage. Since I had taken and passed a special Navy V-6 program test to enter the U.S. Navy Radar School, I was sworn into the Navy, given

Seaman First Class George Corcoran, Jr.,
September 1945.
(Courtesy of George Corcoran)

a serial number, and promoted to seaman first class (radar technician).

Germany surrendered on May 7, 1945, but the U.S. Navy expected the war with Japan would last at least two or three more years, with very high casualties expected when we landed on the Japanese homeland. The United States was transferring U.S. Army and naval forces from Europe to the Pacific theater of war. No one had ever heard of or dreamed of an atom bomb. While I was in radar school training at Great Lakes Naval Training Station in Illinois, two atom bombs were dropped on Japan, and on August 10, 1945, Japan unconditionally surrendered. In November 1945 I transferred to the Naval Base at Lido Beach, Long Island, New York. The Navy kept all of us naval reservists until August 1946, when we were all discharged. I received my honorable discharge from the U.S. Navy on August 23, 1946. I was only nineteen years old, and one month later I entered Villanova College. I had always been a little ashamed that I had not contributed more to the war—but I realize now that my place in this generation was determined by my age and fate. As you can see I certainly was not a hero, but

Army booklet sent by George Corcoran in Florence, Italy, to his parents in Atlantic City, New Jersey.
(Courtesy of George Corcoran)

Victory flag given to George Corcoran upon his return home to Atlantic City.
(Courtesy of George Corcoran)

I am proud that I and all of my friends did not hesitate to join the Navy and do all the right things expected of us. Having served during World War II, I did win one medal, the U.S. Navy World War II Victory Medal. The GI Bill paid for most of my college tuition. I went on to be a special agent in the Bureau of Narcotics and U.S. Customs Service, rising through the ranks to the highest career position of assistant commissioner for investigations. I was a very fortunate young man.

Sincerely yours,
George C. Corcoran, Jr.

—— • ——

Dear Tom:

I was astounded by what I saw and learned on the 50th anniversary celebration of D-Day and about the men and women who served. I was fortunate to lead all the first advance trips for the White House/State Department, and for a student of American history that advance trip was astonishing.

From Italy to Portsmouth, from whence the Allies' armada sailed and where the British admiral gave us a history of D-Day from his perspective, to Normandy, where generals in helicopters took us from beach to beach lecturing on the battles, to Sainte-Mère-Église and Caen, I was stunned into understanding what those men and women did. Where do we get such people?

As I look at our culture today with such narcissism, such consciousness of supposed victimhood, such whining, such apparent need for "self-fulfillment," I join you in applauding our parents' generation and its values: a strong will to survive, a determination to overcome, a refusal to complain, a belief that physical pains will pass if one ignores them and so one does, a reserve of deeply held beliefs, a sturdy sense of personal ethics and of responsibility for self and those one serves, a belief that life goes on after hardships and that it might be engaged and committed to and given back to.

We were fortunate to have such parents, and your book tells why—Thank you.

Best,
Molly Raiser

—— • ——

Dear Mr. Brokaw:

Being born in January 1926, I did not enter the service until March of 1944 and had all stateside service. I did lose friends and high school classmates, and others came back scarred for life.

I agree that a majority of those who endured the Great Depression, World War II and helped rebuild this country, were folks inculcated with a deep sense of honor, duty, patriotism, loyalty, work ethic and respect for God, country and self. I do respectfully disagree, however, that we are the "Greatest Generation." I tip my hat to the generation preceding us, our parents and grandparents, who instilled in us those principles of honor, duty, loyalty, patriotism and respect as well as the work ethic. They taught us to "make do," to get our joy from our companionship and loyalty to and from our friends.

When my 1942 high school graduating class had its 50th reunion, we had former members from virtually all over the country, California, Arizona, Texas, Arkansas, North Carolina, Florida, Ohio, etc., as well as Tennessee. I can honestly state that I have never been in a room that was more filled with more genuine love, consideration and affection than upon that occasion. A number of us had not seen each other since graduation day. There was not one scintilla of jealousy, one-upmanship or braggadocio or egotistical claims that was manifest. I give credit to our parents and grandparents, who instilled those concepts in each of us.

I feel that my generation has fallen short in instilling the same principles in the majority of the "Boomers" and/or Generation X. Far too many of my contemporaries have stated, "I want my child to have all the materialistic advantages that I did not have as a child growing up." Have we given too much of the materialistic aspect of life, and too little of ourselves?

Yours very truly,
F. Evans Harvill

——— • ———

Harvey Clinton Guthrie,
father-in-law of Dana King.
(Courtesy of Dana King)

Dear Mr. Brokaw:

I am not a member of the Greatest Generation, but I like to think I can appreciate them as much as someone born 11 years after the end of the war can.

When I saw *Saving Private Ryan* for the first time, it had just come out. I thought about it for days afterward, about a lot of things. Mostly I thought about being lucky.

Ever since my daughter was born, I have always thought that the single thing in my life I was most grateful for was to be there to see her come into the world. After having seen this movie, I've had to rethink that position. Not that I love my daughter any less. I just can't imagine being more grateful for anything than for not having ever to have gone to war.

When I saw *Private Ryan* again recently, it was different. It af-

Harvey Clinton Guthrie (right) and Army buddies in New York City, 1943.
(Courtesy of Dana King)

fected me on many different levels, and I can't quite get it out of my head. Part of me feels a little foolish because a movie is making me reexamine how I think about some things. Most of me was feeling something different.

Everyone has problems, some worse than others. I've been thinking quite a bit about some of mine lately. When the movie ended that night, most of what I felt was shame, because I don't have any problems.

When I look at what I have to do to get through a day, and I think about what millions of people in this country went through every day for four years, I think less of myself for even having considered complaining. The men overseas, the women who built the instruments of their victory, and the mothers and fathers who lived every minute of every day knowing that today might be the day the telegram came, suffered more in a day, every day, than I wish to imagine. It must have mattered little to read what a fine young man their son had been, how well he had served his country, or how everyone had looked up to him, with all the praises in the past tense because their son would never be any of those things again.

We see them everywhere. When I was in the Army, I must have played taps for fifty funerals. This was when these men began to leave us, and I'm ashamed that I (all of us at the funerals) didn't appreciate them better.

Sincerely,
Dana King

— • —

Dear Mr. Brokaw:

In Jacksonville, Florida, where I was born and raised, I was 18 years old when W.W. II began. A girl with 4 older brothers.

One of my brothers enlisted at 21 in the Air Force and was sent to Italy. The next brother was drafted—a navigator in the Air Force—and sent to the Pacific. My oldest brother was drafted and soon after Basic Training in the 29th Infantry was sent to England.

In those days the telegrams were delivered by Western Union boys on bikes. My parents and I used to sit on the porch hoping the bike would pass our house.

In August of 1944 the "boy" did stop with a telegram saying my brother, Willie Fraden, PFC, was missing in action in France. Needless to say, we were devastated! Two weeks later came the follow-up confirming he was killed in St.-Lô. He didn't get thru the Normandy invasion.

Three weeks later, another telegram!! Another brother was missing—his plane shot down in the Pacific. Fortunately we learned later he was picked up by some Philippine peasants. They fed and hid him for several weeks until he was smuggled to the U.S. troops. For years after the war my brother sent money and clothes to those who saved him. The third brother in Italy got home safely.

After all these years my husband and I went to France last summer, to visit my brother's grave. An ending.

Signed,
Rose Levin

— • —

Dear Tom:

I have just turned 73—probably as young as anyone can be, legally, and still have experienced combat during the war. I enlisted at 17 and served as a dogface with the 10th Inf. Regt., 5th Div., of Patton's 3rd Army and went thru the Bulge. Three of my 6 brothers also served in other branches, and we were all fortunate to have survived. I took a wound and carried two Bronze Star Medals and in the 50-odd years since have not opened to anyone, including my wife and kids, about those months of unreality.

I concur with the majority of your subjects that we didn't feel

like it was a big deal to join in the war effort—but more that it was an obligation to our country and ultimately the world at large.

It often bothers me that the negative attitude of our American people towards veterans has affected our traditions—Veterans Day or Memorial Day parades do not seem to draw much of a population the way they did in the '40s or '50s.

Nathan Futterman

Nathan Futterman (extreme right) and other G.I.s around the time of the Battle of the Bulge. (Courtesy of Nathan Futterman)

———— • ————

Dear Mr. Brokaw:

My daughter has become greatly interested in the WWII era. She lost an uncle she never met. He was my brother, who never lived to be 21, killed in Germany, April 21, 1945. I was almost 15. There were six of us in the Goff family, my brother being the only boy. At the age of 39, my mother lost her husband and then three years later lost her only son.

My oldest sister, Evelyn, and my brother were very close. During the war, as did so many other women, she took over a man's job . . . driving the mail truck for Socony-Vacuum, in Detroit. At this time she kept up a weekly correspondence with a number of servicemen. At Christmastime she was up to about 50 letters a week and decided to send each of them a Christmas box. She bought 50 miniature Christmas trees and decorated each one of them with tiny ornaments and tinsel and then bought 50 pair of G.I. socks and filled them with things like yo-yos, playing cards, etc., and baked dozens of cookies and candy. Christmastime was the only time you didn't have to have a special request

Don Goff, the brother of Ruth Berryman, in Paris, France. (Courtesy of Ruth Berryman)

from the serviceman himself for needed items. She was only 23 at that time.

She and my cousins also entertained a variety of servicemen in our home. There were many who were training in Detroit, mostly British and Canadian. She fed them, during rationing, had a great home party, and took them to church on Sunday.

She and my brother, Don, had a kind of code, and he was able to let her know approximately where he was. It was vague, but she avidly watched the papers for what action was happening in Belgium, France . . . remember, this was not a war that was fought on television, and news was sparse and all letters from military personnel were censored. We will never know how accurate her pins on the globe were. In May we got the letter that turned our Blue Star in the window to Gold. My brother was listed as M.I.A. but only for two days. The second letter came, listing him as killed in action. My mother lost her only son. We lost our only brother, and my daughter, years later, came to know her uncle from reading his always cheerful letters. He was buried in the military cemetery near Maastricht, in Holland.

Sincerely,
Ruth M. Berryman

Newspaper article about Don Goff receiving a posthumous Bronze Star. (Courtesy of the Daily Tribune, *Royal Oak, Michigan)*

———— • ————

Dear Mr. Brokaw:

My husband enlisted the day after Pearl Harbor, left college, served as a fighter pilot for a year in the Aleutians, bombing and strafing Kiska and nearby Amchitka. He was separated on points,* and he arrived home on V-J Day. He finished college on the GI Bill, went to work, moved into a tract house. We've had an exciting, eventful life, three marvelous children and so far 15 years of wonderful retirement. We feel we were fortunate to have grown up in this era despite the Depression and the war.

Dale Mullins

*At the conclusion of the war, a point system (taking into account servicemen's length of service, time spent overseas, campaign stars, Purple Hearts, and children under the age of eighteen) determined the order of military discharge—that is, "separation on points."

ABOVE: *The Eighteenth Fighter Squadron in the Aleutians, 1943. Rev Mullins is in the second row from the top, extreme left.*

LEFT: *Lieutenant Reverdy Mullins with his P-40 in Amchitka, Aleutian Islands, 1943.*
(Both courtesy of Dale Mullins)

——— • ———

Dear Mr. Brokaw:

I am at home here in the Midwest, away from my computer for a month, while I help my mother move into a senior-citizen apartment in Minneapolis. I thought of you while helping my mother with one of the many tasks needing to be done when someone moves out of the family home. Please let me tell you about it.

She and I went to clear out the attic. Hanging among other precious items was a World War II uniform holder. Unzipping it, we found two perfectly cleaned and ironed white Navy dress uniforms. The fabric was still beautiful, and the brass buttons sparkled like new. It had belonged to her adored big brother, Dr. Tom McIntyre, who was killed aboard the USS *Franklin* in 1944. My mother was 30 years old at the time, devastated over the loss of the handsome, dashing young bachelor dentist—the fabulous man about town Tommy McIntyre. Much more important, he was the guardian angel who had watched out for the rest of the family since his father's death five years earlier. He spoiled his mother and treated her like a queen. He looked after his polio-crippled brother, hired his youngest sister as his office secretary, and was extremely close to his other sister (my mother). He was the man so

LEFT: *Tom McIntyre, Kathleen Sharkey's uncle.*
RIGHT: *Tom McIntyre with his mother, 1943.*
(Both courtesy of Kathleen Sharkey)

close to his religion that on Palm Sunday he stayed after to pick up any stray pieces of palm that were blessed by the priest—not to be walked on by people coming to the next mass. He was a glorious mix of glamour boy and altar boy, son and dentist, brother and uncle. Dead at 33 because of a kamikaze jet crashing into his ship. Here it is 1999, 55 years later, and Mom and I stood looking with awe at his uniforms, weeping together. Not only over the unspeakable loss to his family back then but for the world to have been robbed of his potential. My mother told me that it was her mother's birthday (my grandma Jessie) on November 11, 1944, and she was alone in her apartment in Minneapolis. A telegram boy was seen coming up the walk, and Gram (Tom's mother) thought to herself, "That's just like my Tommy. Even though he's away at war he found a way to get a birthday telegram to his mother!" She confidently and eagerly tore open the envelope only to read the unbelievable words: "We regret to inform you that your son, Thomas R. McIntyre, has been killed in action . . ." Mom said she and Gram "wept buckets—we cried for days, until the tears were drained from us. Life was never the same after our beloved Tom was gone."

Sincerely,
Kathleen Sharkey

Mr. Brokaw:

My dad was a waist gunner in a B-17 when he was shot down over Germany on 17 April 1943. He wasn't liberated until 5 May 1945. I never heard my dad complain about his service, and when the Gulf War broke out, he tried to reenlist in the Air Force. Dad and I hold the record of being the only two airmen to not only enlist and serve in the AAF and USAF, in two wars, 25 years apart, but also be assigned as a first assignment to the same unit, the 306th Bomb Group (H) (Dad) and its descendant the 306th Bomb Wing (H).

My father instilled in me a love of country and responsibility to duty that I was to see diminish in many other baby boomers, due to the Vietnam conflict. And, though I too remain bitter about losing my friends, his example, as a citizen soldier and my dad, was my role model throughout my life and, as my HERO, has endured throughout the years. His veracity and patriotism are an inspiration to me, and I would hope to many others that have entered his sphere of influence.

Dad died just recently, 7 February 1999, and I had the opportunity to be the recipient of his casket flag. I was never so proud of him, and to this day, even in an era when we as a society are so lacking in heroes, he is still my hero.

Leo L. Gallegos, Sr. (left), father of Michael Gallegos, in training in Idaho, 1942. (Courtesy of Michael Gallegos)

Michael L. Gallegos, Sr.

———— • ————

Dear Mr. Brokaw:

I'm an identical twin, and my brother and I served with General George Patton in the European Theater of Operation. Now, identical twins serving together in the armed forces is not that unusual. However, identical twins together, as riflemen, in a line outfit is quite another story.

My twin and I were with the 65th Infantry Division, same regiment, same battalion, same company. Just before being shipped to Germany, we both made squad leader. And, that, surprisingly, gave me cause for concern. Would I, inadvertently of course, ever shortchange the squad during a combat situation by thinking first and

Howard and Walter Schultz with their mother, 1944. (All courtesy of Howard Schultz)

foremost of my brother's safety? A persistent thought. And bothersome. My twin confesses he was troubled by the same fear.

Except for a few scratches, the Schultz boys emerged from the war intact. And at the war's conclusion, they received an unexpected bonus; they had the good fortune to be among the first contingent of G.I.s to attend Cambridge University. It was an American project with British blessing. It gave the American serviceman a chance to take some courses and, more important, study, and perhaps learn from the way our British cousins approached education at its highest level.

Now coming from a war-torn country to the hallowed halls of Cambridge was quite a drastic change of climate. A Bertrand Russell lecture was a great contrast to the loud, belligerent bellowing of my topkick. Oh, happy day! *Up* Cambridge!

Well, the years keep rolling by, and my twin, Wally, and I are still very close. After the war we both married and each sired three children. And these children, in turn, produced a gang of grandchildren.

Your book gave me cause to reflect on those days of over half a century ago. My life changed from one of comfort and security to violence and mayhem. But, while in service, there was always that moment where I could find greatness in myself. And it was my moment, and I'll remember it as the one time I was the complete man. I was standing up for something, and that was the thing, sort of justifying my place in history and on this planet Earth. And the cause was a just one. All the yet unborn kids would benefit. Not that the Greatest Generation gave them a bright, shiny new world. But it was a livable one.

Yours truly,
Howard Schultz
Walter Schultz

RIGHT: *Patch of the Sixty-fifth Infantry Division.*
LEFT: *Patch worn by G.I.s attending Cambridge University after the war.*

— • —

Mr. Tom Brokaw:

My husband and I grew up and lived in a good deal of your story. I was born in 1923, he in 1924. Both of our mothers raised us alone—no financial help.

The day of Pearl Harbor we were in the Majestic Theater in Dallas, Texas. Next day he quit high school and joined the U.S. Marines. He was a truly great Marine. A Marine thru and thru. He went from buck pvt. to master gunnery sgt. and then rose to captain. He retired in June 1977, after 35 years. He had a massive heart attack 20 July 1979. At that time we had 2 grown daughters and 2 daughters still at home, a 13-year-old and 14-year-old. We had discussed that when that time came we would be buried in Dallas.

I've had one of our grandsons since he was 3 months, born in 1986. I've tried to make his grandfather alive to him. I've told him of the depression and the sacrifices we and our parents had to make.

Much admiration,
Mrs. Billie B. Bounds

— • —

Dear Sir:

I read your book. I agree it was "the greatest generation." Personally, I owe so much to that elite group!

I owe the greatest generation my freedom and much of my happiness if not all of it. I was a teenager in Europe: Four years of Nazi occupation were a nightmare, and I will never forget the sight of those smiling GIs arriving in my hometown. They had been through plenty before reaching us. You could see that they were happy for all of us.

I will never forget those who did not share that glorious day, and it is with an immense sense of gratitude that I go to the St.-Laurent Cemetery above Omaha Beach every time I go to Normandy. I read the names through my tears, I walk past some of the 9,000+ headstones, thanking them for my freedom and happiness.

Billie Burke on Senior Day at
Dallas Technical High School, 1942.

Jack Bounds in uniform, July 1942.

Jack and Billie Bounds at the
Bicentennial Birthday Ball,
November 1976.
(All courtesy of Billie Burke Bounds)

My husband and I visited other American military cemeteries. They might not have fallen on the Juno or Omaha Beaches, but they were heroes just the same.

Not only did they give me back my freedom but destiny gave me one of those men for forty-six years. He landed on July 6th. Although the fighting was intense, he never talked much about the war. To our questions, he would reply, "I did my duty, nothing more." This was a 19-year-old man who enlisted, went to Officer Candidate School and was discharged with the rank of captain. The same man who decided to get in the Ready Reserve, giving up his Saturdays, his vacations, spending countless hours on his correspondence courses. This son of the Depression was buried in his uniform: he had only his intelligence and a sense of patriotism to guide him through his life.

Sincerely,
Renée M. Stokes

——— • ———

Dear Mr. Brokaw:

In many ways after reading your book and viewing *Saving Private Ryan*, I have been able finally after 54 years to relate to my children and grandchildren. I don't think I ever recall sitting down and telling my children what it was like during the war. I had too many bad memories, especially losing my buddies in arms, who had become like family to me; it was something I wanted to forget. So I'm happy to say that after 54 years I can sit down with my children and grandchildren and tell them what I and millions of other G.I.s had gone thru and how lucky I was that I made it back home alive.

In one part of your book you make mention of the 761 Tank Battalion, an all-Negro outfit that we ran across during the Battle of the Bulge in December of 1944. A great bunch of G.I.s is how I can describe them.

As I look back I now ask myself, why were the Armed Forces segregated. I sincerely feel that had FDR met just one member of the 761 he would have issued a proclamation to desegregate the Armed Forces on December 7, 1941.

It's a shame that it took until 1948 to accomplish.

Sincerely,
Al Cangiano

Dear Mr. Brokaw:

Briefly, I'd like to share with you a couple who have been there and done that. My husband, Ray, from a divorced family, raised himself from an early age. He was in twelve different grade schools due to [moving around to] find a place to bed down for a night. He joined the Army before war to better himself. We met each other at the U.S. Recruiting Office in Peoria, IL. Ray went on to Officer Candidate School, head of a company in the 29th Infantry. We were married June 6, 1943, together one month. Ray went overseas, and I did not see him for 2½ years. On Christmas Eve 1944 I received that yellow telegram saying he was missing in action. He was taken at the Battle of the Bulge.

A little background of his life after he was freed from POW camp in Germany. Becoming a civilian, he went to college; I worked to help. He graduated with honors with a B.S. degree, M.S. degree and several hours towards Ph.D. As all or many young couples then, we never felt anyone owed us anything. We were proud of our accomplishments. We would have it no other way. Ray continued to become manager at Caterpillar Tractor Company. We also raised two children, who are on their own now.

Ray and Peg Regal on their wedding day, June 6, 1943, one month before Ray shipped out to Europe for two and a half years. (Courtesy of Ray and Peg Regal)

*Ray Regal
at Scott Field,
Illinois, 1941.*

*Ray Regal on his first wartime
assignment, Iceland, 1943.*

*Ray Regal in France,
November 1944.*

*Telegram sent to Peg Regal informing
her that her husband was a prisoner
of war.*

ESCAPE
MAP
April 5th 1945

*Escape map drawn by Ray Regal.
(All courtesy of Ray and Peg Regal)*

Ray was in the prime of his life at 52 when he was stricken with Parkinson's disease. Today he is 77, mathematics tells us he's spent 25 years with this disease. He has never given up, believing he'll be the first person to be cured of Parkinson's. Today he is wheelchair bound, on a feeding tube, cannot hold a book or turn pages.

Finally may I add he never complains, has a positive attitude, and a good sense of humor, so appreciates each day we can be together. He has been in the V.A. home in Danville, IL, the past three years. I drive 260 miles twice a week just to be with him and share our marriage vows. Last summer we celebrated our 55th anniversary. All credit goes to God. Thank you for taking the time to read this letter. Ray thanks you also in his way.

God Bless You,
Peg & Ray Regal

——— • ———

Dear Mr. Brokaw:

Just before I read your book, I heard for the first time the details of my father's WWII experience and that of my uncle. They had not talked of these before.

So here I am, in my fifties, just now hearing the real stories; they were amazing and mesmerizing.

I was born on March 17, 1945, in Baltimore, Maryland, almost a baby boomer!

Both of my parents grew up in small towns in Iowa. My father was all German, descended from immigrants in the mid-1800s. Mother's ancestors were from Sweden and England, coming over in the mid to late 1800s.

As those in your book, my father's father lost his farm in 1932 during the Depression. The family suffered greatly. My dad told me these stories only about two or three years ago.

Once they lived in an abandoned house during a snowstorm with three cans of sardines to eat—for a family of four for three or four days!

When Dad was finished telling me about his childhood, he floored me by saying, "But I think these experiences made me a better person!" I only wish my nineteen-year-old son would have any kind of thought like that.

At twenty Dad joined the Navy in 1942. Mom took the train to

Washington, D.C., and became a secretary in the War Office that same year. She was nineteen and a half. They were married in 1943.

After the war they came to California, bought a tract house, and lived the postwar life. Dad was, and is, an Elk, Mason, and Shriner. Mom was a secretary but also active as a Camp Fire leader, etc.

No one in our family had ever gone to college. All I heard growing up was, "When you go to college and become a teacher . . ." Not surprisingly, I did just that. I have a master's degree, and the better life that their generation created for all of us.

I am now fifty-four. My husband, Bill, is sixty and has just retired from teaching. Our only son is nineteen and attends community college. We have a lovely home and an upper-middle-class lifestyle that, I realize now, was a gift from the greatest generation, bought with sacrifice and hardship.

I sat mesmerized as my uncle told tales of being a bomber pilot in the Pacific in 1943–44, and as my dad told of his Navy experiences on the USS *Tennessee* in the Mediterranean. I had heard none of these stories before, and I am so terribly grateful that our family was able to hear them before it was too late.

My father is 76, and my uncle is 75 and has just been diagnosed with Alzheimer's. My mother is now 75. Both my parents have health problems, but I am so thankful for each day they are still here. Their values and work ethic gave us so much that we can never repay.

I pray for our country and our future generations, who will not have the wisdom, values, work ethic, and honesty of our greatest generation to mold and guide them, as we have had.

Most sincerely,
Linda Vallow

Norma and Dale Holle, the parents of Linda Vallow, in Washington, D.C., on their wedding day, June 5, 1943. (Courtesy of Linda Vallow)

———— • ————

Dear Mr. Brokaw:

I just finished reading *The Greatest Generation* and wanted to thank you for allowing me to see my father. Dad died twenty years ago. He was an Army infantryman in the Pacific—hopping from island to island—and later spent a year as an "adviser" in Vietnam. Like your individuals, he never really talked about his wartime experiences. As a teenager during the turbulent '60s and '70s, I came up against a stone wall and resented, even hated, his attitudes and somewhat stern opinions and was certainly not interested in how it was when he was young—boy, was I ever stupid! I simply did not understand then, but I saw him in each of your combat veterans this week.

During the last several years I've become more interested in those times and frequently speak to veterans in my office about their experiences, just to get a glimpse of the times Dad went through. During his lifetime he didn't speak and I didn't ask about those experiences that made him the way he was. When I did want to ask Dad questions, it was too late. Through your book I know him better than I ever did—or could. I even get choked up at the national anthem and the flag. I've been married to the same woman for 18 years, I believe in hard work and responsibility, and I love America. I guess some of Dad and his Greatest Generation have become part of me, too.

Thank you,
Randy J. Buckspan, M.D. FACS

———— • ————

Dear Sir:

As I read your book *The Greatest Generation,* I often thought of my time in the military and especially of my older brother, Wilbur. He was killed in Germany, November 1944, and buried in the Henri-Chapelle Cemetery in Henri-Chapelle, Belgium. I was a 17-year-old and in my senior year in high school in Montebello, California, when I was called into the principal's office and told that my mother wanted to see me at home. I couldn't figure out why. Upon my arrival home she showed me the telegram, and we both cried. My two other brothers were in the service at the time.

I finished out the semester, and then 5 or 6 of us joined the merchant marine, and I was off to help finish something that my brother died for. My mother didn't want me to go, but I really felt that I had to do something, and served two years in the merchant marine.

I married in 1949 and was drafted in 1952 into the Army and served two years in Japan and Korea. It was a good experience, and my first child was born while we were going from Japan to Korea in 1953. Upon my release from the Army I worked and went to night school and raised a family of four children.

After forty-plus years of marriage, we were divorced. I re-met an old high school sweetheart, and eventually we were married. While we were on vacation at the Punchbowl in Hawaii, I looked at that cemetery and said something like "I wonder if this is what the Henri-Chapelle Cemetery, where my brother is buried, looks like." Her answer was that we will never know if we don't go there. This was in September of 1995, and we started to plan our trip to Belgium. In April of 1996 we were there, and the 51-plus years since my brother's death came rolling down my cheeks in the form of tears. As I looked at that cross with his name on it and the flowers that I had ordered lay on his grave, I was crying like a baby and not ashamed of it one bit. Here was a 68-year-old man, crying. My wife just hugged me. Thanks to the American Battle Monuments Commission for their help in seeing that we had a pleasant visit.

Sincerely,
Cecil H. Wilkie

———— • ————

Dear Mr. Brokaw:

Today was my second visit to the USS *Arizona*, Pearl Harbor and Punchbowl National Cemetery. It was extremely emotional this time. I realized how fortunate my life has been. This generation has given values to the baby boomers (as myself) so much, including sometimes their lives (as those on the USS *Arizona*). The Greatest Generation men and women have given the baby boomers et al. the challenge, the pride and the conscience of their lives. They made enormous sacrifices for their family, the country.

Today, standing on the USS *Arizona* and walking in Punchbowl Cemetery, I talked to a woman from Japan my age. She also said "thank God" for this generation. Her grandfather was a bomber on Dec. 7th. It was mixed conversation with hand gestures, broken English and extremely long embraces at the end of the boat ride.

Thank you again,
Mrs. Nancy J. Constantino

To Tom Brokaw:

My husband, Jacob H. Wingard, a sergeant in the 501st Parachute Infantry, in the 101st Airborne, was killed September 19, 1944, after he had been ordered up into the only windmill in the village for observation of the Germans in control. He was directing mortar fire onto the Germans when a sniper picked him off. The Van Riell family, whose windmill Jake was killed in, told me after he was killed the Germans used howitzers and blasted the top of the windmill. Jake was brought down and laid on a wheelbarrow for 3 days before he could be moved to a temporary burial point. (He was moved twice, until the national cemetery was made ready in Margraten, the Netherlands). The Dutch were so grateful to the Americans and the British for their liberation after more than 4 years, many adopted graves.

Jacob Wingard in England, 1944.
(Courtesy of Evelyn Wingard Boehms)

I became a pen pal to Dinike Dorries, who adopted Jake's grave—and we corresponded for years and years. They moved to northern Holland, and another couple, the Post-Bickers, re-adopted Jake's grave. The Van Riells owning the windmill tried for years to find Jake's family—without success 'til 1987.

They tried the American Embassy, War Department, other agencies and couldn't locate me. They thought Pa. was where they'd find the Wingard family. Jake enlisted in Pa., met me in N.J., where he was living with an aunt—we married in Dec. 1943, in NYC—in the Little Church Around the Corner. Went overseas in England in Jan. 1944—went to France D-Day—survived—sent back to England to prepare for Holland in Sept. and killed the next morning.

Many paratroopers have revisited Eerde and the Van Riells' home. They saw the memorial they have to him with plaques and pictures and a small attractive parklike area adjacent and the remaining bottom of the windmill. It's a shrine, sort of, to Jake and the British soldiers killed there on their property.

One of the paratroopers from the 501st told Van Riells he'd try to locate me. He finally reached another trooper, Jim McKearney (the one who ordered Jake up into the windmill), who knew I was in Florida but had shoved my address into a drawer and had for-

*Grave of Jacob Wingard in the American military cemetery in
Margraten, the Netherlands.
(Courtesy of Evelyn Wingard Boehms)*

gotten. At last contact was made between Glen Bartlett (the
searcher), Jim McKearney, Van Riells and me.

Josef Van Riell invited me over to Eerde, Holland, in 1997. I of
course saw the windmill and all else they had done. They also took
me to the national cemetery to visit Jake's grave. We've kept in
touch, of course, by telephone and mail. The language barrier is a
bit of a problem, but we manage. I'll be 78 in Sept.—Josef Van Riell
is in his early 60s. He and his older sister live in the same home-
stead directly across—a few feet from the windmill.

They have invited me again for Sept. of this year—as the entire
village is commemorating the 55th year of the drop.

Josef Van Riell said to me, "Your husband gave his life for us,
all I can do to help repay some of the terrible loss to you is to invite you here, completely as a guest—all expenses paid." I am widowed again.

If all goes well I leave Orlando for Amsterdam from September
12th to the 27th.

Sincerely,
Evelyn Wingard Boehms

———— • ————

Dear Mr. Brokaw:

My name is Warren Illing. During World War II I was an instructor pilot flying B-25 and A-20 type aircraft. I went to New Guinea as an A-20 pilot with the 5th Air Force, 417th Bomb Group. I came home after the Philippine Campaign, having flown 49 combat missions.

The reason I'm writing is because of the letter I received from my grandson (copy enclosed). He's a doctor serving as a captain in the U.S. Army Medical Corps.

My generation is getting close to the end of the line, but with a new generation like my grandson and many other young men and women like him, our country will still be in good hands.

God Bless America
Warren J. Illing

Dear Big Daddy:

I wanted to write to you today, because I don't know if I ever expressed to you how truly proud I am of you. I know that we have talked about your service in the military several times, but I just had to let you know how I feel being your grandson. Words can hardly do justice to the pride I feel when I think of the commitment and sacrifice that you gave to our country during World War II. I love the picture of you with your plane that you gave me, and it hangs with pride in my hallway. I tell everyone who sees it about you and your military career. I often think of you during the war and know how scared you must have been yet never once hesitated to carry out the duty you swore to uphold and complete your mission. A mission that I and every other American will always be in debt to you for. We can never truly repay this debt to you or any of the other brave men and women who sacrificed everything, many their lives, so that our country would remain free. I am so proud to call myself the grandson of Major Warren Illing. As a captain in the United States Army, I hope and pray that I am able to follow in your footsteps and serve my country honorably and make you proud. Having never been in combat, I cannot truly empathize with the sacrifice and bravery that you demonstrated, but if I am ever called upon to serve my country in a similar way, I hope that I will be able to serve my country with that same honor and bravery and make you proud. I love you very much, Big Daddy, and I wanted you to know how proud I will always be of you. My children and my children's children will never forget the sacrifice that you made for them, and they will always know of your bravery and honor, that I promise you!

My Big Daddy, Major Warren Illing, I salute you with pride, love and admiration.

I love you,
Beau
Cpt. Joseph W. Olivere, U.S. Army

—— • ——

Dear Tom:

It was 54 years ago. We sailed through the Golden Gate in the very early morning hours of December 16, 1945. It was very cold and very windy, but neither seemed to matter as the great bridge guided our ship home. One thousand GIs were aboard, most jamming the ship's railings to witness that wonderful sight. We were three weeks out of Manila, and it was rough as hell most of the way, which made that famous harbor all the more welcome.

The San Francisco Bay ferries were all busy moving shiploads of troops from unloading transports docked along the San Francisco waterfront to Angel Island for the first stage of processing that moved the troops on their respective ways to discharge camps and bases everywhere across the country, in each case the nearest to each GI's home. The massive effort to get as many home for Christmas [as] possible was, as I have looked back on that day many times, a daunting task, but the army and the navy together with the many civilian agencies involved got it done with magnificent organization in the true spirit of the times.

For a busload of Californians the mighty undertaking paid off handsomely. We were on our way that night to Camp Beale up near Sacramento, and by noon of the 19th the discharge process was completed. Along with my discharge certificate and service ribbons, I received discharge pay of $300, for almost three years' service to the day with no leave time offered or taken. Four of us hired a taxi for the trip back to San Francisco's bus station, where I took a Greyhound bus to Marin County across that same Golden Gate Bridge that had ushered our ship home only three days before.

We lived in the quiet residential town of Ross, near San Rafael. The Ross bus stop was on the San Francisco–San Rafael route. By the time my bus got there it was evening and very dark, as a rural street can be in the dead of winter. I remember my big duffel bag didn't seem heavy that night in spite of the half-mile walk home. My mother was at the door when I walked up the driveway. Home at last at the ripe old age of 21. It had been a very long time.

Jack Kirkwood on police duty, Rome, 1945. (Courtesy of Jack Kirkwood)

In these later years I have come to realize how lucky I was. Drafted at 18 years old on New Year's Eve 1942 if you can imagine. Never been away from home. Assigned to the Army's Corps of Military Police for training in Georgia and Mississippi. Almost 29 months overseas, including duty in North Africa, Italy and the Philippines, and seven ocean crossings aboard troopships in 1943 and 1945. Nineteen of those months in Italy. Support of the line outfits but never committed to combat. Numerous German air raids early in 1944 against port operations in Naples, in particular during the loading for the Anzio landings and during the eruption of Mount Vesuvius, which ignored blackout regulations and guided the enemy planes to their targets. All of this and unscratched. Lucky indeed.

In 1992 my wife and I visited Normandy and the American military cemetery overlooking Omaha Beach. If one has never walked upon that hallowed ground, it would be quite impossible fully to understand its place in our time or to grasp its awesome impact on the mind and the heart of the visitor.

We were so moved by the experience that we felt compelled to pay our respects again when we too attended the 1994 50th-anniversary ceremonies.

Each time I see those crosses row after row after row, I clearly remember more vividly what happened then and where I was at that time and what it has meant since.

Respectfully,
Jack Kirkwood

———— • ————

Dear Mr. Brokaw:

An experience I recently had in France has haunted me and kept coming to mind as I read your book.

In the town of Périgueux, near Bordeaux, I was wandering in

the weekly open-square vegetable market, taking pictures and en-joying the scene. A very old man, leaning on a cane, stood near me, and he spoke to me in French. I responded, "I speak English. I am American." He looked at me closely and slowly said, "America." Then he took my hand, stood in front of me (the brim of his base-ball cap touched my forehead) and said, with great emphasis, "*Je . . . soldat . . . la guerre.*" I could understand only the words quoted here, and translated them as "I . . . soldier . . . the war." I said, "*Oui.*" He then said, with great emphasis on each word, "*Merci. Merci beaucoup, America.*"

Tears started down my cheeks and then down his. We cried a little, laughed a little, squeezed hands, but we couldn't talk with each other. After a couple of minutes, he hobbled away, leaning on his cane.

He had found an American lady in her 70s who might under-stand his memories and emotions about the events of 1944 in France. He had an overwhelming need to thank our generation for rescuing France from dictatorship.

I have no way to tell the thousands of men and women who fought in that war that this old French man is, more than fifty years later, compelled to thank us for what we did to bring peace to Europe.

It was a wonderful moment, and I thought you would like to hear about it.

Sincerely,
Marie Pooler

CONTRIBUTORS

—•—

The following people generously contributed letters
and memorabilia to *An Album of Memories:*

Barbara Adelman (pp. 268–270), Mike Ahlstrom (pp. 63–67), Mary
Ahlstrom (pp. 63–67), Mary O'Hearn Armitage (pp. 242–245), Kay
Atkinson Ball (pp. 61–63), Carl Barger (pp. 246–247), Esther Barger
(pp. 246–247), Irma L. Barrigan (pp. XII,19–21), Jackie Barron (pp. 90,
92–93), Armand J. Beauchesne (pp. 13, 15), Ruth M. Berryman (pp.
292–203), Barbara A. Birra (pp. 79–82), Evelyn Wingard Boehms (pp.
307–308), Ebby Bolger (pp. 121–124), Billie B. Bounds (pp. 298–299),
James D. Branch (pp. 83–86), Jane M. Branston (pp. 249–250), Jack L.
Brimm (pp. 273–275), Donal Brody (pp. 227–229), Randy J. Buckspan
(pp. 304–305) Al Cangiano (p. 300), W. L. Chilcote (pp. 167–168),
Ernest E. Coffman (pp. 176–177), Malinda Colwell (p. 278), Nancy J.
Constantino (p. 306), Nancy Cope (p. 230), George C. Corcoran, Jr.
(pp. 285–287), Robert Cromer (pp. 8–10), Karen Cummins (pp.
30–32), Mary Ellen De La Torre (pp. 233–234), Hendrika DeRonde
(pp. 101–102), Marie Knight Dion (pp.117–118), Irma Dryden (pp.
76–79), Robert Eberle (pp. 115–117), Frona C. Faulkner (pp. 164–165),
Edgar Fergon (pp. 129–132), Douglas G. Fish (pp. 89–91), Glenn D.
Frazier (pp. 209–213), Nathan Futterman (p. 291–292), Michael L.
Gallegos, Sr. (p. 296), George Galo (pp. 67–68), Charlene Nicholls
Gamble (pp. 47–59), James M. Garvin (pp. 175–176), Victor Goehring
(pp. 187–191), Ted Gurzynski (pp. 170–173), John A. Hammond (pp.
236–237), Frances Hamrick (pp. 247–249), Harold Hart (p. 168),
F. Evans Harvill (pp. 288–289), Dana Boyle Hawa (p. 229), Elias
Hellerstein (pp. 10–11), Edward Herold (pp. 180–183), Merle J. Hill
(pp. 168–170), William Holton (pp. 199–201), Maureen Honey (pp.
230–231), Robert Howard (pp. 270–272), Barbara Howell (p. 278–281),
David R. Hubbard (pp. 135–138), Claire Ignacio (pp. 231–232), Warren
J. Illing (p. 309), Fred Irwin (p. 208), Carol E. Isselian (p. 234),
Trinidad S. Jiménez (pp. 234–235), Fay I. Key (pp. 158–159), Dana King

(pp. 289–290), Jack Kirkwood (pp. 310–311), Steve A. Kish (pp. 17–18), Robert A. Kleinsmith (pp. 186–187), Edna Luella Lappas (pp. 29–30), Robert W. Lawrence (pp. 73–76), Dolores Leathers (pp. 238–240), Doris Lee (pp. 32–33), Rose Levin (p. 291), Stanley Lewin (pp. 251–252), Dorothy Lingenfelter (pp. 178–180), Al Loveless (pp. 232–233), Dawn Lowenhaupt (pp. 69–73), Alice K. Lusby (p. 161), Lorne J. MacDonald (pp. 183–185), Stan Makielski (pp. 16–17), Cliff Mathews (pp. 283–285), Archie F. McDole, Sr. (pp. 82–83), Earl Dean Mitchell (pp. 213–216), Marie Mobley (pp. 185–186), Ed Mooney (pp. 95–98), Beverly Moore (pp. 33–34), Betty J. Morrill (pp. 93–95), Dovie Morrison (pp. 21–28), Madelenne Moyer (p. 178), Dale Mullins (pp. 293–294), John L. Murphy (pp. 161–163), Harold D. Muth (pp. 60–61), Rosa Lee Newkirk (p. 281–282), Helen Nielsen (pp. 203–206), Mary Norton (pp. 127–129), P. Thomas Oberholtzer (pp. 282–283), Joseph W. Olivere (pp. 308–309), Barbara Olson (pp. 174–175), Hazel R. Parks (pp. 241–242), John Pensabene (pp. 98–100), Don Perna (pp. 275–277), Richard Peterburs (pp. 114–126), Joesph Peterburs (pp. 114–127), Marie Pooler (pp. 311–312), Myrna Saunders Qualls (pp. 235–236), Molly Raiser (p. 288), Peg Regal (pp. 301–303), Ray Regal (pp. 301–303), Mark Robb (pp. 142–144), Virginia Robinson (pp. 191–194), Janet E. Rodgers (pp. 174–175), Herrick S. Roth (pp. 206–208), Dorothy A. Rump (pp. 240–241), Helen L. Ryan (pp. 14–15), Kemal Saied (pp. 119–121), Howard Schultz (pp. 296–297), Walter Schultz (pp. 296–297), Jack Schwartz (pp. 196–199), Kathleen Sharkey (pp. 294–295), Margaret F. Sheffield (p. 195), Jim Shenton (pp. 59–60), Zelpha Simmons (pp. 11–12, 235, 236), Ardelle Sorenson (pp. 165–167), Richard E. Stafford (pp. 87–88), Joyce Merrifield Steele (p. 250), Renée M. Stokes (pp. 298–300), I. Harold Storey (pp. 110–115), Jane Sunderbruch (pp. 132–135), Klaus Theisen (pp. 138–142), Madeline Fenton Thomas (p. 237), Linda Vallow (pp. 303–304), L. J. Varnell, Jr. (pp. 102–110), Charles G. Westwater (pp. 201–203), Robert White (pp. 156–158), Beatrice Wiegand (pp. 118–119), Cecil H. Wilkie (pp. 305–306).

ABOUT THE AUTHOR

TOM BROKAW, a native of South Dakota, graduated from the University of South Dakota with a degree in political science. He began his journalism career in Omaha and Atlanta before joining NBC News in 1966. Brokaw was the White House correspondent for NBC News during Watergate, and from 1976 to 1981 he anchored *Today* on NBC. He's been the sole anchor and managing editor of *NBC Nightly News with Tom Brokaw* since 1983. Brokaw has won every major award in broadcast journalism, including two DuPonts, a Peabody Award, and several Emmys. He lives in New York and Montana.

ABOUT THE TYPE

This book was set in Fairfield, the first typeface from the hand of the distinguished American artist and engraver Rudolph Ruzicka (1883–1978). Ruzicka was born in Bohemia and came to America in 1894. He set up his own shop, devoted to wood engraving and printing, in New York in 1913 after a varied career working as a wood engraver, in photoengraving and banknote printing plants, and as an art director and freelance artist. He designed and illustrated many books, and was the creator of a considerable list of individual prints—wood engravings, line engravings on copper, and aquatints.